Richard C. Hallgren, Ph.D., is an assistant professor at Michigan State University. He has written numerous articles and is the author of *Interface Projects for the Apple II* (Prentice-Hall, Inc.).

Prentice-Hall, Inc., Englewood Cliffs, New Jersey 07632  A SPECTRUM BOOK

RICHARD C. HALLGREN

INTERFACE PROJECTS FOR THE TRS-80

Library of Congress Cataloging in Publication Data

Hallgren, Richard C.
    Interface projects for the TRS-80.

    "A Spectrum Book"
    Includes bibliographical references and index.
    1. Computer interfaces—Amateurs' manuals. 2. TRS-80 (Computer)   I. Title.
TK9969.H254   621.3819'592   82-343
ISBN 0-13-469437-6   AACR2
ISBN 0-13-469429-5

This Spectrum Book can be made available to businesses and organizations at a special discount when ordered in large quantities. For more information, contact:
    Prentice-Hall, Inc.
    General Publishing Division
    Special Sales
    Englewood Cliffs, N.J. 07632

© 1982 by Prentice-Hall, Inc., Englewood Cliffs, New Jersey 07632. All rights reserved. No part of this book may be reproduced in any form or by any means without permission in writing from the publisher. A Spectrum Book. Printed in the United States of America.

ISBN 0-13-469437-6
ISBN 0-13-469429-5 {PBK.}

10 9 8 7 6 5 4 3 2 1

Editorial/production supervision by Alberta Boddy
Page layout by Gail Collis
Manufacturing buyer: Barbara A. Frick

Prentice-Hall International, Inc., *London*
Prentice-Hall of Australia Pty. Limited, *Sydney*
Prentice-Hall Canada Inc., *Toronto*
Prentice-Hall of India Private Limited, *New Delhi*
Prentice-Hall of Japan, Inc., *Tokyo*
Prentice-Hall of Southeast Asia Pte. Ltd., *Singapore*
Whitehall Books Limited, *Wellington, New Zealand*

CONTENTS

1
INTRODUCTION 1

2
REVIEW OF DATA TRANSFER FORMATS 3

3
SAMPLING THE EXTERNAL WORLD 19

4
DIGITAL-TO-ANALOG CONVERSION 62

5
UTILIZATION OF THE MOD III IN SERIAL APPLICATIONS 68

6
BIOFEEDBACK 84

7
CONTROLLING A VIDEO PLAYBACK DEVICE 100

8
DATA ANALYSIS 122

APPENDICES 133

INDEX 149

INTRODUCTION

The rapid expansion of the electronics industry, along with its ability to mass produce reliable, large-scale integrated circuits, has given us scientific calculators and multifunctional digital watches for under $20, as well as "personal computers" starting from $200. In 1971 the Intel Corporation had the honor of initiating this revolution by introducing the first commercially available microprocessor. While the performance of this device was limited by its relatively slow central processing unit and by its use of a 4-bit data bus, its acceptance was so dramatic that, within a two-year period, the cost of a single unit had dropped from $200 to under $20. Today, it is a rare individual who does not have a microprocessor of some type in their home.

As I have talked to owners of personal computers, it has become apparent that a certain group of them would like to utilize their machines as extensively as possible, both at home and at their places of employment. This desire inevitably results in the need for interface circuitry that connects the computer to external devices and then allows users to monitor and control their environment. Based on the response of readers to several articles that I have written, I have come to the conclusion that there is a great need for a book not only that covers the theory behind interfacing a computer to external devices, but that also gives a broad selection of interface circuits that can be built and expected to work. So what I have attempted to do in this book is to provide a number of examples of interface circuits, ranging from the very simple to the somewhat complicated. I have included software for each circuit and can assure you that both the hardware and the software have not only been tested together, but have been used in some practical applications.

The result is a document that explains the theory behind computer interfacing and that gives you the choice of either building the circuit as is, or of modifying it to meet your specific needs. The hardware for these projects was designed and the components selected so that construction and check-out would be a straightforward matter. The circuits have been chosen to offer something of interest and application to a broad range of individuals: the hobbyist, the experimenter, the manager of a manufacturing plant, and the engineer or scientist in a research facility. The intent is to enable people to more fully utilize the computers in practical and interesting ways.

The book assumes that readers have a fairly good understanding of the commands in TRS-80, Model III BASIC, and have written some of their own programs. Since some of the supporting software will be using Z-80, machine code, you are encouraged to become familiar with the Z-80 instruction set. Programming examples using both Model III BASIC and Z-80 machine language have been provided throughout the book. While construction of the circuits is straightforward, it should be understood that a certain amount of experience and a certain level of expertise are expected. Previous construction of a commercial kit would probably qualify most individuals. So, with all this in mind, let's get started with the job of connecting your Mod III to the outside world.

REVIEW OF DATA TRANSFER FORMATS

Before we get into actual circuit designs, we need to spend some time reviewing basic interface concepts. I would recommend that even experienced circuit designers read this section to familiarize themselves with the terminology that I use.

We can define an *input/output (I/O) port* as a collection of electronic circuits, under the control of the computer, which route data to and from an external peripheral device. The key words in this definition are "data" and "external." The route by which the data flow to or from the external device is called the *port*. A line printer is a common example of an external device; the computer sends characters to be printed to the printer, and, in some cases, the printer sends control signals back to the computer. The purpose of these signals is to regulate the flow of the data, the interaction being called *handshaking*.

Ports can be constructed so that data are handled in either a serial or a parallel format (Figure 2.1).

Parallel transfer of data involves the mass transfer, at a given point in time, of several bits of data, where the number of bits being transferred is usually equal to the word size of the computer. For the case of the Model III this is equal to 8 bits. In general, the number of bits transferred at one time will be equal to the size of the data bus. For example, if we were working with a Z8000, which has a 16-bit data bus, a parallel transfer would involve 16 bits. For ap-

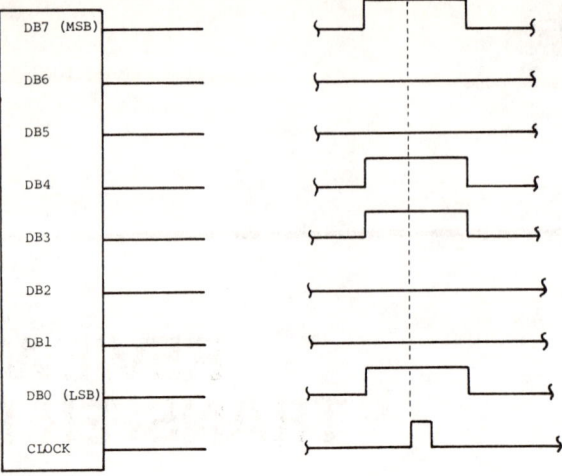

a) Parallel format

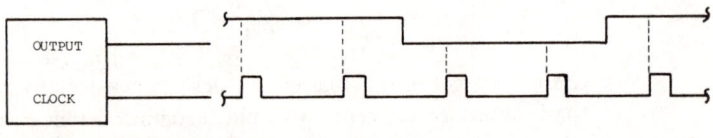

b) Serial format

FIGURE 2-1 Comparison of parallel and serial out format. The clock pulse is used to signal the external device that the signals are stable. For both examples, the data word being transmitted is binary 10011001.

plications where high rates of data transfer are desired, such as data transfer between a computer and a floppy disk, the transfer is usually handled with a parallel format. Computers handle parallel communication relatively easily, and even though multiconductor cables are required, the total expense is not too great because the distance between devices is usually quite short.

Serial transfer of data involves transmitting individual bits of data, one bit at a time. Microcomputers do not normally communicate in a serial format, so there is usually no single machine language command that facilitates this type of operation. As a result, we need to add either a software subroutine or an additional piece of hardware to accomplish a serial transfer of data. This adds to the system expense, but it gives us the capability of transferring data over increased distances at relatively high data rates. The Electronics Industry Association (EIA) RS-232C electrical specification for serial transfer of data is the standard for industrial applications. This specification defines the following voltage levels: a logic level 1 is called a *mark* and is considered to be any voltage level more negative than −3V. A logic level zero is called a *space,* and it is considered to be any voltage level more positive than +3V. In general, designers use +12 and −12-V levels for the logic 0 and 1 states. In addition to specifying voltage levels, the EIA also defines the standard RS-232C connector to be a 25-pin, D subminiature type (commonly referred as a DB-25). The pin assignments and their functions are listed in Table 2.1

Before we look at specific examples, we should take a look at the architecture of the Z-80 to determine how we can communicate in an orderly manner with several peripheral devices that may be connected to the same data bus and to the same address bus. The Model III computer used a Z-80 type of microprocessor to perform the logical, mathematical, and decision-making operations necessary for high-speed operation of the computer. This microprocessor is an 8-bit device that combines the bus structure of the 8080 with an instruction set that includes 644 differant commands. The bidirectional data bus is used to transfer information both to and from the central processing unit. The address bus has 16 lines that can be used to uniquely define 65,536 addressable locations. The Z-80 generates several signals that are used both internally and externally to supervise and manage the flow of information. Since data can flow in only one direction at a time, and since the data are usually directed to a specific

TABLE 2-1 EIA standards for DB-25 connector pin assignments when used for communication between RS-232C systems.

Pin 1	PGND - Protective Ground This is chassis or equipment ground. It may also be tied to signal ground.
Pin 2	TD - Transmit Data This is the serial data from the terminal to the remote receiving equipment. When no data is being sent it is in a marking (1) condition.
Pin 3	RD - Receive Data This is the serial data from the remote equipment which is transmitted to the terminal.
Pin 4	RTS - Request to Send Controls the direction of data transmission. In full-duplex operation an "on" sets transmit mode and an "off" sets non-transmit mode. In half-duplex operation an "on" inhibits the receive mode and an "off" enables it.
Pin 5	CTS - Clear to Send Signal from the modem to the terminal indicating ability to transmit data. An "on" is "Ready" and an "off" is "not ready."
Pin 6	DSR - Data Set Ready Signal from the modem to the terminal. An "on" condition indicates that the modem is ready.
Pin 7	SGND - Signal Ground
Pin 8	CD - Carrier Detect An "on" indicates reception of a carrier from the remote data set; "off" indicates no carrier is being received.
Pin 20	DTR - Data Terminal Ready "On" connects the communication equipment to the communications channel; "off" disconnects the communications equipment from the communications channel.
Pin 22	RI - Ring Indicator An "on" indicates that a ringing signal is being received on the communications channel.

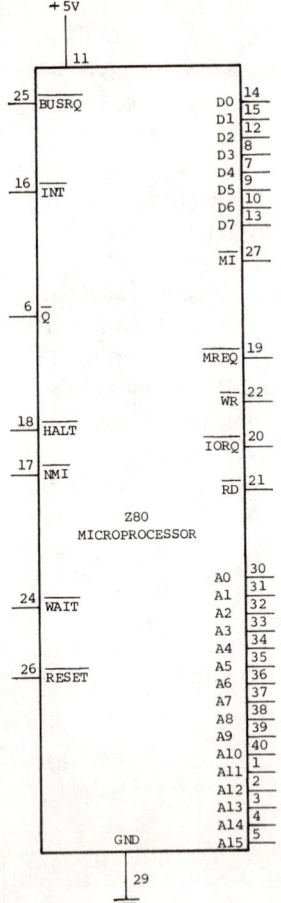

FIGURE 2-2
Z-80 pin configuration.

device or memory location, these control lines provide an essential coordinating function.

Figure 2.2. shows the pin configuration for the Z-80, and Table 2.2 lists the control signals used when communicating with external devices. The Z-80 belongs to the one-address architectural class of microprocessors; that is, most memory-related instructions reference a single memory location. While the computer is officially an 8-bit device, several instructions treat pairs of 8-bit registers as a single, 16-bit word. These 16-bit registers are advantageous for handling some complex calculations.

When the microprocessor is reading a data byte from memory, the address of the desired memory location is placed on the address bus. Information stored in that particular memory location is strobed onto the data bus and flows from

Signal Name	Description
A0	Address Output
A1	Address Output
A2	Address Output
A3	Address Output
A4	Address Output
A5	Address Output
A6	Address Output
A7	Address Output
D0	Bidirectional Data Bus
D1	Bidirectional Data Bus
D2	Bidirectional Data Bus
D3	Bidirectional Data Bus
D4	Bidirectional Data Bus
D5	Bidirectional Data Bus
D6	Bidirectional Data Bus
D7	Bidirectional Data Bus
MREQ	Memory Request
RD	Read
WR	Write
IORQ	Input/Output Request

TABLE 2-2 Microprocessor input/output. There are eight address lines which will be used to select a specific external device. There are eight bidirectional data lines which will carry data to and from the CPU and the external devices whether the CPU is going to send data or is expecting to receive data.

memory to a data register in the central processor. Data being written to memory is handled by a reversed set of operations.

The Z-80 has a specific set of instructions that are unique to input and output operations. The operation of these instructions is similar to that of the memory-referenced instructions, with the exception that a different set of control lines is used to indicate to external devices that the central processor wishes to communicate with them and not with the memory. The least significant 8-bits of the address bus are used to uniquely address 256 possible I/O ports. Various methods can be used to decode these lines to signal a specific device that it is being addressed. Figure 2.3 shows a simple but effective method for decoding the four least significant bits of the address bus into 16 unique control lines. For normal operation, the INHIBIT control line would remain low. Upon execution of an input or output command, a processor control signal (IN* or OUT*) would be connected to the STROBE control line, used to strobe the current contents of the address bus into the decoder. The decoded output would then be used to indicate to a specific external device that the data bus was available for its specific use. This particular circuit allows up to 16 devices to be uniquely addressed; if increased addressing capability is required, the circuit of Figure 2.4 can be used.

Four control signals that we will be particularly interested in keeping track of are MREQ*, I/O REQ*, RD*, and WR*. Any memory-referenced command is accompanied by the MREQ* line going to the low state; an I/O command is accompanied by the I/O REQ* line going to the low state. The central processor indicates to the external device whether a read or a write operation is occurring by causing either the RD* or the WR* line to go low. As you might have ex-

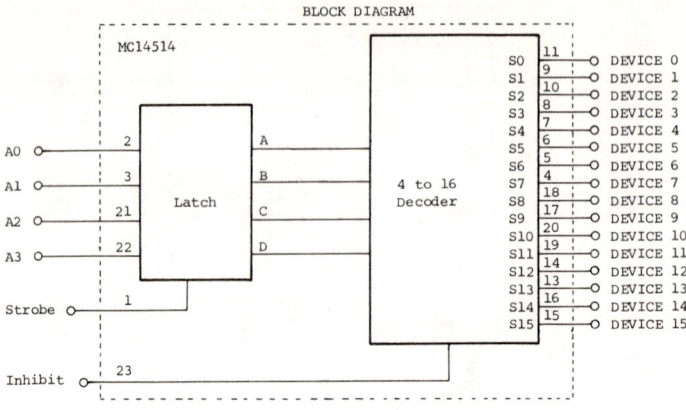

DECODE TRUTH TABLE (Strobe = 1)

INHIBIT	DATA INPUTS				SELECTED OUTPUT
	A3	A2	A1	A0	LOGIC "1"
0	0	0	0	0	Device 0
0	0	0	0	1	Device 1
0	0	0	1	0	Device 2
0	0	0	1	1	Device 3
0	0	1	0	0	Device 4
0	0	1	0	1	Device 5
0	0	1	1	0	Device 6
0	0	1	1	1	Device 7
0	1	0	0	0	Device 8
0	1	0	0	1	Device 9
0	1	0	1	0	Device 10
0	1	0	1	1	Device 11
0	1	1	0	0	Device 12
0	1	1	0	1	Device 13
0	1	1	1	0	Device 14
0	1	1	1	1	Device 15
1	X	X	X	X	All Outputs = 0

X = Don't Care

FIGURE 2-3 4-16 line address decoder. Each device is selected by a unique combination of the address lines A0-A3.

pected, when the RD* line goes low, the computer is transferring data from the external device to the central processor. Likewise, when the WR* line is low, the computer is transferring data from the central processor to the external device. Figure 2.5 shows how three of these control lines could be decoded to give signals that will assist us in controlling the flow of data to and from the computer. Fortunately, the designers of the Mod III have decoded these signals for us, making our life a little easier. Our strategy, as we design interface circuits, will be to use the address lines to select a particular device and to use the decoded control lines to tell the device whether the computer is going to send data to it or receive data from it.

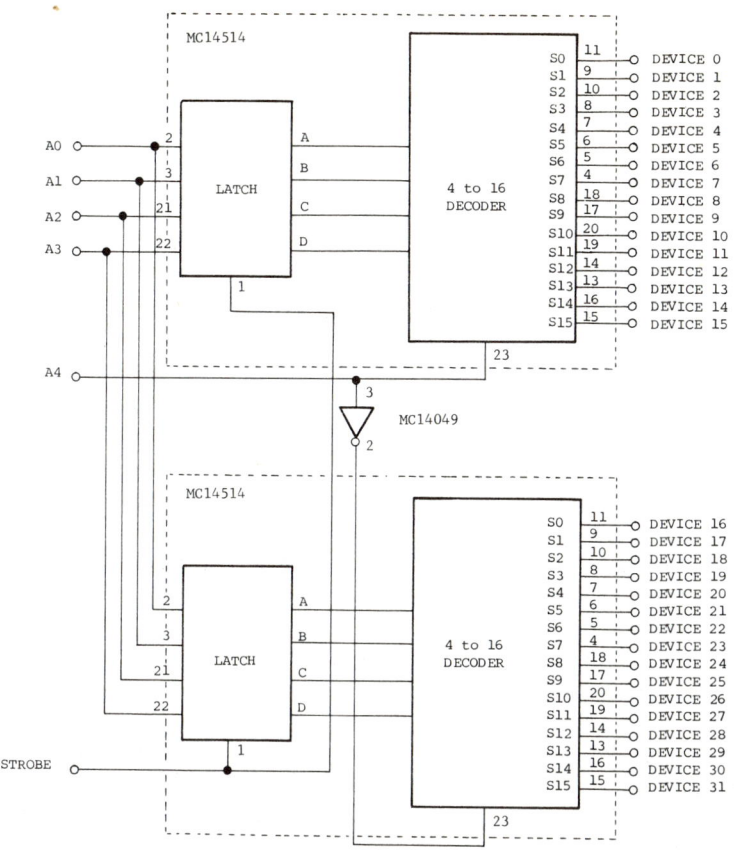

FIGURE 2-4
Extension of a 16 device address decoder into a 32 device decoder.

FIGURE 2-5 Control signals on the Z-80 microprocessor. The Z-80 uses a variety of control signals to keep data flowing at the right time and in the right direction. Three control signals are used as follows: the I/O REQ line goes to a low state when an input/output (I/O) operation is in progress; the RD line goes low when the processor is reading data from memory or from a peripheral device; the WR line goes low when the processor is writing data to memory or to a peripheral device. The RD and WR signals control the direction that data flows along the bidirectional data bus. Monitoring these three lines gives us all the information necessary to support I/O decoding functions.

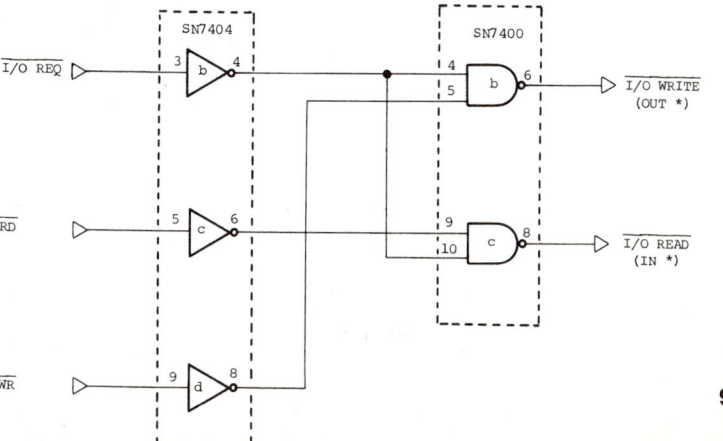

9

PARALLEL DATA FORMAT

Transmission and reception of data in a parallel format combines the advantages of high transfer rates and low cost. As mentioned earlier, parallel data transfer involves the mass movement of several bits of data at one time. It becomes a relatively straightforward task to construct both input and output ports since all the control, data, and address lines that we will need are available on the Model III I/O bus connector (Figure 2.6). Table 2.3 lists the signals appearing on this connector and their functions. Figures 2.7a and 2.7b show examples of practical circuits that could be connected directly to the I/O bus connector, providing one 8-bit, latched output port and one 8-bit input port. To access the I/O port bus, it is necessary to first perform the BASIC statement, OUT 236,16 or the assembly language command, OUT (OECH), 10H. After this, whenever you perform the BASIC statement, OUT N,D or the assembly language command, OUT (N), A, the following happens:

1. The device address (N) is strobed onto the address bus.
2. The contents of the accumulator (D) are strobed onto the data bus.

Since the data are valid for only a few clock cycles (perhaps 500 ns) a set of clocked flip-flops (IC3 and IC4) is provided so that the data are latched and consequently stable, until the next OUT command to this port is executed. The circuit works in the following manner:

1. Whenever address line A0 and A1 are high and low respectively and the OUT* line is low, an output strobe pulse will appear on pin #12 of IC1.
2. Whenever this strobed output pulse appears, the contents of the data bus will be transferred into the clocked flip-flops and will appear on the latched data output lines.
    will appear on the latched data output lines.

External devices transferring data into the computer can be connected directly to the data bus. But, to add an additional margin of safety (that is, to help keep you from "smoking" your computer), I have included a 3-state buffer. The 3-state buffer is used as a gate that allows signals from the peripheral device to be placed on the data bus at an appropriate time. The Model IIIrequires that the

FIGURE 2-6   Output pin configuration for the Model III I/O bus connector. Refer to Table 2-3 for a description of each pin.

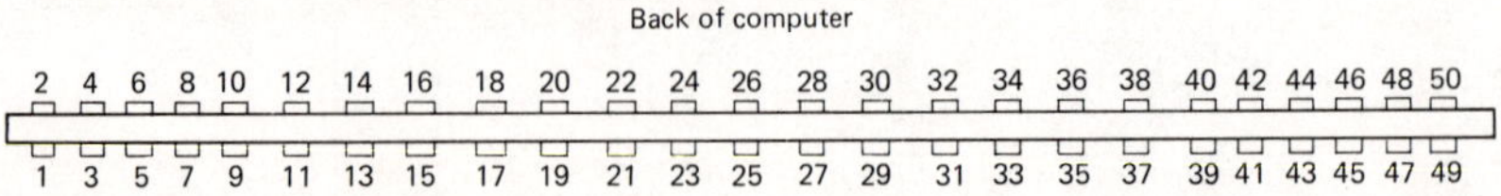

P/N	SIGNAL NAME	DESCRIPTION
1	D0	Bidirectional Data Bus
2	GND	Signal Ground
3	D1	Bidirectional Data Bus
4	GND	Signal Ground
5	D2	Bidirectional Data Bus
6	GND	Signal Ground
7	D3	Bidirectional Data Bus
8	GND	Signal Ground
9	D4	Bidirectional Data Bus
10	GND	Signal Ground
11	D5	Bidirectional Data Bus
12	GND	Signal Ground
13	D6	Bidirectional Data Bus
14	GND	Signal Ground
15	D7	Bidirectional Data Bus
16	GND	Signal Ground
17	A0	Address Output
18	GND	Signal Ground
19	A1	Address Output
20	GND	Signal Ground
21	A2	Address Output
22	GND	Signal Ground
23	A3	Address Output
24	GND	Signal Ground
25	A4	Address Output
26	GND	Signal Ground
27	A5	Address Output
28	GND	Signal Ground
29	A6	Address Output
30	GND	Signal Ground
31	A7	Address Output
32	GND	Signal Ground
33	IN*	Peripheral Read Strobe Output
34	GND	Signal Ground
35	OUT*	Peripheral Write Strobe Output
36	GND	Signal Ground
37	RESET*	System Reset
38	GND	Signal Ground
39	IOBUSINT*	Interrupt Input
40	GND	Signal Ground
41	IOBUSWAIT*	I/O Bus Wait
42	GND	Signal Ground
43	EXTIOSEL*	I/O Bus Select
44	GND	Signal ground
45	N.C.	No Connection
46	GND	Signal Ground
47	XMI*	Standard Z-80 Signal
48	GND	Signal Ground
49	IORQ*	Input/Output Request
50	GND	Signal Ground

NOTE: "*" means logical "0" true input or output

TABLE 2-3 Functional description of pins on the Model III I/O bus connector.

device being interfaced pull the EXTIOSEL* line (pin #43) down to a 0 during the execution of an IN command. This tells the bidirectional data bus to strobe data into the accumulator. To access the I/O port, it is necessary to first perform the BASIC statement, OUT 236,16 or the assembly language command, OUT (0ECH), 10H, After this, whenever you perform the BASIC statement, INP (N) or the assembly language command, IN A, (N), the following happens:

1. The device address (N) is strobed onto the address bus.
2. The contents of the data bus are strobed into the accumulator (A).

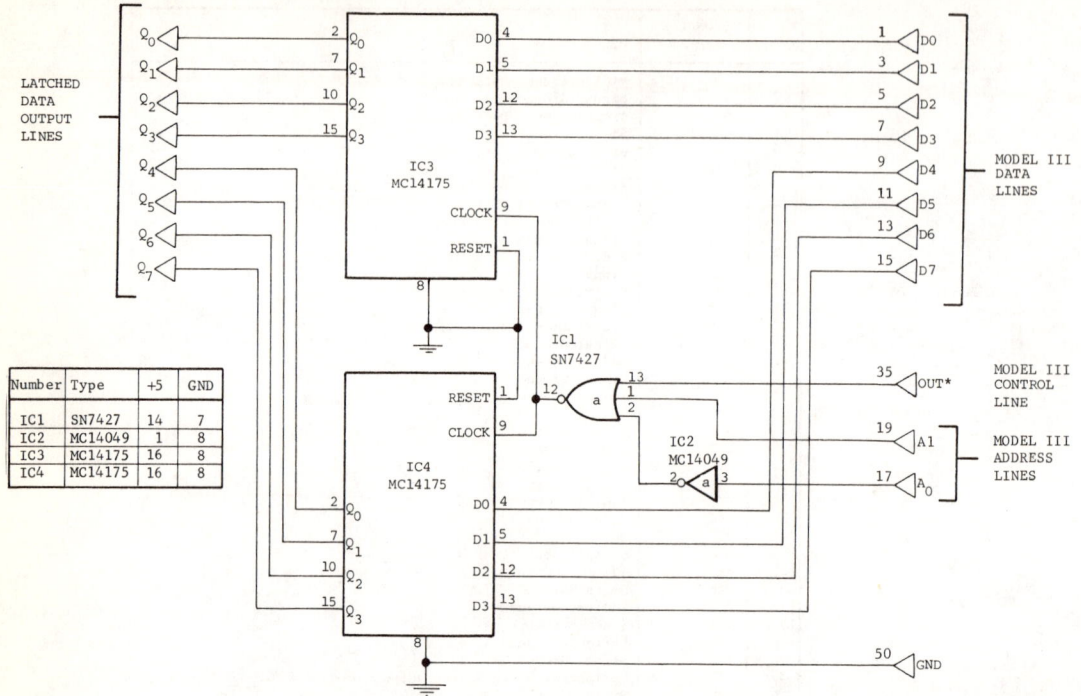

FIGURE 2-7a Circuit diagram of a typical parallel output port. Performing an OUT 236,16 to initialize the Model III I/O circuitry followed by an OUT 1,16 would cause the OUT* control line to go low, address lines A_0 and A_1 to go high and low respectively, and 16_{10} to be latched into the output register.

The circuit works in the following manner:

1. Whenever address line A0 and A1 are high and low respectively and the IN* is low, an input strobe pulse will appear on pin #12 of IC1.
2. Whenever this strobed input pulse appears, the 3-state buffer will connect the data input lines to the data bus.
3. The EXTIOSEL* line will go low, allowing the input data to be transferred into the accumulator.

SERIAL DATA FORMAT

When considering a computer interface project involving a fairly large distance between the computer and the device to be interfaced, we begin to encounter problems when trying to use a parallel data transfer scheme. Among the first of

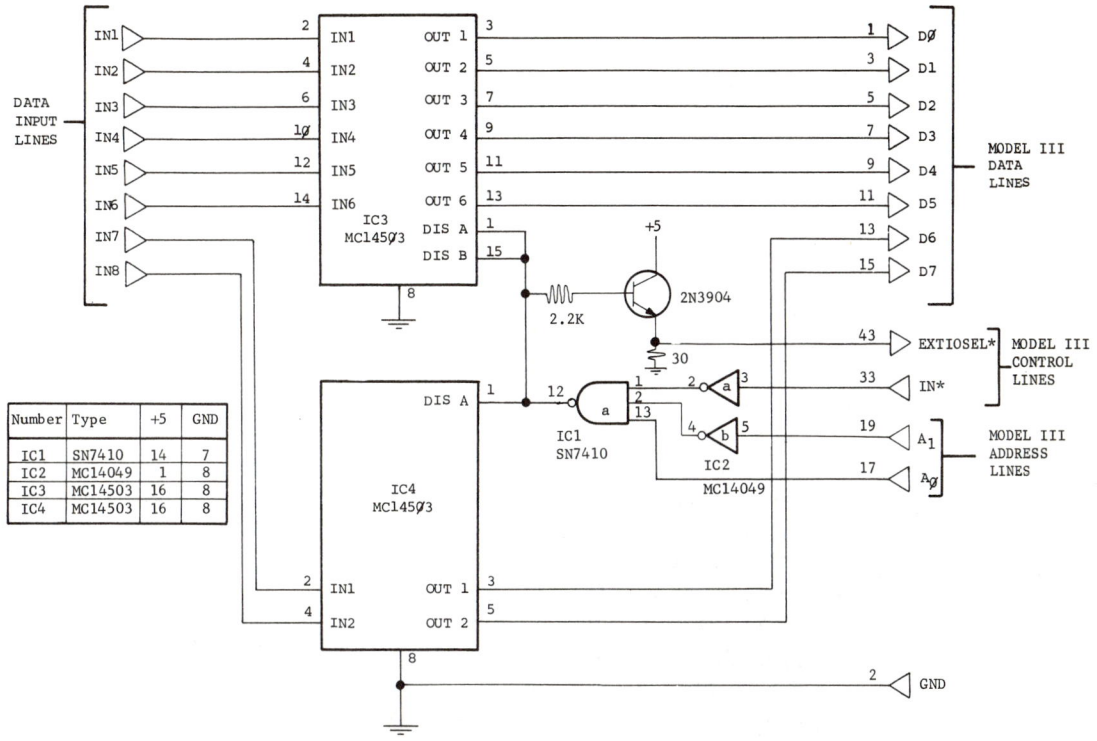

FIGURE 2-7b   Circuit diagram of a typical parallel input port. Performing an OUT 236,16 to initialize the Model III I/O circuitry followed by an INP (1) would cause the IN* control line to go low, address lines A_0 and A_1 to go high and low respectively, and the data on the input lines to be transferred into the accumulator.

these are the expense and inconvenience of running a multiconductor cable over some long distance. There is also the problem of the noise that gets into the data, control, and address lines. This noise can be reduced with filters, or current level signals can be used, but it is often more convenient to use a serial format for the transmission of control and data bits. With serial transmission, individual bits are transmitted over a pair of wires one bit at a time. The receiving device collects the bits and reconstructs them into a single computer word, which for the Model III is equal to 8-bits. Since the computer normally processes data in a parallel format, the transmitting device must perform a parallel-to-serial conversion, and the receiving device must perform a serial-to-parallel conversion.

Obviously, the transmission speed and the bit format must be well defined, and there must be some way to synchronize the serial bit flow so that the receiving device knows where each data word begins. The most common format for serial transmission is called *asynchronous-serial*. Because the data format is self-clocking, that is, it contains a special bit pattern that allows the receiving

13

device to know exactly where a new data word begins, the cable connecting a peripheral device with the computer needs only two signal lines and one ground line. Figure 2.8a shows the format for the transmission of a data word in an asynchronous-serial format. The START bit, a logic-1-to-logic-0 transition, is used to alert the receiving circuitry that a new data word is going to be sent. The receiver waits for one-half of a bit period and then samples the input again. If the input line is still a logic 1 or a logic 0, the receiver assumes it has detected a "real" start bit, and not a fluctuation due to noise on the line. The receiving device then waits one bit period and samples the input line to determine whether data bit 1 is a logic 1 or a logic 0. By periodically waiting one bit period and sampling the input line, the remainder of the data bits are obtained. The two STOP bits then signal the receiving device that it has reached the end of the data word. Having transferred the data word into the computer, the device starts looking for the next START bit.

Figure 2.8b shows the actual bit pattern that results when the data word 10011101 is transmitted. The asynchronous-serial protocol allows the use of either 5-, 6-, 7-, or 8-data bits along with either 1 or 2 STOP bits. The examples we will be using will be formatted so as to transmit and receive 1 START bit, 8 data bits, and 2 STOP bits. The bit transfer rate can be set to 110, 150, 300, 600, 1,200, 2,400, 4,800, and 9,600 bits per second (bps), the actual value depending on the application.

Figure 2.9 shows a circuit that converts TTL voltage levels to RS-232C voltage levels, and that can be used with the program shown in Listing 2.1 to accomplish a parallel-to-serial output. When an OUT (01),A machine language command is executed, the contents of the accumulator are latched into the output of the D-type flip-flop (IC2). Figure 2.10 shows a flow chart for the TTL to RS-232C program.

Figure 2.11 shows a circuit that can be used to convert RS-232C voltage

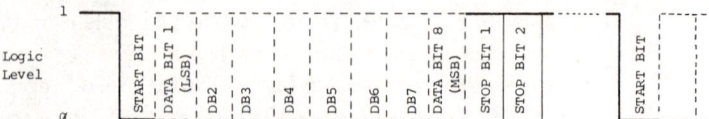

FIGURE 2-8a Typical asynchronous-serial bit pattern for the transmission of an 8-bit data word with 2 stop bits.

FIGURE 2-8b Logic levels plotted as a function of time during the asynchronous-serial transmission of the 8-bit data word, 10011101$_2$.

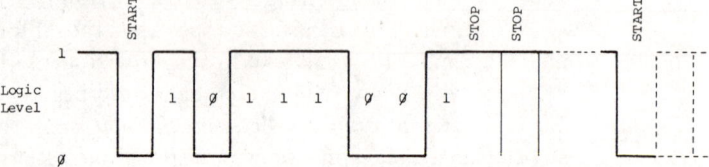

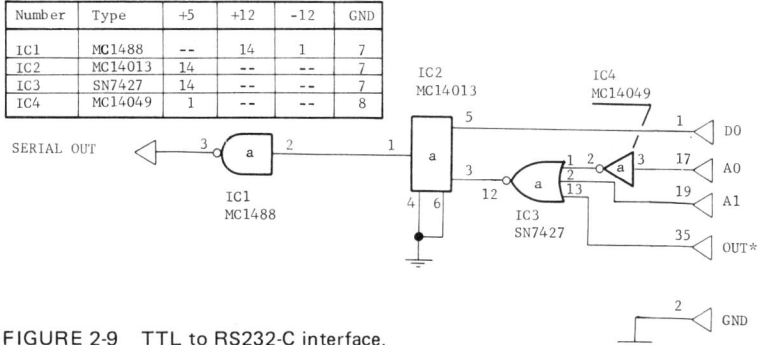

FIGURE 2-9 TTL to RS232-C interface.

levels to TTL levels, and that can be used with the program shown in Listing 2.2 to accomplish a serial-to-parallel conversion. When an IN A, (01) machine language command is executed, the voltage level appearing on the SERIAL IN line will be strobed into data bit D7 of the accumulator. Figure 2.12 shows a flow

LISTING 2-1 Subroutine for parallel-to-serial output. Program assumes that the character to be sent will be in the memory storage location labeled TEMP.

```
7F00            00120          ORG     7F00H
7F4F            00130   TEMP   EQU     7F4FH           ;CHARACTER STORAGE
7F00 F3         00140   RS     DI                      ;DISABLE INT
7F01 3A4F7F     00150          LD      A,(TEMP)        ;GET CHARACTER
7F04 1609       00160   SEND   LD      D,09H           ;1 START BIT, 8 DATA BITS
7F06 37         00170          SCF
7F07 3F         00180          CCF                     ;CLEAR CARRY (START BIT)
7F08 324F7F     00190   DATA   LD      (TEMP),A        ;SAVE DATA
7F0B DA187F     00200          JP      C,MARK          ;IF CARRY, SEND MARK
7F0E 3E01       00210          LD      A,01H
7F10 D301       00220          OUT     (01H),A         ;SEND SPACE
7F12 D4907F     00230          CALL    NC,DELAY        ;JUMP IF SPACE SENT
7F15 C31F7F     00240          JP      NEWD
7F18 3E00       00250   MARK   LD      A,00H
7F1A D301       00260          OUT     (01H),A         ;SEND A MARK
7F1C CD907F     00270          CALL    DELAY
7F1F 3A4F7F     00280   NEWD   LD      A,(TEMP)        ;GET DATA
7F22 1F         00290          RRA                     ;LSD INTO CARRY
7F23 15         00300          DEC     D
7F24 C2087F     00310          JP      NZ,DATA         ;JUMP IF ALL BITS NOT SENT
7F27 3E00       00320   STPBIT LD      A,00H
7F29 D301       00330          OUT     (01H),A         ;SEND MARK
7F2B CD907F     00340          CALL    DELAY
7F2E C9         00350          RET
7F90            00360          ORG     7F90H
7F90 0E02       00370   DELAY  LD      C,02H
7F92 3EE6       00380   DEL    LD      A,0E6H
7F94 3D         00390          DEC     A
7F95 C2947F     00400          JP      NZ,$-1
7F98 0D         00410          DEC     C
7F99 C2927F     00420          JP      NZ,DEL
7F9C C9         00430          RET
```

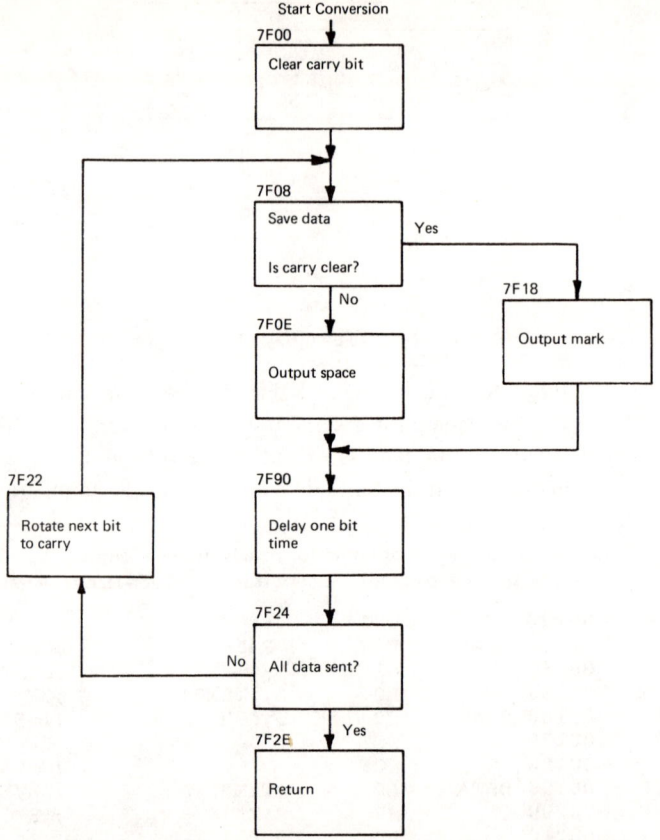

FIGURE 2-10   Flow chart for the TTL to RS232-C program.

LISTING 2-2   Subroutine for serial-to-parallel input. Program will display the input character on the video display.

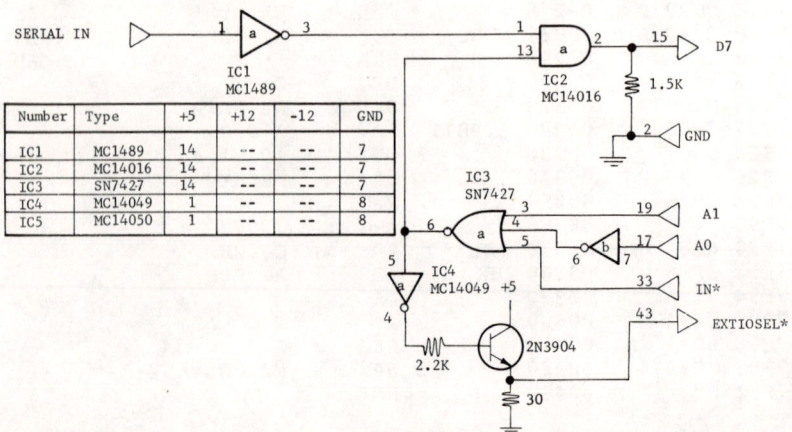

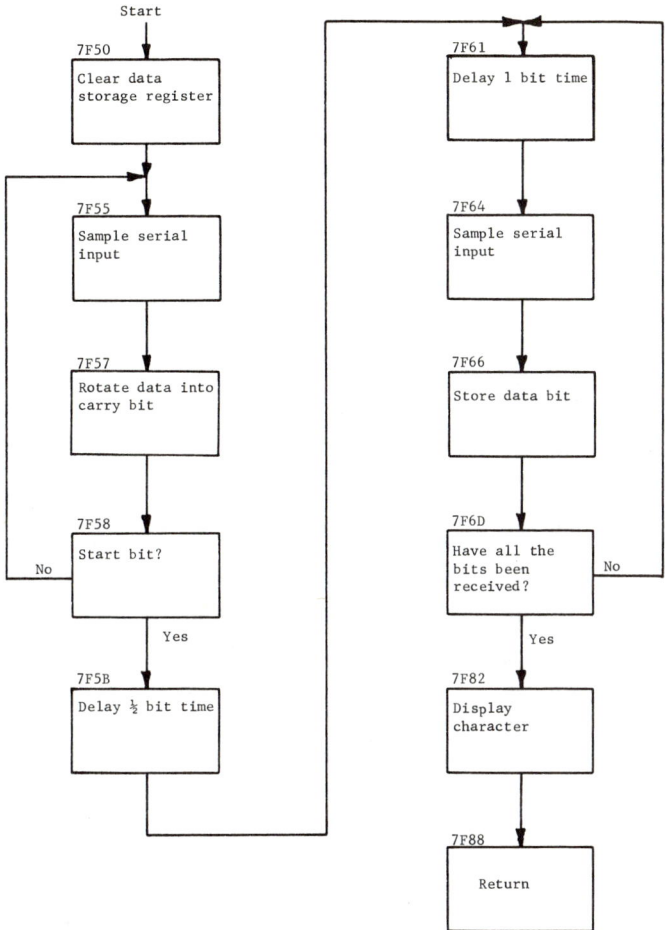

FIGURE 2-11 RS232-C to TTL interface.

chart for the RS-232C-to-TTL program. Timing for both subroutines results in a baud rate of 300 bps. The serial output subroutine (listing 2.1) expects the character that is to be sent to be stored in the memory location labeled TEMP. The serial input subroutine (Listing 2.2) will display the received character on the video display. We will put both of these circuits to use when we get to Chapter 5 and see how to use the Mod III in serial applications.

17

FIGURE 2-12 Flow chart for the RS232-C to TTL converter.

```
7F50             00360           ORG     7F50H
7F50 F3          00370 RECV      DI
7F51 0600        00380           LD      B,00H
7F53 1608        00390           LD      D,08H           ;8 DATA BITS
7F55 DB01        00400 SAMP      IN      A,(01H)         ;SAMPLE INPUT
7F57 17          00410           RLA                     ;ROTATE BIT INTO CARRY
7F58 DA507F      00420           JP      C,RECV
7F5B 3EE6        00430           LD      A,0E6H
7F5D 3D          00440           DEC     A
7F5E C25D7F      00450           JP      NZ,$-1
7F61 CD937F      00460 AGAIN     CALL    DELAY
7F64 DB01        00470           IN      A,(01H)
7F66 E680        00480           AND     80H             ;SAVE MSB
7F68 B0          00490           OR      B               ;ADD NEW BIT TO DATA
7F69 47          00500           LD      B,A
7F6A CB08        00510           RRC     B               ;ROTATE BITS
7F6C 15          00520           DEC     D
7F6D C2617F      00530           JP      NZ,AGAIN
7F70 CB10        00540           RL      B
7F72 78          00550           LD      A,B             ;TRANSFER DATA INTO ACC.
7F73 E67F        00560           AND     7FH
7F75 47          00570           LD      B,A
7F76 FE40        00580           CP      40H
7F78 CA507F      00590           JP      Z,RECV
7F7B 78          00600           LD      A,B
7F7C FE0D        00610           CP      0DH
7F7E CA507F      00620           JP      Z,RECV
7F81 78          00630 CR        LD      A,B
7F82 CD3300      00640           CALL    33H
7F85 C9          00650           RET
7F90             00660           ORG     7F90H
7F90 CD937F      00670           CALL    DELAY
7F93 0E02        00680 DELAY     LD      C,02H
7F95 3EE6        00690 DEL       LD      A,0E6H
7F97 3D          00700           DEC     A
7F98 C2977F      00710           JP      NZ,$-1
7F9B 0D          00720           DEC     C
7F9C C2957F      00730           JP      NZ,DEL
7F9F C9          00740           RET
```

SAMPLING THE EXTERNAL WORLD

Now that we have covered some background material on the operation of the Mod III computer, we can proceed to what I consider to be the "fun" part of computer operation—the part that involves the evaluation of a need, along with the construction of a circuit to meet that need. We will progress from examples that are very simple to examples that are somewhat complicated, with the confidence that, once you can build and use simple circuits, you will be able to build and use the more complicated ones. In Appendix A, I have made an appraisal, based on personal prejudice, of several construction techniques that you may want to consider, it may be to your advantage to review that material at this time.

STATUS OF A BINARY SIGNAL

For some applications we will want to be able to sample an input port to determine the status or state of an external device. For example, we might want to know whether a device was turned on, a valve open, or a switch closed. Figure 3.1 shows a schematic of a circuit that will allow you to test the state of six switches. When an X=INP (01) BASIC command is executed, a voltage level,

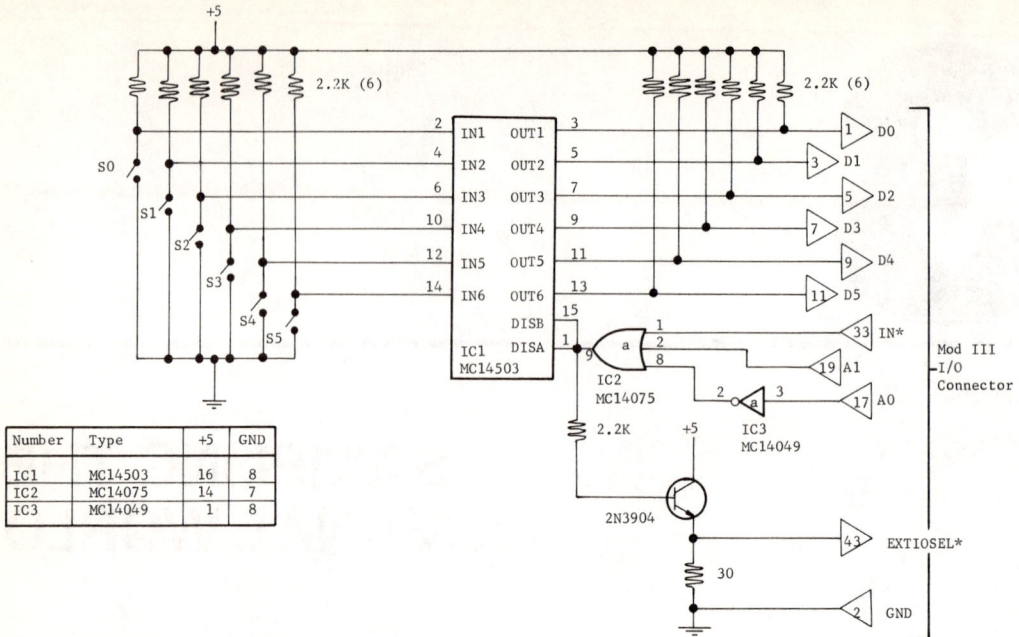

FIGURE 3-1   Schematic of switch status input port.

which is a function of whether each individual switch is open or closed, will be strobed into the computer. The variable X can then be decoded to determine the status of each switch.

You might use such a circuit for the external control of a program that is being executed, that is, to take an action that would be consistant with the state of the switch. The switches might be simple toggle switches mounted on a panel, or they might be relay switches associated with some automated process that you want to monitor.

Figure 3.2 shows a flow chart for a **BASIC** program that will test the status of each switch and display that status on the video display. Listing 3.1 shows the program with comments. This program is intended to be called as a subroutine, and it is set up so that, if the status has not changed, control will return to the calling routine.

While I have used mechanical toggle switches for this example, the application could be easily extended to:

1. water level sensing switches,
2. displacement sensing microswitches,
3. light-sensitive photoswitches,
4. temperature-sensitive, bimetalic switches, or
5. motor relay switches.

An advantage of using the computer to sense and respond to the status of a switch lies in its ability to be reprogrammed easily, when the application changes.

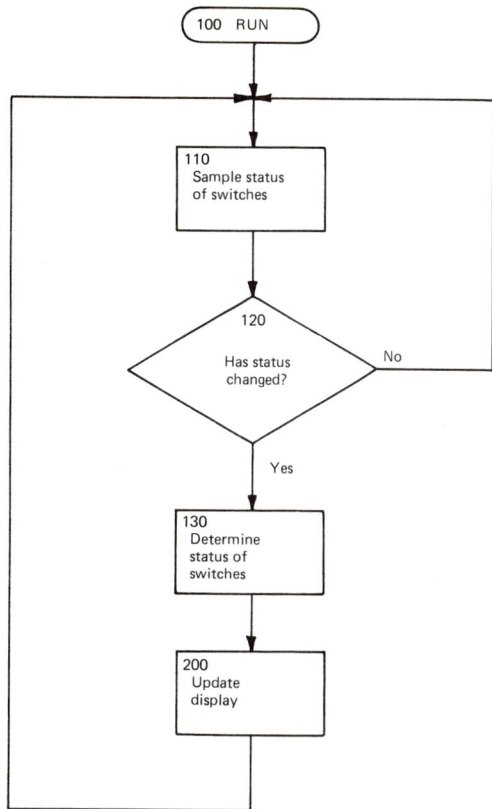

FIGURE 3-2 Flow chart of switch status program.

ANALOG-TO-DIGITAL CONVERSION

Background

In many applications we will want to have our computer system "measure" some parameter that varies as a function of time. In most cases, we will be using some type of transducer which takes a physical parameter such as temperature, pressure, strain, or position and converts it into an electrical voltage or current. While computers are quite proficient when handling binary voltages, they are not directly able to handle the type of analog voltages that come from the transducers we will be using. To resolve this problem we need only to build an interface called an *analog-to-digital (A/D) converter*. Our design criteria will be primarily concerned with determining appropriate values, based on our particular application, for resolution (dR), relative system error, and sampling frequency (F_S). We will be taking a look at three examples of A/D converters, which are very different in design, using separate and distinct processes to perform the analog-to-digital conversion. I will spend the rest of this section making general comments that will apply to each example, saving specific comments for the individual circuits.

LISTING 3-1 Basic program for determining and displaying switch status.

```
100 REM SWITCH STATUS ROUTINE
102 REM MOD III, R. HALLGREN, 6-10-81
104 X1=0
110 REM SAMPLE SWITCH STATUS
112 OUT 236,16
114 X=INP(01)
120 REM STATUS CHANGED?
122 IF X>127 THEN X=X-128
124 IF X>63 THEN X=X-64
126 IF X=X1 THEN GOTO 110
130 REM DETERMINE SWITCH STATUS
132 X1=X
134 IF X>31 THEN D5=1:X=X-32:GOTO 140
136 D5=0
140 IF X>15 THEN D4=1:X=X-16:GOTO 150
142 D4=0
150 IF X>7 THEN D3=1:X=X-8:GOTO 160
152 D3=0
160 IF X>3 THEN D2=1:X=X-4:GOTO 170
162 D2=0
170 IF X>1 THEN D1=1:X=X-2:GOTO 180
172 D1=0
180 IF X=1 THEN D0=1:GOTO 184
182 D0=0
184 IF D0=1 THEN D0$="ON"
185 IF D0=0 THEN D0$="OFF"
186 IF D1=1 THEN D1$="ON"
187 IF D1=0 THEN D1$="OFF"
188 IF D2=1 THEN D2$="ON"
189 IF D2=0 THEN D2$="OFF"
190 IF D3=1 THEN D3$="ON"
191 IF D3=0 THEN D3$="OFF"
192 IF D4=1 THEN D4$="ON"
193 IF D4=0 THEN D4$="OFF"
194 IF D5=1 THEN D5$="ON"
195 IF D5=0 THEN D5$="OFF"
200 REM UPDATE DISPLAY
210 CLS
212 PRINT CHR$(23)
220 PRINT "******************************"
222 PRINT "*"
226 PRINT "*      SWITCH S0 IS ";D0$;"
228 PRINT "*"
230 PRINT "*      SWITCH S1 IS ";D1$;"
232 PRINT "*"
234 PRINT "*      SWITCH S2 IS ";D2$;"
236 PRINT "*"
238 PRINT "*      SWITCH S3 IS ";D3$;"
240 PRINT "*"
242 PRINT "*      SWITCH S4 IS ";D4$;"
244 PRINT "*"
246 PRINT "*      SWITCH S5 IS ";D5$;"
248 PRINT "*"
250 PRINT "******************************"
299 GOTO 110
```

For our purposes, we define an *analog signal* as being generally smooth, continuous, and analytical. Examples are the output voltage from a pressure transducer, the output voltage from some analytical instrument, and the voltage resulting from some physiological phenomenon such as the electrocardiogram. We shall define a *discrete signal* as one that is constrained to specific voltage levels; where the interval between levels is determined by dividing the maximum voltage range (V_{max}) by the number of possible intervals (k). Consequently, any analog voltage within the maximum voltage range can be represented as a discrete quantity, the magnitude being equal to some multiple of dR, where dR is defined by equation 3.1:

$$dR = \frac{V_{max}}{k} \qquad (3.1)$$

Resolution

The function of an A/D converter is to transform an analog quantity into a digital quantity, which can then be handled by a computer. This transformation usually involves sampling the continuous voltage, representing the voltage as a discrete value, and then formatting this quantity so that the computer can process it. An example of a signal represented in both continuous and discrete forms is shown in Figure 3.3. In general, we will assume that y-axis values depend on x-axis values such that y can be expressed as some function of x.

$$y = f(x) \qquad (3.2)$$

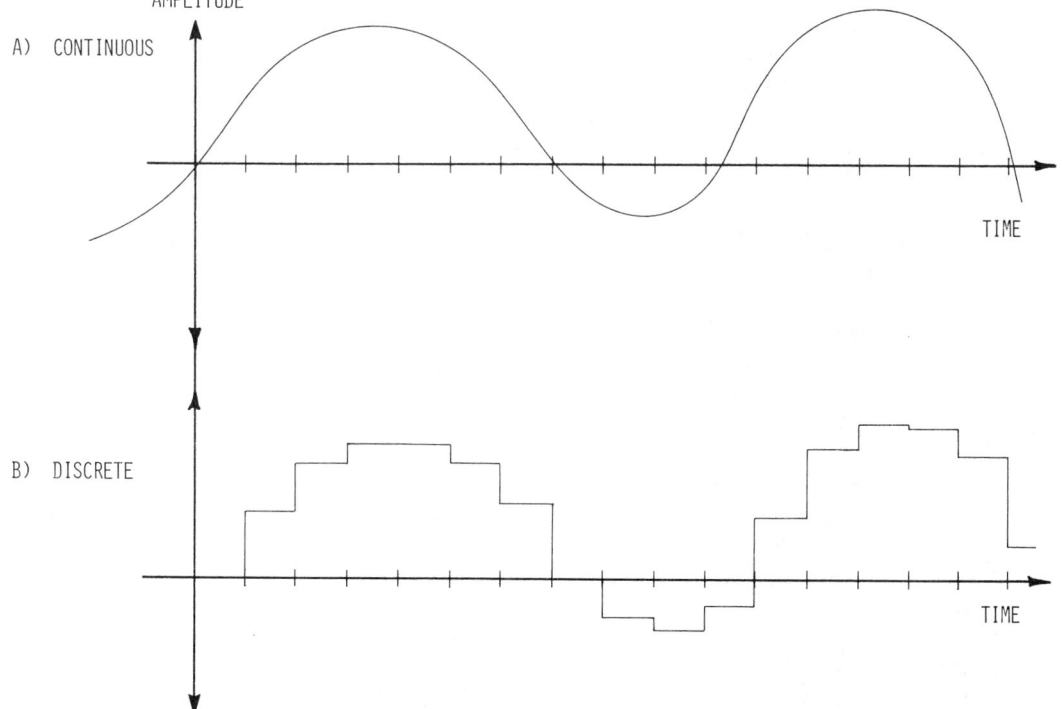

FIGURE 3-3 Continuous and discrete waveforms.

Resolution, as we will be using the term, is related to our ability to distinguish between two voltages having magnitudes that are very close together. The smallest magnitude difference that we can detect will define the resolution of our system. For each of the analog-to-digital systems which we will discuss, the resolution will be equal to the magnitude of a unit change in the least significant digit of the output of the converter.

Relative System Error

Accuracy is related to our ability to determine the actual value of an unknown input voltage. Accuracy will be a function of the linearity of the system, gain and offset errors, resolution, and the magnitude of the signal that we are measuring. In general, most system inaccuracy usually results from the necessity to represent the analog voltage by a discrete quantity. If we assume that this is true for the circuits that we will be building, we can define *relative system error* as the ratio of system resolution to the magnitude of the voltage being measured. Obviously, for a given system, relative system error will be minimized when the unknown input voltage is equal to the maximun value that the system can handle.

Sampling Theory

Since an A/D converter samples an input signal sequentially with respect to time, the output voltage (y) can be expressed in the form $y(1), y(2), \ldots, y(n)$, where n is equal to the sample number. The rate (F_S) at which we sample the input signal determines the maximum frequency component that can theoretically be detected. The sampling rate can be expressed as a function of the time between samples by the following equation:

$$F_S = \frac{1}{dt} \text{ samples per second}$$

where $dt = [t(n+1) - t(n)]$

The *sampling theorem* states that we should sample at a rate that is at least twice the frequency (F_C) of the highest significant frequency component present in the waveform that we will be digitizing. In practice, the sampling frequency should be ten times F_C to allow you to reconstruct the complex waveform from the digital data without having to be overimaginative. Remember that you can always throw out data points once you have them if you find that you have sampled at a higher rate than necessary.

In some applications, you might not be interested in the highest frequency component that was contained in the input signal, but only in lower frequency components. *Aliasing,* which is the impersonation of a low-frequency signal by a high-frequency signal, results from choosing a sampling rate that is

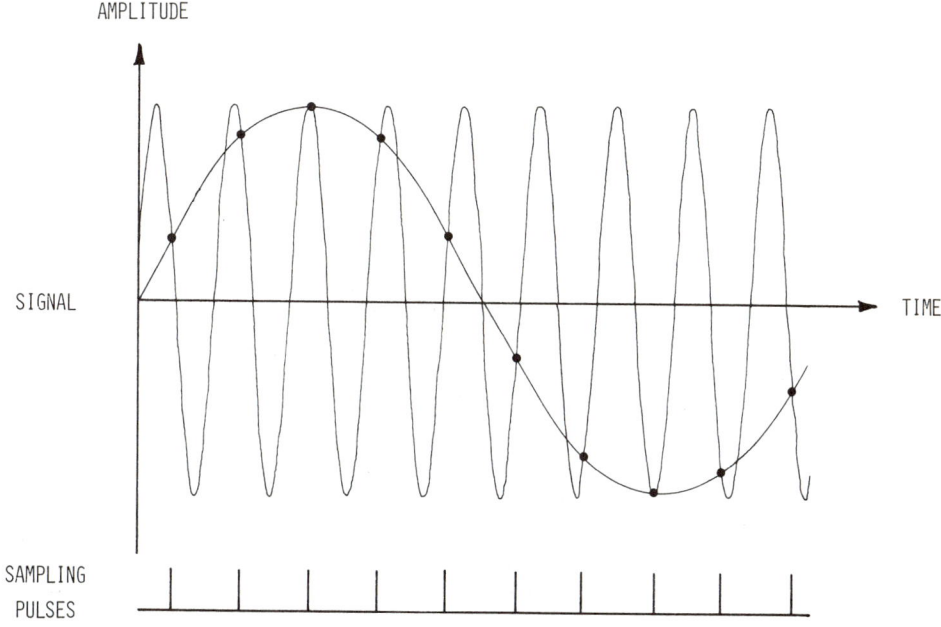

FIGURE 3-4 Aliasing error caused by inadequate sampling rate.

too low for the frequency components that make up the input signal. Figure 3.4 shows how a relatively high-frequency signal and a relatively low-frequency signal can share identical sample points, thus making it impossible to differentiate between the two signals. For applications where you will be sampling at rates that are less than $2F_C$, you must insert a low-pass filter at the input of the A/D converter to limit the frequency content and to ensure faithful reproduction of the input signal.

Low-Cost Analog Interface

Devices that interface analog signals to the digital world of computers can range from complex and expensive analog-to-digital converters to inexpensive circuits that provide an indirect measurement of an analog quantity. We are going to look at a device that actually measures resistance, but that can be used to indirectly measure analog quantities. This device is inexpensive in terms of cost, construction time, and skill involved, but the sacrifice for these positive qualities comes in terms of accuracy and stability. In spite of these limitations, the device will be adequate for interpreting the position of a joystick, for measuring the resistance of a thermistor, or for gauging other slowly varying physical quantities that can be related to a change in resistance.

Many applications, towards which we can direct our attention, require only the ability to measure the value of a resistance. For example:

1. The joystick, which is so often used with arcade-type games, is made up of two potentiometers that relate the position of a level to a value of resistance. Successfully interfacing a joystick to the Mod III will allow you to control the position of a point on the video display. If you are blessed with a large amount of talent and time, you may want to develop a space war game. In such a game the joystick might control the throttle of your craft. Pulling back slows the spaceship down, while pushing forward moves you ahead at increasing speed.
2. Thermistors are usually constructed from temperature-sensitive resistors that have been selected to vary in a predictable manner as a function of temperature. Incorporating one of these inexpensive devices in the following circuitry will allow you to monitor and record the ambient temperature of your greenhouse. With a little initiative, you should be able to control the speed of a fan in order to maintain the temperature within acceptable limits.
3. A wind direction indicator could be constructed from a potentiometer and a movable vane. Connected to the analog interface, it would allow you to convert the physical quantity of wind direction into a value of resistance, which could then be displayed as wind direction on the video display.
4. A float could be mechanically attached to a potentiometer to allow the computer to monitor the level of some fluid within a container.

Figure 3.5 shows a simple circuit that we are going to use as an example of how to interface a joystick to the Mod III. The main component in this circuit is the NE556 dual timer, configured as two monostable multivibrators. If you provide a monostable multivibrator with a trigger signal, you will find that the output will go high for a period of time that depends on the ratio of a resistor/capacitor combination. If the value of capacitance is fixed, and if the joystick potentiometer is used for the resistor, the duration of the output pulse will be proportional to the position of the joystick lever.

Normally, the 556 will initiate an output pulse on the high-to-low transition of an input trigger signal. For the device to function properly, it is necessary to return the trigger input to its normal high state before the output can "timeout." In other words, before the output can return to the low state, the trigger input must have returned to the high state. The 556 has provision for resetting its output before it would normally timeout; this feature is not required for this project, and consequently the reset line has been tied to +5V. Executing an OUT(01),A machine language command causes a trigger signal to be applied to both of the NE556 timers. By executing a machine language INA,(01), the output of timer #1 (ICIa) will be strobed into data bit D0 of the accumulator, and the output of timer #2 (IC1b) will be strobed into data bit D1 of the accumula-

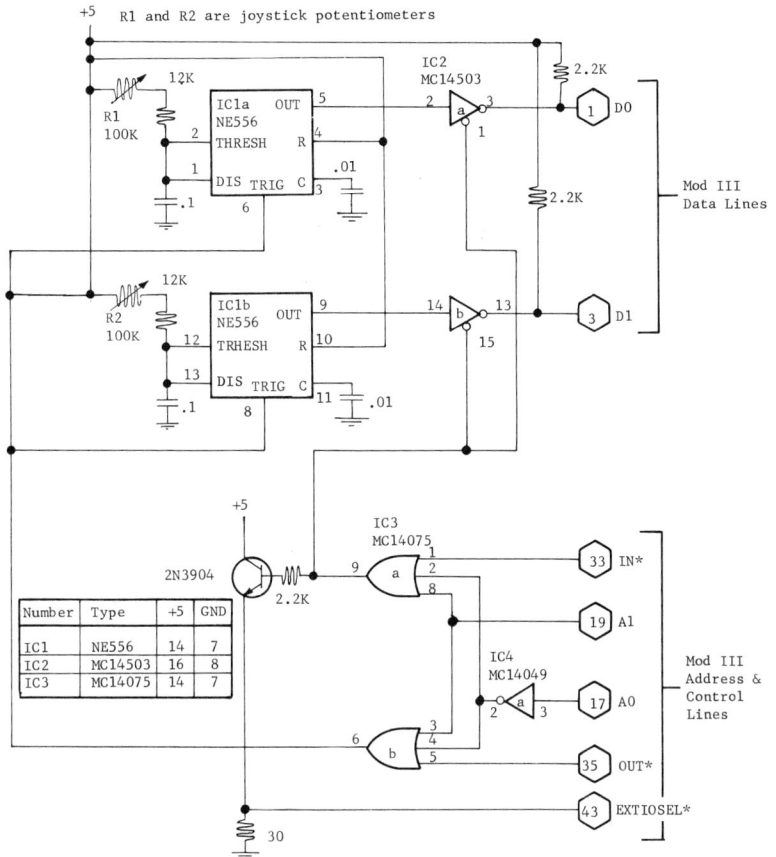

FIGURE 3-5 Joystick interface circuit for the Mod III.

tor. Both of these bits can be tested to determine when the respective timer outputs return to the 0 state.

I decided to use the joysticks that are available for the Radio Shack Color Computer. If you decide to do the same, you will need to make an internal modification to the wiring connections. Figure 3.6a shows the original connections, and Figure 3.6b shows the modified connections. Connect the black wire to the +5V supply, connect the yellow wire to the 12K resistor connected to pin #2 on IC1, and connect the green wire to the 12K resistor connected to pin #12 on IC1.

Once you have constructed the interface, connect it to the computer and perform the following tests to make sure that it is working correctly:

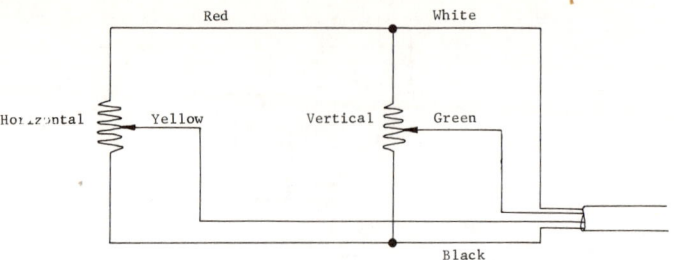

FIGURE 3-6a Schematic of Radio Shack Color Computer joystick.

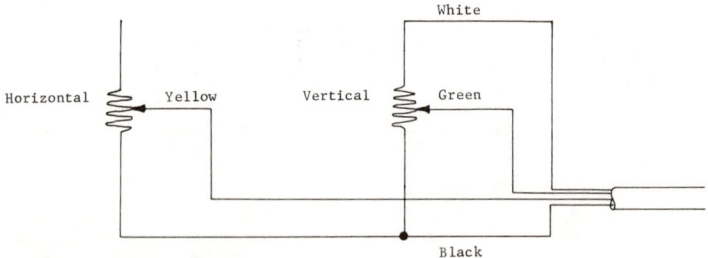

FIGURE 3-6b Schematic of modified joystick.

1. If you execute the following BASIC statements, the output of each timer should go to +5V and return to 0V.
   100 OUT 236,16
   110 OUT 1,0
2. The time that the signal is at +5V should be a function of the joystick position. If you execute the following BASIC statements, you should be able to see the output pulse width change as you move the joystick.
   100 OUT 236,16
   110 OUT 1,0
   120 GOTO 100

Figure 3.7 shows the flow chart for the software driver and Listing 3.2 shows the actual program with comments. The software is very straightforward. Upon entering the subroutine, the I/O bus is initialized and both timers are triggered. The program then samples the output of each timer and increments a count held in separate registers if the respective output is high. After both of the monostable multivibrators have timed out, the program stores the respective counts and returns to the main program.

Figure 3.8 shows the flow chart for a demonstration program written in BASIC, and Listing 3.3 shows the actual program with comments. The BASIC routine first loads the machine language routine by using the READ and POKE statements. Next the machine language routine is called to determine the position

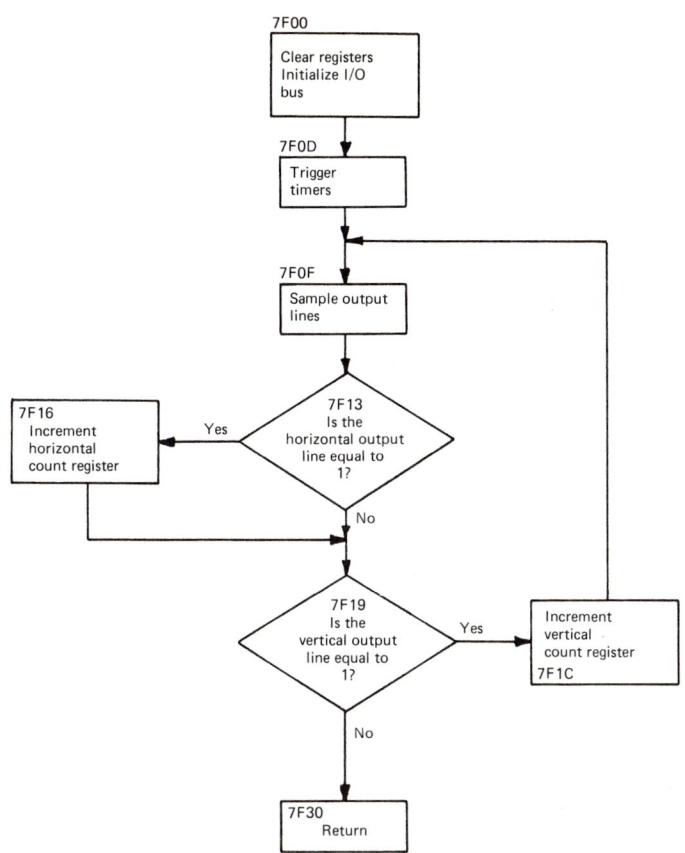

FIGURE 3-7
Flowchart for the machine language program for the joystick interface.

LISTING 3-2 Machine language program with comments.

```
                00100  ;R. HALLGREN
                00110  ;MOD III, JOYSTICK INTERFACE, 6-15-81
7F00            00120         ORG     7F00H
7FA0            00130  HORIZ  EQU     7FA0H           ;HORIZONTAL POSITION
7FA2            00140  VERT   EQU     7FA2H           ;VERTICAL POSITION
7F00 F3         00150  START  DI
7F01 3E10       00160         LD      A,10H
7F03 D3EC       00170         OUT     (0ECH),A        ;INITIALIZE I/O
7F05 210000     00180  TRIG   LD      HL,00H          ;CLEAR HL
7F08 010000     00190         LD      BC,00H          ;CLEAR BC
7F0B 3E00       00200         LD      A,00H
7F0D D301       00210         OUT     (01H),A         ;TRIGGER MONOSTABLE
7F0F DB01       00220  INPUT  IN      A,(01)          ;READ POTENTIOMETERS
7F11 CB47       00230         BIT     0,A             ;TEST LSB
7F13 CA207F     00240         JP      Z,TWO
7F16 23         00250         INC     HL
7F17 CB4F       00260         BIT     1,A
7F19 CA0F7F     00270         JP      Z,INPUT
7F1C 03         00280         INC     BC
7F1D C30F7F     00290         JP      INPUT
7F20 CB4F       00300  TWO    BIT     1,A
7F22 CA297F     00310         JP      Z,BACK
7F25 03         00320         INC     BC
7F26 C30F7F     00330         JP      INPUT
7F29 22A07F     00340  BACK   LD      (HORIZ),HL
7F2C ED43A27F   00350         LD      (VERT),BC
7F30 C9         00360         RET
```

29

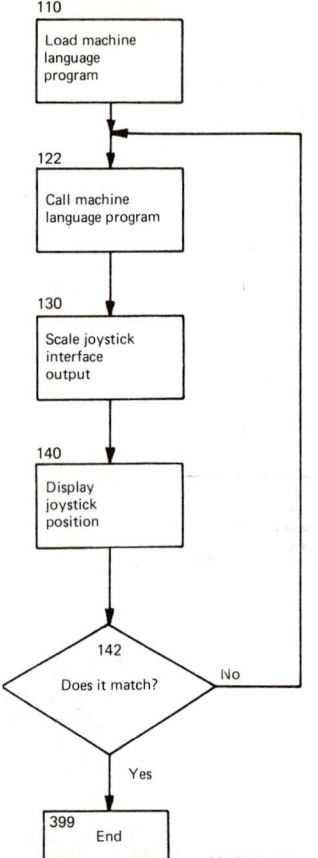

FIGURE 3-8
Flowchart for the BASIC program for the joystick demonstration.

of the joystick potentiometers. Upon returning from the machine language routine, the potentiometer position is converted into a graphic location on the video display and a point is plotted. The demonstration program then checks to see if the position of the joystick matches the position of a flashing point on the screen. If the points match, execution is terminated. If the points do not match, the program returns to sample the joystick position. Load and execute the demonstration program. Move the joystick point around until the points match to see if the interface hardware and software are working correctly.

Resolution of the interface is a function of the efficiency of the timing loop. Its accuracy is a function of the time that can be spent sampling the joysticks. The timing loops have been optimized to the point of providing good accuracy and repeatability. When you incorporate the interface into your projects, you will want to maximize the amount of time that can be spent sam-

LISTING 3-3 BASIC program with comments.

```
100 REM JOYSTICK ROUTINE
102 REM R. HALLGREN, MOD III, 6-15-81
110 FOR I=1 TO 49:READ K:POKE (32511+I),K:NEXT I
112 J=0:K=0
114 CLS
120 POKE 16526,0:POKE 16527,127
122 X=USR(0)
130 X=256*PEEK(32673)+PEEK(32672)
132 Y=256*PEEK(32675)+PEEK(32674)
134 X=X/5
135 Y=Y/12
136 RESET(J,K)
140 SET(X,Y)
141 J=X:K=Y
142 IF POINT(64,24) THEN GOTO 300
150 GOSUB 200
152 GOTO 122
199 END
200 REM DEMONSTRATION ROUTINE
210 SET(64,24):FOR I=1 TO 20:NEXT I:RESET(64,24)
299 RETURN
300 REM POINT HAS BEEN COVERED
310 CLS
312 PRINT CHR$(23)
314 PRINT @512,"YOU HAVE MATCHED THE POINT"
316 PRINT "";"";"";""
399 END
10000 DATA 243,62,16,211,236,33,0,0,1,0,0,62,0,211,1,219,1,203,71,202
10001 DATA 32,127,35,203,79,202,15,127,3,195,15,127,203,79
10002 DATA 202,41,127,3,195,15,127,34,160,127,237,67,162,127,201
```

pling the position of the joysticks so that the time lag between when you move the joystick and when the movement is displayed is minimized.

I have included a game program to serve as a simple illustration of the usage of joysticks. Listing 3.4 shows this program.

8-Bit, Low-Speed A/D Converter

The MC14433 (Motorola Semiconductor Products Inc., Austin, Texas 78721) is a high-performance, low-power, 3-1/2 digit A/D converter combining both linear CMOS and digital CMOS circuitry. This device, when combined with two external resistors and two external capacitors, forms a dual-slope A/D converter featuring automatic zero correction and automatic polarity. By using an indirect conversion technique, the dual-slope system realizes some of the following positive characteristics:

1. Conversion accuracy is independent of component values and the clock frequency.

LISTING 3-4   Joystick game.

```
100 REM JOYSTICK ROUTINE
102 REM R. HALLGREN, MOD III, 6-15-81
104 RESTORE
110 FOR I=1 TO 49:READ K:POKE (32511+I),K:NEXT I
112 J=0:K=0
114 CLS
116 PRINT @256,"MATCH THE JOYSTICK POSITION WITH THE FLASHING SQUARE"
117 GOSUB 120
118 GOTO 142
120 POKE 16526,0:POKE 16527,127
122 X=USR(0)
130 X=256*PEEK(32673)+PEEK(32672)
132 Y=256*PEEK(32675)+PEEK(32674)
134 X=INT(X/5)
135 Y=INT(Y/12)
136 RESET(J,K)
141 RETURN
142 SET(X,Y)
144 J=X:K=Y
145 IF POINT(20,24) THEN GOTO 300
150 GOSUB 200
152 GOTO 117
199 END
200 REM INITIAL JOYSTICK POSITION
210 SET(20,24):FOR I=1 TO 20:NEXT I:RESET(20,24)
299 RETURN
300 REM GAME GRAPHICS
310 CLS
320 FOR I=1 TO 768:PRINT @(127+I),CHR$(191);CHR$(28):NEXT I
330 FOR I=1 TO 15:RESET(15+I,24):RESET(15+I,23):RESET(15+I,25):NEXT I
334 FOR I=1 TO 10:RESET(30,22+I):RESET(31,22+I):NEXT I
336 FOR I=1 TO 4:RESET(29+I,34):RESET(29+I,35):RESET(29+I,33):NEXT I
338 FOR I=1 TO 10:RESET(34,36-I):RESET(35,36-I):RESET(36,36-I):NEXT I
340 FOR I=1 TO 20:RESET(35+I,26):NEXT I
342 FOR I=1 TO 12:RESET(54,25+I):RESET(55,25+I):RESET(56,25+I):NEXT I
344 FOR I=1 TO 30:RESET(53+I,38):RESET(53+I,37):NEXT I
346 FOR I=1 TO 20:RESET(83,39-I):RESET(84,39-I):NEXT I
348 FOR I=1 TO 5:RESET(82+I,19):NEXT I
400 REM START GAME
412 X=USR(0)
420 GOSUB 120
430 IF POINT(X,Y) THEN GOTO 800
432 SET(X,Y)
434 J=X:K=Y
450 GOTO 420
800 REM HIT THE SIDE OF THE WALL
810 IF X=88 THEN GOTO 900
812 CLS:PRINT CHR$(23)
820 PRINT "TOO BAD!!!"
821 PRINT ""
822 PRINT "YOU ONLY MADE IT TO SQUARE ";INT(X)
824 PRINT "":PRINT ""
826 PRINT "WANT TO TRY AGAIN?"
830 PRINT "PRESS Y IF YES, N IF NO"
832 K$=INKEY$
834 IF K$="N" THEN END
```

```
836 IF K$="Y" THEN GOTO 100
838 GOTO 832
900 REM FINISHED
910 CLS
929 PRINT CHR$(23)
940 PRINT @512,"YOU MADE IT ALL THE WAY"
950 PRINT ""
960 PRINT "WANT TO PLAY AGAIN?"
970 PRINT "PRESS Y IF YES, N IF NO"
972 K$=INKEY$
980 IF K$="N" THEN END
982 IF K$="Y" THEN GOTO 100
984 GOTO 972
999 END
10000 DATA 243,62,16,211,236,33,0,0,1,0,0,62,0,211,1,219,1,203,71,202
10001 DATA 32,127,35,203,79,202,15,127,3,195,15,127,203,79
10002 DATA 202,41,127,3,195,15,127,34,160,127,237,67,162,127,201
```

2. Differential linearity is excellent.
3. The integration process provides rejection of high-frquency noise and averages of small voltage changes that may occur during the conversion process.

The main disadvantage to the dual-slope technique is that the analog-to-digital conversion process takes a relatively long time, consequently limiting the sampling rate. In spite of this drawback, the device is ideal for digital voltmeters, digital thermometers, and other such devices not requiring sampling rates over 100 samples per second.

Figure 3.9 has been included to help you understand the dual-slope conversion process. The actual configuration of the analog circuitry depends on the polarity of the input voltage during the previous conversion cycle, and it is automatically switched by the internal logic circuits. I have chosen to show the analog circuit configuration that would be used when a negative voltage is connected to the input. When performing an A/D conversion, the MC14433 internal control logic first connects the unknown input voltage to the input of an integrator for a fixed period of time determined by an internal clock. (Figure 3.10 shows a plot of the integrator output as a function of time.) This results in the voltage across the integrator capacitor increasing to a value that is proportional to the input voltage averaged over the time interval that the input is connected. At the end of this interval, the input to the integrator is switched from the unknown voltage to a reference voltage. The purpose of the reference voltage is to cause the integrator capacitor to discharge at a known rate while the counter keeps track of the lengh of time it takes the voltage to return to 0. Note that the count associated with a given input voltage is a function of the reference voltage and the ratio of the time that it takes to charge and discharge the integrator capacitor. In summary, the MC14433 uses a *ratiometric measurement scheme* that produces an output reading that is a function of the

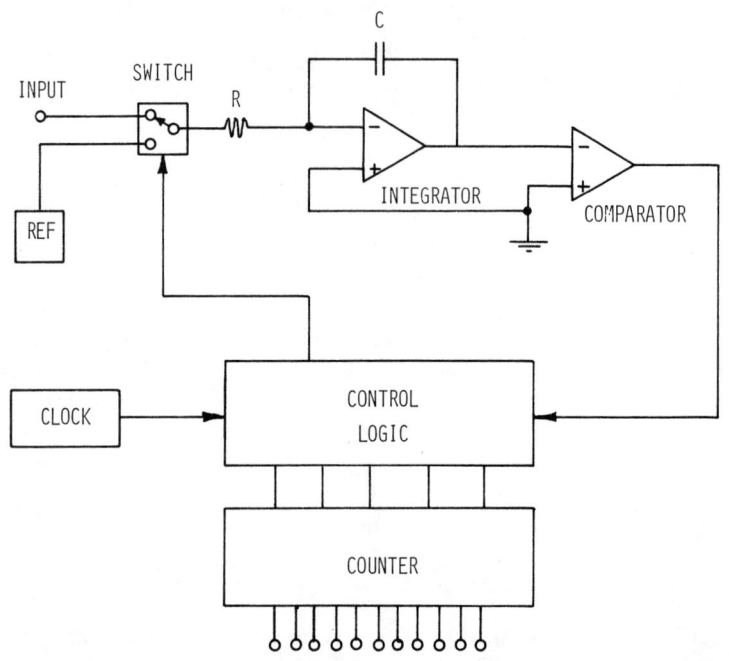

FIGURE 3-9 Simplified block diagram for a typical dual slope A/D converter.

FIGURE 3-10 Integrator output plotted as a function of time for two different input voltages converted by the dual slope process.

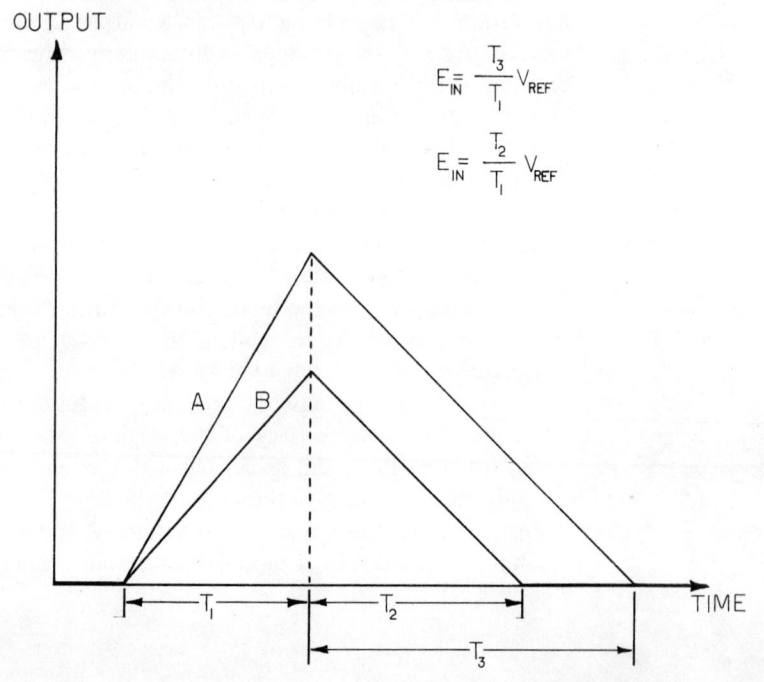

$$E_{IN} = \frac{T_3}{T_1} V_{REF}$$

$$E_{IN} = \frac{T_2}{T_1} V_{REF}$$

ratio of the unknown input voltage to the reference voltage, where a ratio of 1 equals a count of 1.999. Obviously, absolute stability of the reference voltage is necessary to ensure reproducible readings from sample to sample.

Figure 3.11 shows the actual block diagram and Figure 3.12 shows the pin assignment for the MC14433. This integrated circuit operates from standard 5-V positive (pin #24) and 5-V negative (pin #12) supplies. (See Appendix C for power supply circuit configurations.) The absolute value of the input voltage can vary between 0 and 1.999V. If the magnitude of the input voltage is greater than the upper limit of 1.999V, you can use the voltage divider circuit shown in Figure 3.13 to reduce the voltage to an acceptable value. On the other hand, if the input voltage is less than 0.2V, you will achieve greater accuracy by using a circuit similar to the one shown in Figure 3.14 to increase the magnitude of the input voltage. Appendix B has been included to explain the operation of amplifier circuits such as the one shown in this figure. The frequency of the internal system clock of the MC14433 is controlled by the selection of the resistor connected between pins #10 and #11. Figure 3.15 shows typical values for the frequency as a function of resistance, and the following equation relates the conversion rate (samples per second) to the clock frequency:

FIGURE 3-11   Block diagram of the Motorola MC 14433 3½ digit A/D converter.

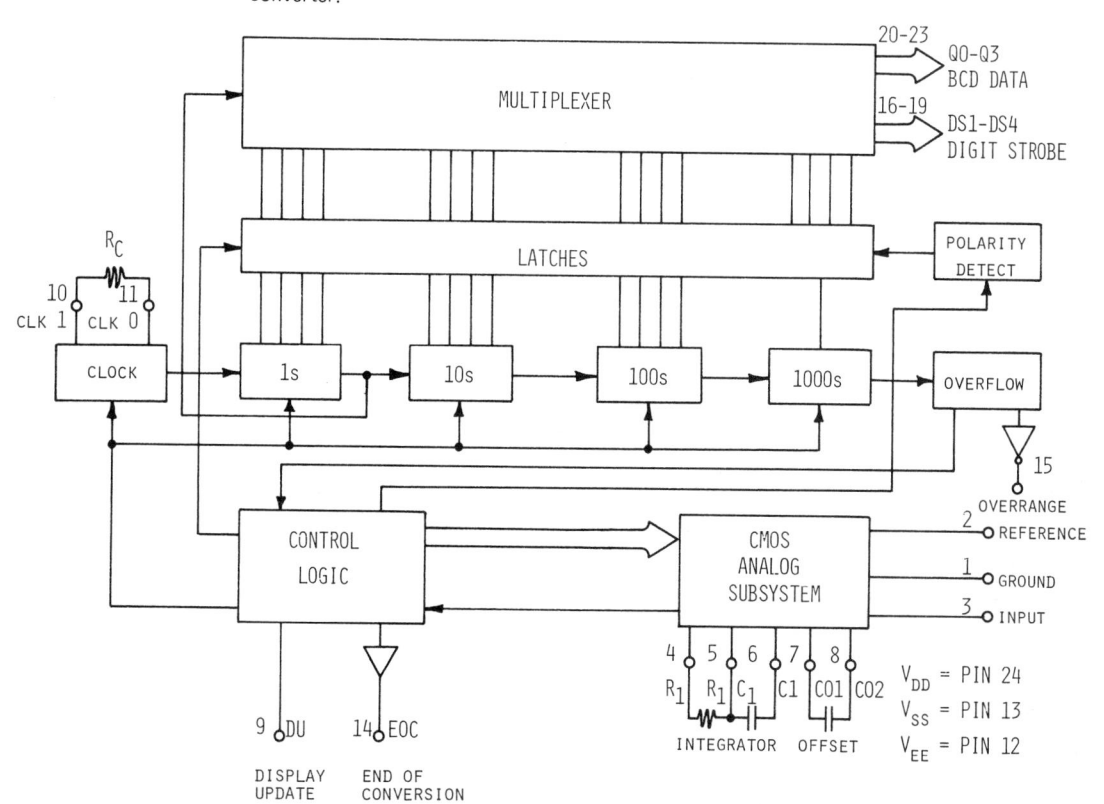

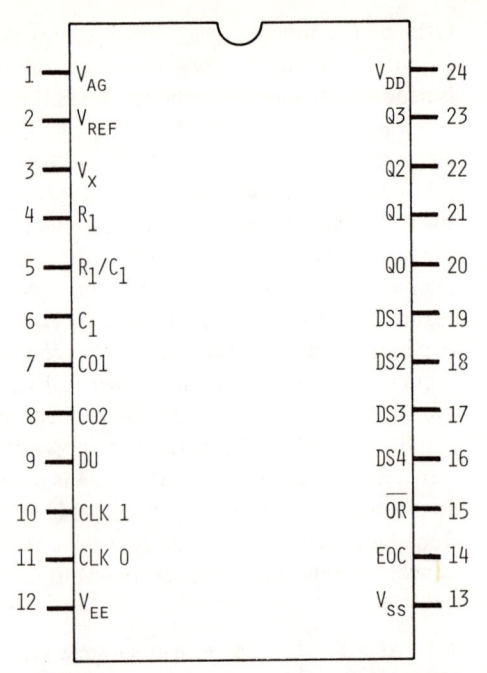

```
 1 ─ V_AG        V_DD ─ 24
 2 ─ V_REF        Q3  ─ 23
 3 ─ V_X          Q2  ─ 22
 4 ─ R_1          Q1  ─ 21
 5 ─ R_1/C_1      Q0  ─ 20
 6 ─ C_1          DS1 ─ 19
 7 ─ CO1          DS2 ─ 18
 8 ─ CO2          DS3 ─ 17
 9 ─ DU           DS4 ─ 16
10 ─ CLK 1        OR  ─ 15
11 ─ CLK 0        EOC ─ 14
12 ─ V_EE         V_SS ─ 13
```

FIGURE 3-12 Pin assignment for the MC14433.

$$V_{OUT} = \frac{R_2}{R_1 + R_2} V_{IN}$$

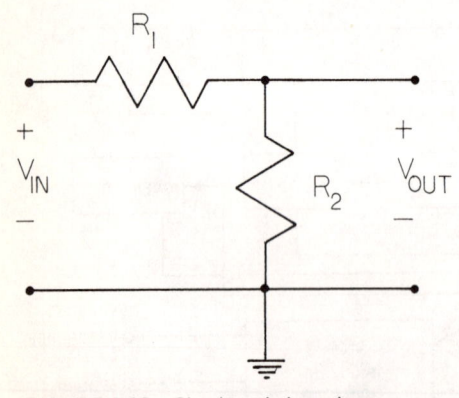

FIGURE 3-13 Simple resistive voltage divider network.

FIGURE 3-14 Simple noninverting amplifier.

$$V_{OUT} = \left[1 + \frac{R_2}{R_1}\right] V_{IN}$$

36

$$\text{Conversion rate} = \frac{\text{Clock frequency}}{16,400}$$

The normal operation of the MC14433 permits the conversion of an analog signal to a digital signal on a continuous basis, but the results of each conversion are transferred to the output latches only when an appropriate logic pulse is applied to the DISPLAY UPDATE (DU) (pin #9) control line. We can control this transfer of data by providing a positive going pulse to the DU line prior to the ramp-down segment of the conversion cycle. The data that are strobed into the output latches will then be equal to the digital quantity that was obtained from the last A/D conversion.

During the time that the conversion is being performed, the status line, END OF CONVERSION (EOC) (pin #14), is low indicating that the converter is busy. Upon completion of the conversion cycle, this line produces a pulse whose width is equal to one-half of the period of the system clock. When this output is wired directly into the DU input, the result of every conversion is

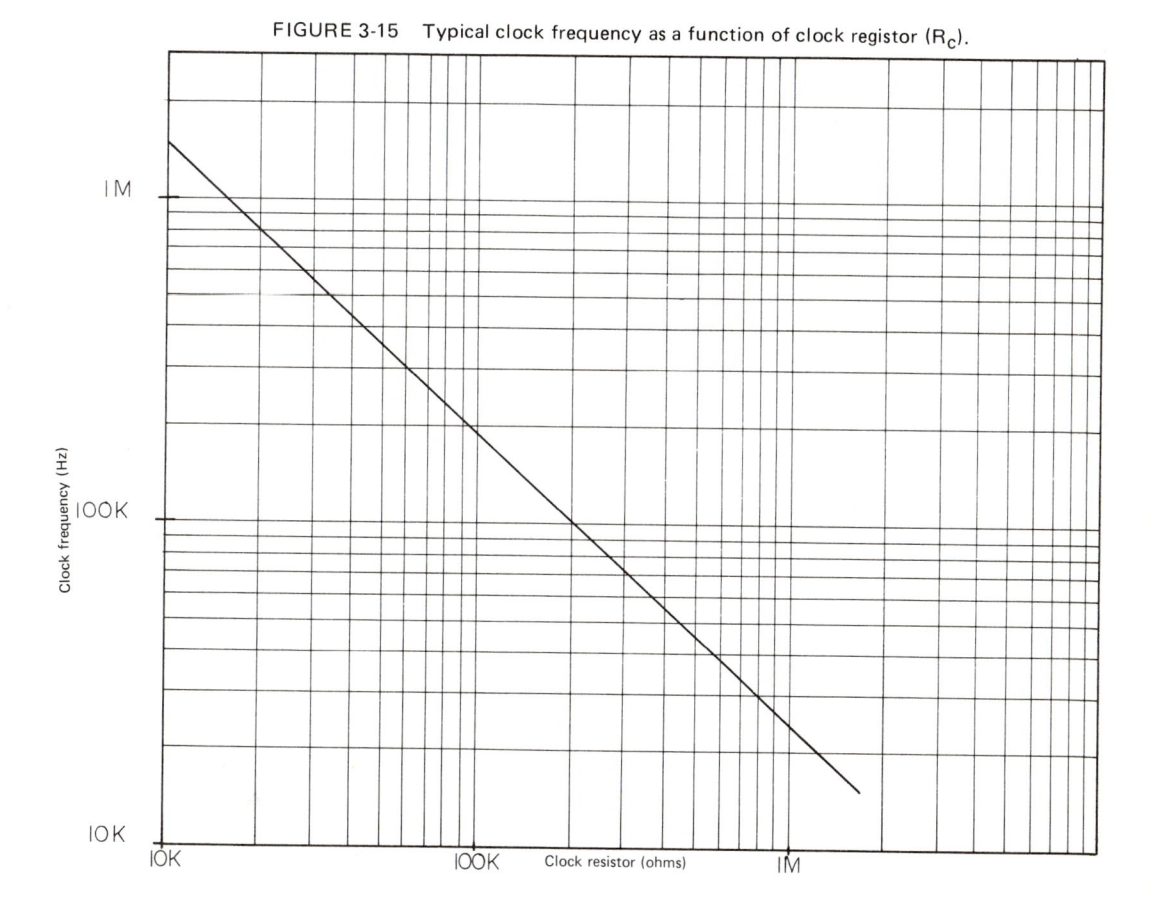

FIGURE 3-15 Typical clock frequency as a function of clock registor (R_c).

strobed into the output latches. I will use the EOC status line to indicate to the computer when a conversion has been completed, and consequently when new data have been strobed into the output latches.

The result of an analog-to-digital conversion is contained in the internal output latches in a binary format. However, the data are sent to the external world over the data lines (pins #20−#23) in a multiplexed, BCD format. Eight bits of information are used to transfer the results of a conversion. The four most significant bits (pins #16−#19) contain the code for a particular digit, and the four least significant bits (pins #20−#23) contain the binary value of the digit that is selected. The digit select output lines (pins #16−#19) go high when the respective digit is selected, and the data lines then contain the value of the selected digit. The digit select timing sequence is arranged so that the most significant digit (MSD) (½ digit) is selected immediately after an EOC pulse. The remaining digits are sequenced as shown in Figure 3.16. When the MSD is multiplexed, the data lines contain not only the value of that digit but also coded information relating to overrrange, underrange, and polarity as shown in Table 3.1.

Figure 3.17 shows the low-speed, A/D converter circuit configured for the Model III. The Model III uses a port-based addressing scheme, which allows it to specify up to a maximum of 256 unique I/O address locations that the central processor can address. The least significant 8 bits of the address bus are used to specify the port. The IN* and OUT* control lines determine whether an input or an output operation is occurring, and the data bus is used to pass information back and forth between the converter and the computer.

FIGURE 3-16   Digit select timing diagram for the MC14433.

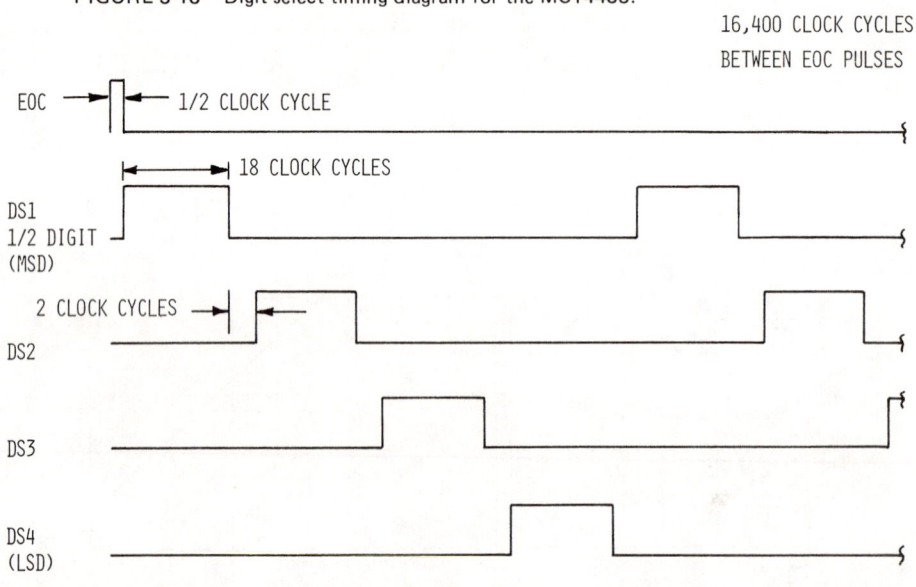

Coded Condition of MSD	Q3	Q2	Q1	Q0	BCD to 6 Segment Decoding	
+0	1	1	1	0	Blank	
-0	1	0	1	0	Blank	
+0 UR	1	1	1	1	Blank	
-0 UR	1	0	1	1	Blank	
+1	0	1	0	0	4 → 1	Hook up
-1	0	0	0	0	0 → 1	only seg b
+1 OR	0	1	1	1	7 → 1	and c to
-1 OR	0	0	1	1	3 → 1	MCD

Notes for Truth Table

Q3 - ½ digit, low for "1", high for "0"
Q2 - Polarity: "1" = positive, "0" = negative
Q0 - Out of range condition exists if Q0 = 1. When used in conjunction with Q3 the type of out of range condition is indicated, i.e., Q3 = 0 → OR or Q3 = 1 → UR.

The overrange indication (Q3 = 0 and Q0 = 1) occurs when the count is greater than 1999, e.g., 1.999 V for a reference of 2.000 V. The underrange indication, useful for autoranging circuits, occurs when the count is less than 180, e.g., 0.180 V for a reference of 2.000 V.

TABLE 3-1 Truth table showing the information format on the multiplexed data lines during selection of DS1.

Looking at the upper portion of Figure 3.17, you will see the MC14433 A/D converter. The clock resistor (RC) has been selected, and the EOC and DU control lines connected together so that 15 conversions per second are being performed on a continuous basis. All data and status lines to the TRS-80 are isolated through the MC14503 3-state buffers (IC7 and IC8). IC4, configured as an R/S flip-flop that is initially reset by the computer, is set by the MC14433 after an analog-to-digital conversion has been completed. When the TRS-80 senses this change in status, it starts the decoding and data transfer process. The Z-80 processor speed is high enough to enable one conversion to be decoded and stored before another conversion is initiated. A stable reference voltage source is obtained from the output of the Analog Devices AD580 voltage regulator (IC6).

The right, lower section of Figure 3.17 shows the control logic that is used to coordinate the transfer of signals to and from the computer. The least significant 3 bits of the address bus are decoded by IC1 and are used for on-board addressing. By executing an OUT (02H,A machine language command, the status control line (SC) is forced high, resetting IC4. Performing an IN A, (01H) maching language command transfers the end of conversion (EOC) and overrange (OR) status information into the accumulator. Performing an IN A, (03H) machine language command transfers the digit select code and the binary-coded decimal (BCD) value of the selected digit into the accumulator.

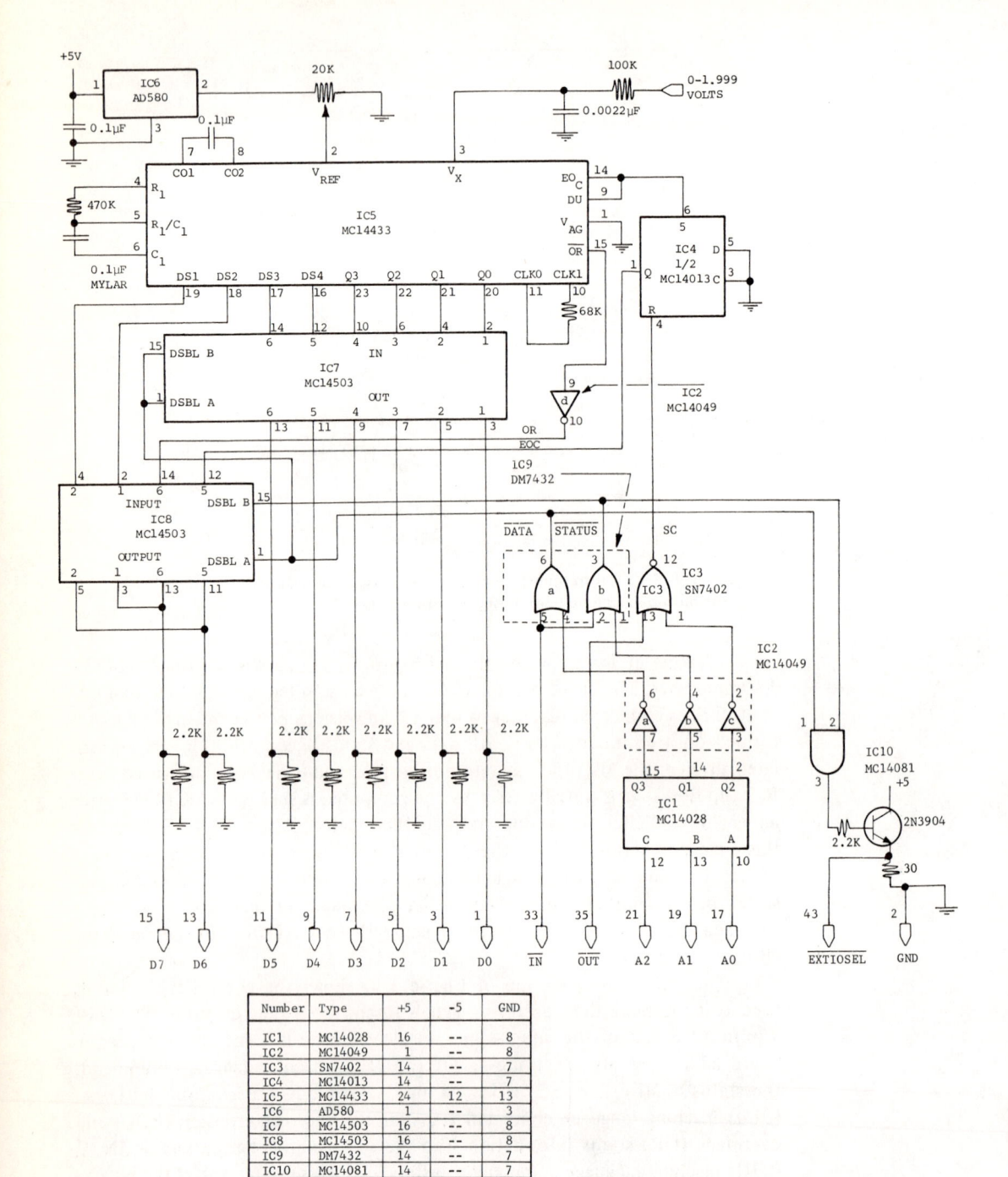

FIGURE 3-17 Schematic diagram of the low speed analog-to-digital converter.

The software portion of the low-speed A/D converter has been divided into two parts:

1. A machine language routine was written to control the MC14433, and to provide the high-speed transfer of data from the MC14433 to a specific location in computer memory.
2. A TRS-80, Model III BASIC routine was written to take the data in memory and format it into a voltage that can be displayed as a decimal quantity on the video display.

Figure 3.18 shows the flow chart of the machine language program, and Listing 3.5 shows the coded program with comments. Upon entering the subroutine, the end of conversion (EOC) flip-flop is reset, and the program loops until

FIGURE 3-18 Flow chart for the machine language program #1.

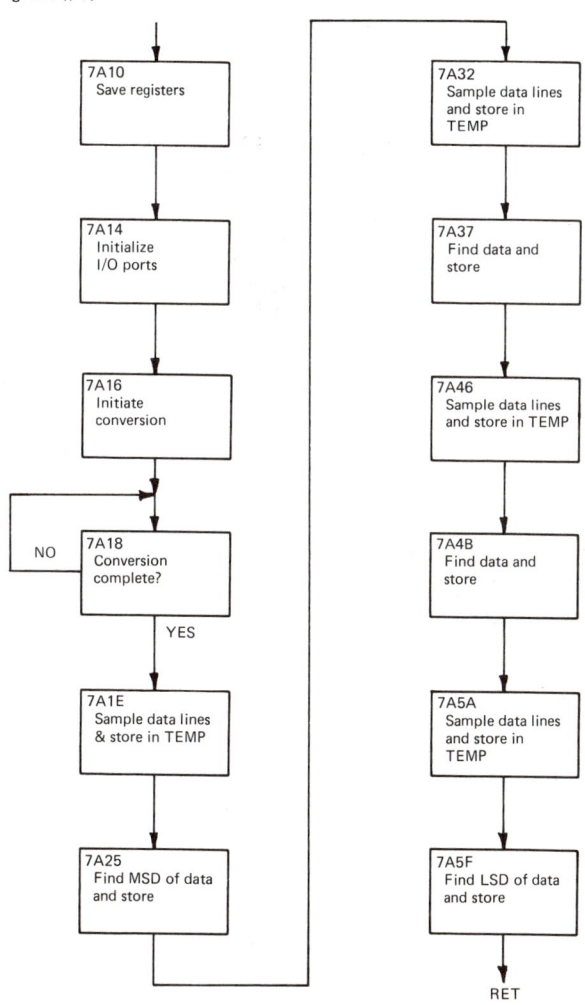

```
7A10                         7A32
Save registers               Sample data lines
                             and store in
                             TEMP

7A14                         7A37
Initialize                   Find data and
I/O ports                    store

7A16                         7A46
Initiate                     Sample data lines
conversion                   and store in TEMP

7A18                         7A4B
NO  Conversion               Find data and
    complete?                store
    YES

7A1E                         7A5A
Sample data lines            Sample data lines
& store in TEMP              and store in
                             TEMP

7A25                         7A5F
Find MSD of data             Find LSD of data
and store                    and store

                             RET
```

LISTING 3-5 Machine language program #1 for the low speed A/D converter.

```
                  00100  ;LOWSPEED A/D CONVERTER #1, SINGLE SAMPLE
                  00110  ;CALL FROM BASIC PROGRAM
                  00120  ;R. HALLGREN
7A00              00130  D1      EQU     7A00H           ;MOST SIGNIFICANT DIGIT
7A01              00140  D2      EQU     7A01H
7A02              00150  D3      EQU     7A02H
7A03              00160  D4      EQU     7A03H           ;LEAST SIGNIFICANT DIGIT
7A04              00170  TEMP    EQU     7A04H           ;TEMPERARY DATA STORAGE
7A10              00180          ORG     7A10H           ;INTERRUPT ENTRY POINT
7A10 08           00190  CONVRT  EX      AF,AF'
7A11 D9           00200          EXX
7A12 3E10         00210          LD      A,10H
7A14 D3EC         00220          OUT     (0ECH),A        ;INITIALIZE I/O PORTS
7A16 D302         00230          OUT     (02H),A         ;START CONVERSION
7A18 DB01         00240  SAMP    IN      A,(01H)         ;SAMPLE STATUS LINE
7A1A 17           01050          RLA
7A1B D2187A       00260          JP      NC,SAMP
7A1E DB03         00270  INPT1   IN      A,(03H)         ;SAMPLE DATA LINES
7A20 32047A       00280          LD      (TEMP),A        ;STORE DATA
7A23 E680         00290          AND     80H
7A25 FE80         00300          CP      80H
7A27 C21E7A       00310          JP      NZ,INPT1
7A2A 3A047A       00320          LD      A,(TEMP)
7A2D E60F         00330          AND     0FH             ;PEEL OFF DIGIT CODE
7A2F 32037A       00340          LD      (D4),A          ;STORE MSD OF DATA
7A32 DB03         00350  INPT2   IN      A,(03H)
7A34 32047A       00360          LD      (TEMP),A
7A37 E640         00370          AND     40H
7A39 FE40         00380          CP      40H
7A3B C2327A       00390          JP      NZ,INPT2
7A3E 3A047A       00400          LD      A,(TEMP)
7A41 E60F         00410          AND     0FH
7A43 32027A       00420          LD      (D3),A
7A46 DB03         00430  INPT3   IN      A,(03H)
7A48 32047A       00440          LD      (TEMP),A
7A4B E620         00450          AND     20H
7A4D FE20         00460          CP      20H
7A4F C2467A       00470          JP      NZ,INPT3
7A52 3A047A       00480          LD      A,(TEMP)
7A55 E60F         00490          AND     0FH
7A57 32017A       00500          LD      (D2),A
7A5A DB03         00510  INPT4   IN      A,(03H)
7A5C 32047A       00520          LD      (TEMP),A
7A5F E610         00530          AND     10H
7A61 FE10         00540          CP      10H
7A63 C25A7A       00550          JP      NZ,INPT4
7A66 3A047A       00560          LD      A,(TEMP)
7A69 E60F         00570          AND     0FH
7A6B 32007A       00580          LD      (D1),A          ;STORE LSD OF DATA
7A6E 08           00590          EX      AF,AF'
7A6F D9           00600          EXX
7A70 C9           00610          RET
```

the MC14433 completes the next conversion and sets the flip-flop. The progam then samples the data lines and decides whether the most significant digit of data was sampled. If it was not, the program continues to sample the data lines until this digit is obtained. Once this digit is found, it is transferred to memory and the program looks for the second digit. After the 4 digits representing the digitized input voltage have been stored, the program executes a RET and returns to the BASIC program.

The BASIC routine has the task of calling the machine language routine and assembling the 4 digits from each conversion back into a single number, which is equal to the measured voltage. This program has been written using the X=USR (0) command to call the machine language routine. A flow chart for the BASIC program is shown in Figure 3.19. Listing 3.6 shows the coded program with comments, and it also has the machine language program included in it as a series of DATA statements that are read in at line #22. You only have to

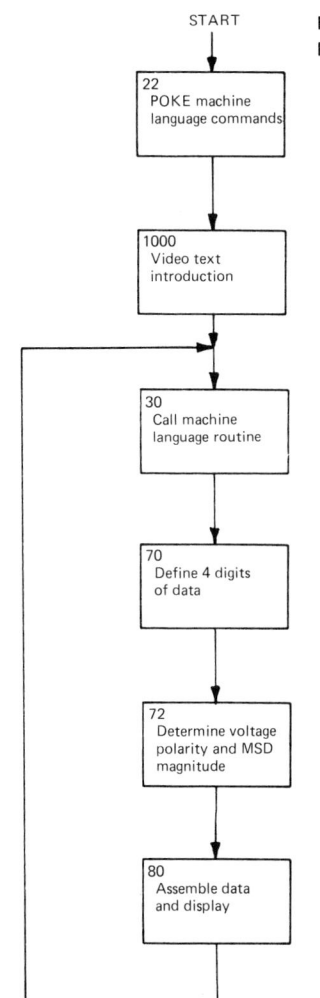

FIGURE 3-19
Flow chart for the BASIC program #1.

LISTING 3-6 BASIC program #1 for the low speed A/D converter.

```
10 REM LOWSPEED A/D CONVERTER #1
20 REM R. HALLGREN
22 FOR I=31248 TO 31344:READ K:POKE I,K:NEXT I
24 GOSUB 1000
30 REM CONVERT ONE SAMPLE
50 POKE 16526,16:POKE 16527,122
60 X=USR(0)
70 X1=PEEK(31232):X2=PEEK(31233):X3=PEEK(31234):X4=PEEK(31235)
71 W4=X4
72 IF X4>7 THEN X4=0
73 IF X4=0 THEN GOTO 80
74 X4=1
80 X$=STR$(X4)+STR$(X3)+STR$(X2)+STR$(X1)
81 X=-VAL(X$)/1000
82 IF X4=0 THEN W4=W4-8
83 IF W4>3 THEN X=-X
84 CLS
86 PRINT @256,"THE MAGNITUDE OF THE INPUT VOLTAGE EQUALS ";X;" VOLTS"
90 GOTO 30
1000 REM INTRODUCTION
1010 CLS
1020 PRINT "",""
1030 PRINT "THIS IS A DEMONSTRATION PROGRAM FOR THE LOW SPEED A/D CONVERTER."
1040 PRINT "",""
1050 PRINT "THE A/D CONVERTER EXPECTS THE MAGNITUDE OF THE INPUT VOLTAGE TO"
1060 PRINT "BE LESS THAN 1.999 VOLTS."
1070 PRINT "",""
1080 PRINT "THE INPUT VOLTAGE WILL BE SAMPLED AND THE MAGNITUDE WILL BE"
1090 PRINT "DISPLAYED ON THE VIDEO DISPLAY."
1100 PRINT "",""
1110 PRINT "PRESS THE SPACE BAR TO CONTINUE, PRESS THE BREAK KEY TO STOP."
1120 K$=INKEY$
1130 IF K$<>" " THEN GOTO 1120
1140 RETURN
2000 DATA 8,217,62,16,211,236,211,02,219,01,23,210,24,122,219,3
2010 DATA 50,04,122,230,128,254,128,194,30,122,58,04,122,230,15
2020 DATA 50,3,122,219,3,50,4,122,230,64,254,64,194,50,122,58,4,122
2030 DATA 230,15,50,2,122,219,3,50,4,122,230,32,254,32,194,70,122,58,4,122
2040 DATA 230,15,50,1,122,219,3,50,4,122,230,16,254,16,194,90,122
2050 DATA 58,4,122,230,15,50,0,122,8,217,201
```

load the BASIC program to get the A/D converter to work. This program performs A/D conversions on a continous basis, displaying the value of the analog input voltage on the video monitor.

Once the circuitry has been built, you still have the job of finding any errors that may have been made during construction. To assist you in this process, I am including the following checks for you to make:

1. The voltage at pin #2 on IC5 should be set to 2.00 V.
2. Using an oscilloscope attached to pin #10 in IC5, you should see a 150,000-Hz distorted square wave varying between + and −2V.

3. The voltage at pin #1 on IC4 should be equal to +5V. Run the following program to repeatedly reset the flip-flop.
   100 OUT 236,16
   110 FOR I=1 TO 20
   120 OUT 2,0
   130 FOR J=1 to 20
   140 NEXT J
   150 NEXT I

4. After you have loaded the BASIC program, connect a 1.5-V battery to the input and execute the program. You should see a video introduction and, after pressing the space bar, you should see the value of the battery voltage (1.54V) displayed on the CRT.

The MC14433 circuitry has been set up so that it is performing an analog-to-digital conversion approximately every 0.067 seconds (15 samples per second). For many applications we will want to take data less frequently and to know fairly precisely the sampling rate, so that the data can be plotted as a function of time. The real-time clock in the Model III can be used to indirectly control the data sample rate. Since the clock information is stored in memory, the program can be written to sample the clock memory location containing seconds, jumping to the data sample routine when the value is incremented. Obviously, slower rates could be obtained by having the program jump after several increments, or by sampling the minutes or hours memory storage locations. Listing 3.7 shows a program that takes one sample every second for a total of 60 seconds and then plots the data, 20 points at a time. Figure 3.20 shows a flow chart for the program.

LISTING 3-7   BASIC program #2.

```
10 REM LOWSPEED A/D CONVERTER #2
12 REM R. HALLGREN    4-15-81
20 DIM K(100)
22 FOR I=31248 TO 31344:READ K:POKE I,K:NEXT I
24 GOSUB 1000
30 REM CONVERT ONE SAMPLE
32 FOR I=1 TO 60
40 L=PEEK(16919)
42 IF L=J THEN GOTO 40
44 J=L
50 POKE 16526,16:POKE 16527,122
60 X=USR(0)
70 X1=PEEK(31232):X2=PEEK(31233):X3=PEEK(31234):X4=PEEK(31235)
71 W4=X4
72 IF X4>7 THEN X4=0
73 IF X4=0 THEN GOTO 80
74 X4=1
80 X$=STR$(X4)+STR$(X3)+STR$(X2)+STR$(X1)
82 K(I)=-VAL(X$)/1000
83 IF X4=0 THEN W4=W4-8
84 IF W4>3 THEN K(I)=-K(I)
```

LISTING 3-7 (continued)
```
85 CLS
86 PRINT @256,"THE MAGNITUDE OF VOLTAGE SAMPLE";I;"EQUALS ";K(I);" VOLTS"
90 NEXT I
99 GOTO 5000
1000 REM INTRODUCTION
1010 CLS
1020 PRINT "",""
1030 PRINT "THIS IS A DEMONSTRATION PROGRAM FOR THE LOW SPEED A/D CONVERTER"
1032 PRINT "AND THE DATA PLOT ROUTINE."
1040 PRINT "",""
1050 PRINT "THE PLOT ROUTINE EXPECTS THE INPUT VOLTAGE TO BE POSITIVE."
1070 PRINT "",""
1080 PRINT "THE INPUT VOLTAGE WILL BE SAMPLED AND THE MAGNITUDE WILL BE"
1090 PRINT "DISPLAYED ON THE VIDEO DISPLAY."
1100 PRINT "",""
1102 PRINT "SIXTY SAMPLES WILL BE TAKEN, AT A RATE OF 1 PER SECOND."
1104 PRINT "",""
1105 PRINT "",""
1110 PRINT "PRESS THE SPACE BAR TO CONTINUE, PRESS THE BREAK KEY TO STOP."
1120 K$=INKEY$
1130 IF K$<>" " THEN GOTO 1120
1140 RETURN
2000 DATA 8,217,62,16,211,236,211,02,219,01,23,210,24,122,219,3
2010 DATA 50,04,122,230,128,254,128,194,30,122,58,04,122,230,15
2020 DATA 50,3,122,219,3,50,4,122,230,64,254,64,194,50,122,58,4,122
2030 DATA 230,15,50,2,122,219,3,50,4,122,230,32,254,32,194,70,122,58,4,122
2040 DATA 230,15,50,1,122,219,3,50,4,122,230,16,254,16,194,90,122
2050 DATA 58,4,122,230,15,50,0,122,8,217,201
5000 REM DATA PLOT ROUTINE
5002 L=0
5008 CLS:J=0
5009 L=L+1
5010 PRINT @993,"SAMPLE";CHR$(28)
5015 PRINT @512,"VOLTAGE";CHR$(28)
5016 PRINT @576,"(VOLTS)";CHR$(28)
5020 PRINT @907,"0";CHR$(28):PRINT @912,"2";CHR$(28):PRINT @917,"4";CHR$(28)
5021 PRINT @927,"8";CHR$(28):PRINT @932,"10";CHR$(28):PRINT @937,"12";CHR$(28)
5022 PRINT @942,"14";CHR$(28):PRINT @947,"16";CHR$(28):PRINT @952,"18";CHR$(28)
5024 PRINT @957,"20";CHR$(28):PRINT @922,"6";CHR$(28)
5030 FOR I=1 TO 53:PRINT @(842+I),CHR$(176);CHR$(28):NEXT I
5100 REM SCALE PLOT
5101 FOR I=0 TO 13
5102 PRINT @(11+64*I),CHR$(191);CHR$(28)
5103 NEXT I
5104 FOR I=0 TO 7
5105 PRINT @(4+64*I),2-.15*I;CHR$(28)
5106 NEXT I
5107 FOR I=10 TO 13
5108 PRINT @(4+64*I),2-.15*I;CHR$(28)
5109 NEXT I
5110 REM DATA PLOT
5111 M=2:DM=.15
5112 FOR I=0 TO 20
5113 K=20*(L-1)+I
5114 IF K(K)=0 THEN GOTO 5200
5116 IF K(K)<0 THEN GOTO 5200
5122 Y=M-J*(DM/3)
5130 IF Y<K(K) THEN Y=J:GOTO 5180
5140 J=J+1
5142 IF J>40 THEN GOTO 5180
```

```
5144 GOTO 5122
5180 X=(22+5*I)
5182 IF Y<0 THEN Y=0
5184 SET (X,Y)
5190 J=0
5200 NEXT I
5250 SET (23,3):SET (23,4):SET (23,5):SET (22,3):SET (22,4):SET (22,5)
5290 L1=15429
5292 POKE L1,49
5293 POKE L1+1,46
5294 POKE L1+2,56
5295 POKE L1+3,53
5300 REM END MESSAGE
5301 POKE 16148,80:POKE 16149,82:POKE 16150,69:POKE 16151,83:POKE 16152,83
5302 POKE 16153,32:POKE 16154,42:POKE 16155,32:POKE 16156,84:POKE 16157,79
5303 POKE 16158,32:POKE 16159,80:POKE 16160,76:POKE 16161,79:POKE 16162,84
5304 POKE 16163,32:POKE 16164,78:POKE 16165,69:POKE 16166,87:POKE 16167,32
5305 POKE 16168,68:POKE 16169,65:POKE 16170,84:POKE 16171,65:POKE 16172,32
5306 POKE 16173,83:POKE 16174,69:POKE 16175,84
5307 IF L=3 THEN END
5400 K$=INKEY$
5402 IF K$<>"*" THEN GOTO 5400
5404 GOTO 5008
5499 END
```

FIGURE 3-20   Flow chart for the BASIC program #2.

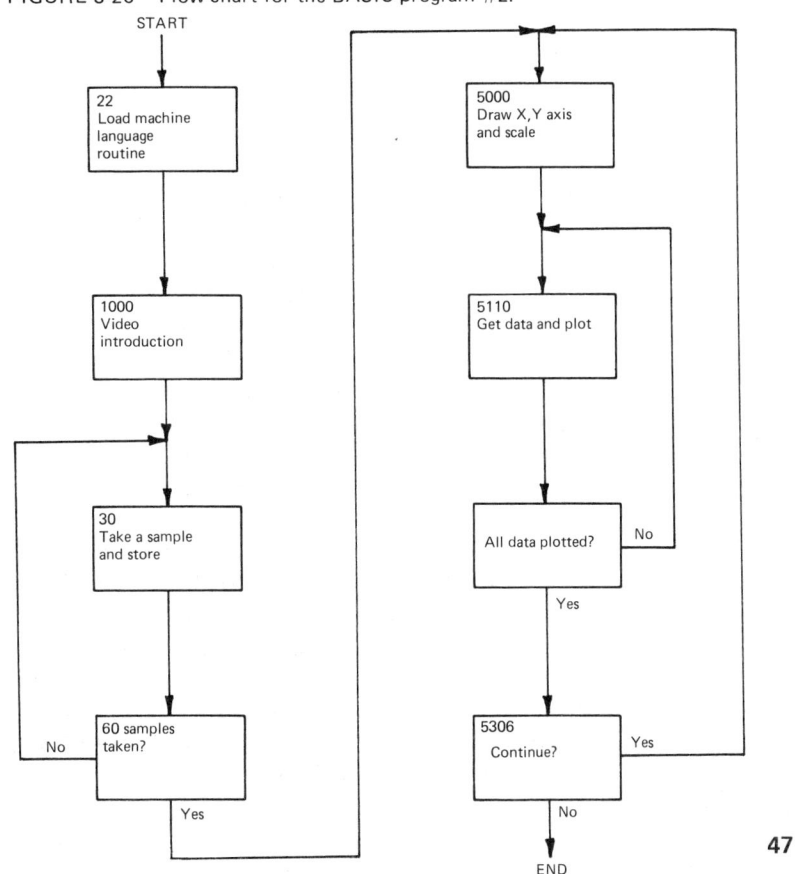

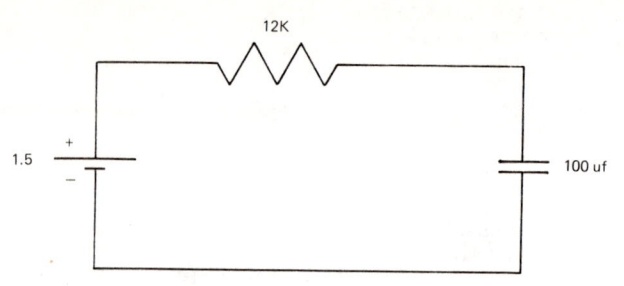

FIGURE 3-21 Series RC circuit for low speed A/D converter demonstration.

Hooking the 1.5-V battery to the input should give a straight-line plot. Figure 3.21 shows a simple resistor, capacitor, and battery combination that can be used to demonstrate the capability of the system. Initially, disconnect the battery and connect the input of the A/D converter across the capacitor. Begin executing the program. Connect the battery to the circuit. The plot should show an exponential rise in voltage across the capacitor (exactly what you would expect).

10-Bit, High-Speed A/D Converter

The AD571 (Analog Devices, Norwood, Massachusetts 02062) is a 10-bit, successive-approximation, A/D converter consisting of an internal D/A converter, voltage reference, clock, comparator, approximation register, and output buffers. With this device, an analog voltage can be converted into a quantity represented by 10 binary bits in approximately 25 ms, the conversion rate not being a function of the magnitude of the input voltage. Figure 3.22 shows the block diagram and pin assignment for the AD571. This integrated circuit can operate from a positive supply voltage (pin #10), which can be set between +5 and +15V depending on whether you need TTL or CMOS compatibility. The negative supply voltage (pin #12) is intended to be set at −15V, but it can be set as low as −12V if necessary. The AD571 gives the designer the option of being able to configure the internal circuitry for either unipolar (0 to +10V) or bipolar (−5 to +5V) operation. If your application involves only positive signals, then the greatest resolution can be realized by operating the circuit in the unipolar mode. Grounding the Bipolar Offset Control (pin #15) puts the chip in the unipolar mode, while leaving this pin "open" puts the chip in the bipolar mode. Figure 3.23 shows a way to have logic control of pin #15. When it is operated in the unipolar mode, 0V gives an output code of 10000000000 and +10V gives an output code of 1111111111. When it is operated in the bipolar mode, 0V gives an output code of 1000000000, −5V gives an output code of 0000000000, and +4.99V gives an output code of 1111111111. For

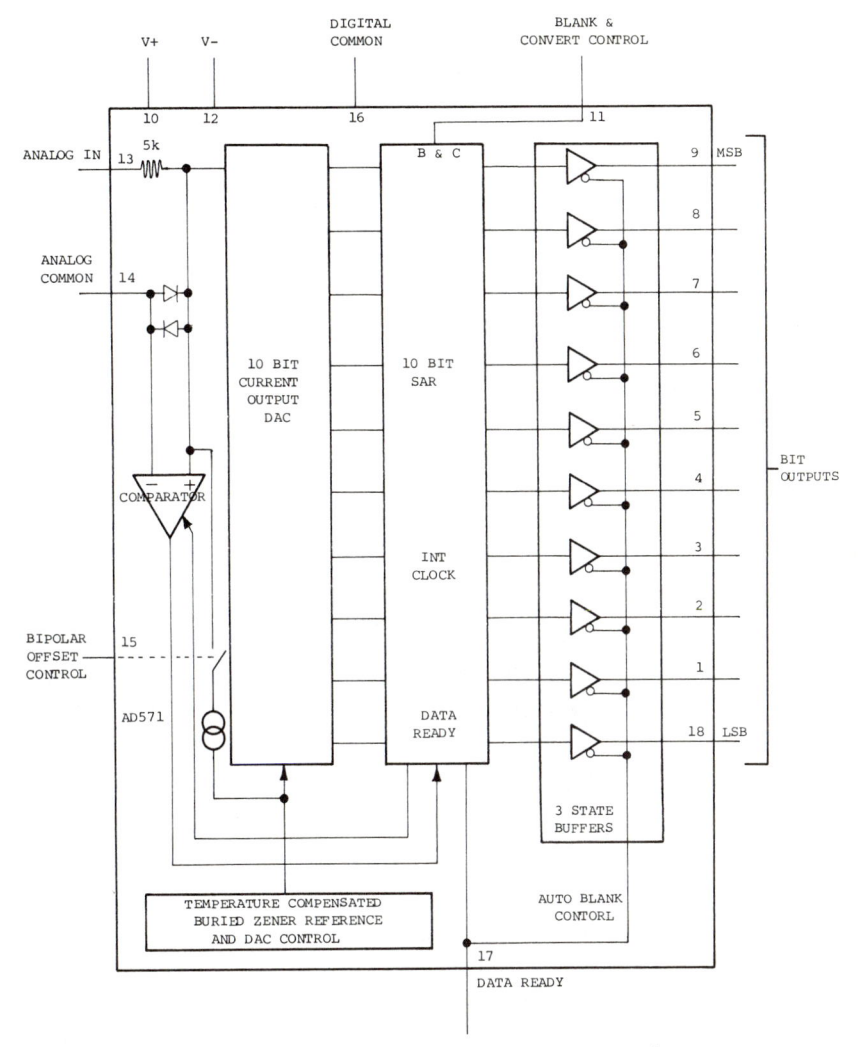

FIGURE 3-22   Block diagram of the Analog Devices AD571 A/D converter.

our application, bipolar operation was desired; consequently pin #15 was left "open."

The AD571 uses a conversion scheme known as "successive-approximation" to achieve the high resolution and speed necessary for some computer applications. *Successive-approximation* involves comparing the unknown input voltage to a preset series of voltages that are binary fractions of the maximum voltage that may be measured. Initialization of the conversion process is accomplished by providing a pulse to the control line CONVERT*. Upon receipt of the convert pulse, the internal D/A converter is sequenced from its most

49

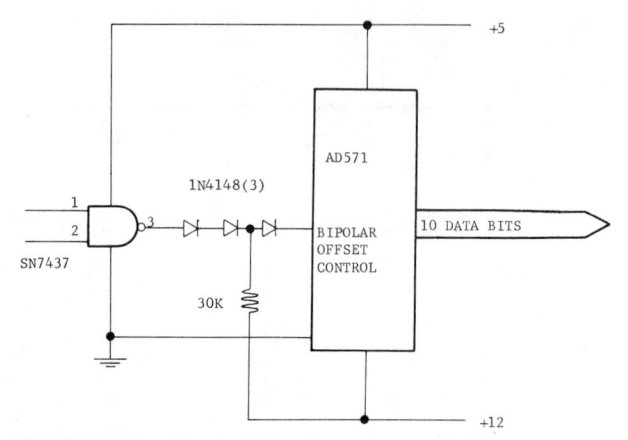

FIGURE 3-23 Bipolar Offset Control controlled by logic gate.

significant bit to its least significant bit. The internal comparator determines whether the addition of each successively-weighted bit creates a voltage that is greater or less than the input voltage. If the voltage is greater, the bit is turned *off*, if the voltage is less, the bit is left *on*. After the sequence is completed, the conversion is complete, and the internal successive approximation register contains the 10-bit binary code that represents the input signal. Thus for a circuit that measures an input varying between 0 and 10.0V, the comparisons would be made between voltage levels that varied in 9.766×10^{-3} volt increments (10V divided by 1,024 discrete levels). When an unknown input voltage is to be converted, the **MSB** of the D/A converter's output (half full scale) is turned on and the input voltage is compared to 5V. If the input voltage is less than 5V, the **MSB** is turned off, the next bit (quarter full scale) is turned on, and the input voltage is compared to 2.5V. If the unknown voltage is greater than 2.5V, the second bit is left on, the next bit (eighth full scale) is turned on, and the input voltage is compared to 3.75V. If the unknown voltage is less than 3.75V, the third bit is turned off, the next bit (sixteenth full scale) is turned on, and the input is compared to 3.125V. This process continues in order of descending bit weight until all the bits have been tried. The conversion process is thus completed, and the 10-bit binary number representing the unknown input voltage is ready to be read by the computer. Figure 3.24 shows the timing relationship between the start of a conversion and the test sequence that we have just described.

During the time that the conversion is being performed, the status line, **DATA READY*** (pin #17), goes high indicating that the converter is busy. Upon completion of the conversion, the status line goes low bringing the 3-state buffers out of their "open" state and activating the bit output lines.

The typical input resistance of the AD571 is equal to 5,000Ω. Since this is low enough to excessively load some circuits, I would recommend that

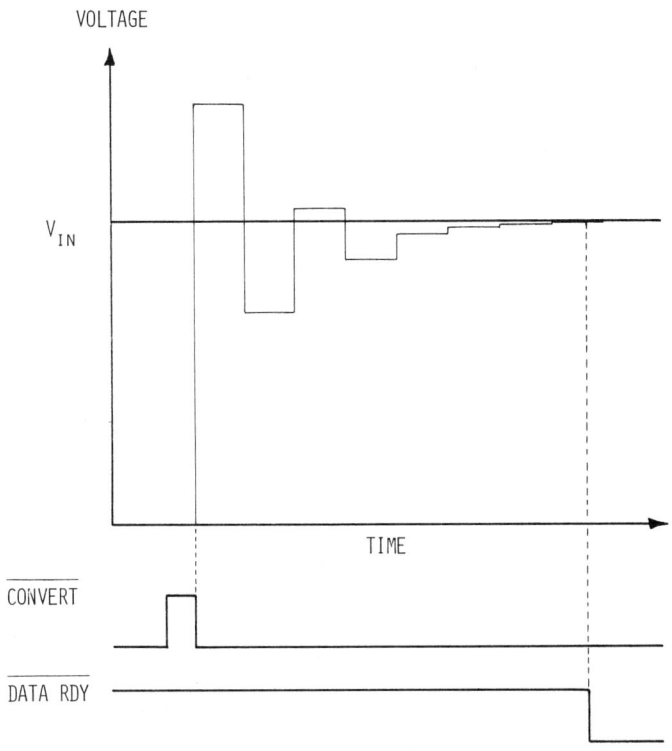

FIGURE 3-24 Typical test sequence for a successive approximation A/D converter.

you use a buffer circuit to provide the necessary impedance matching. If your input voltage approaches the maximum capability of the A/D converter, then the simple unity gain, voltage follower shown in Figure 3.25 should be adequate. If your input voltage is much less than the maximum that the converter is capable of measuring, then the inverting amplifier shown in Figure 3.26 should be used. Notice that the gain of this amplifier configuration is variable, depending on the ratio of the resistor combinations that are used. Appendix B has been provided to explain the operation of amplifier circuits, and to provide you with enough information so that you could design a specific circuit to satisfy your design requirements, if you should need to do so.

While we have discussed the definition of resolution in an earlier section, some additional comments will help you determine the resolution that your particular application will require. In the process of A/D conversion, we are representing a continous analog voltage in terms of a certain number of binary bits. We have already stated that the number of binary digits that are available to represent the analog signal is going to determine the resolution of the system.

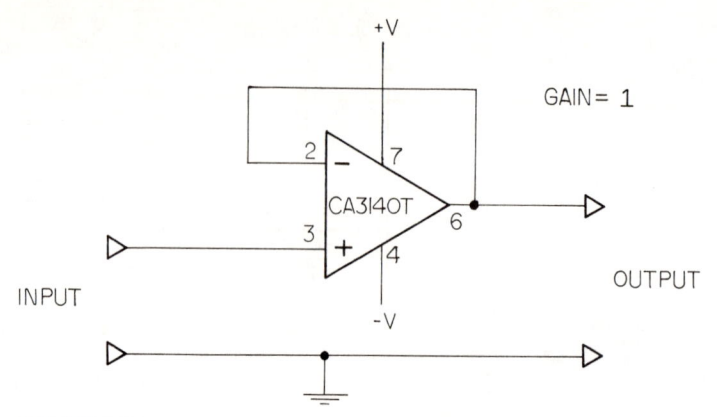

FIGURE 3-25 Noninverting, unity gain, buffer amplifier.

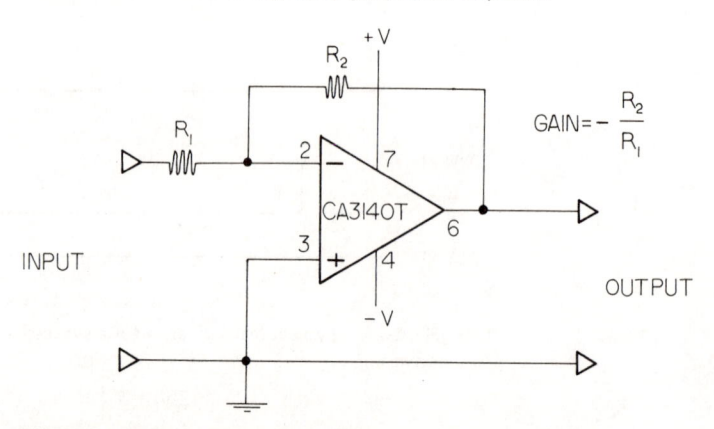

FIGURE 3-26 Inverting, adjustable gain, buffer amplifier.

Resolution gives a measure of the converter's ability to distinguish between two voltages separated by some small voltage increment *(dR)*. For example, in Figure 3.27 we have the block diagram of a typical 8-bit A/D converter. Functioning correctly, this device will convert an analog input voltage, V_{IN}, into a discrete voltage represented by the 8-bit binary number at the output. If a 0V signal is represented by a bit configuration equal to 00000000, and a +10V signal is represented by a bit configuration equal to 11111111, then any magnitude of voltage between these extremes will be equal to a multiple of 0.039V (10V divided by 256 discrete levels). The converter will by necessity introduce an uncertainty, and consequently inaccuracy, into the measurement, since the actual input voltage has to be represented by a discrete quantity at the output, and only so many bits are available.

It should be easy to see that we should be able to increase the accuracy of the A/D converter by increasing the resolution—that is, by increasing the number

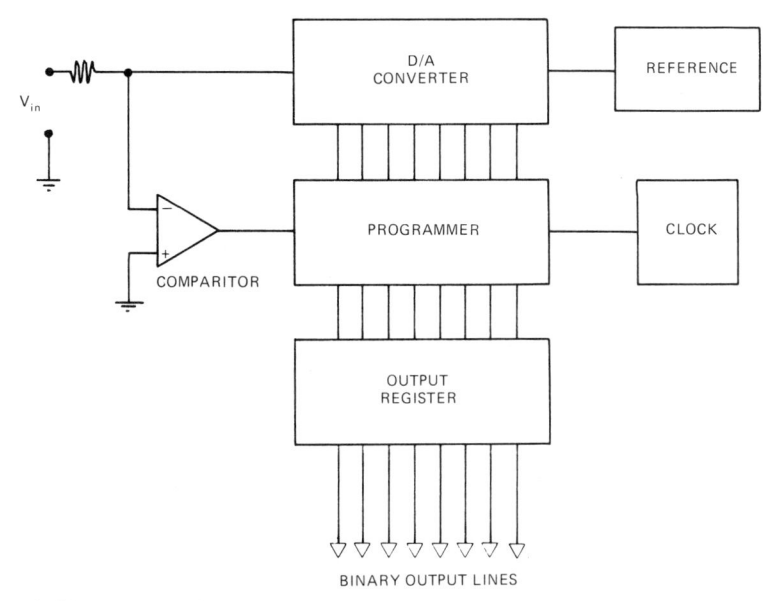

FIGURE 3-27 Block diagram of an 8-bit, successive approximation type A/D converter.

of binary output bits available to the represent the input voltage. For example, if we were using a 10-bit A/D converter, we could expect the device to represent the input voltage as one of 1,024 possible values. This would mean that an 0V signal would be represented by 0000000000, a +10V signal would be represented by 1111111111, and values in between these two extremes would be assigned values in steps of 0.00977V (10V divided by 1,024 discrete levels). This is obviously an improvement over the 8-bit device.

Increased resolution usually means increased circuit cost, increased conversion time, and increased memory requirements, so we need to chose the number of output bits wisely so as to satisfy our particular design requirements without providing excessive capability. How then do we determine the resolution (dR) that we will need to meet the requirements of our application? Suppose we needed to determine the magnitude of the input voltage and be reasonably certain that the apparent magnitude was within 1 percent of the actual magnitude. To achieve this, we would have to have a resolution of at least 1 part in 100. To attain this resolution, we will need at least 7 binary bits at the output. If both positive and negative quantities are to be represented, the converter will need one extra bit to represent the sign, making a total of 8 bits. While 1 percent sounds pretty good, remember that this is in reference to the maximum voltage that the converter can handle; this means that for a maximum input voltage of 10V, you will be able to distinguish signals that are 0.1V apart. If the input voltage is varying between 0 and +1V, you will still have a resolution equal to

53

0.1V, but your accuracy will have decreased to 10 percent (1/0.1). Keep in mind that for this discussion, I am assuming that the primary source of inaccuracy in our system is due to a lack of resolution.

To determine a measure of your system's ability to differentiate between the magnitude of two voltages, follow these steps:

1. Determine the magnitude of the signal that you will be measuring.
2. Determine the maximum resolution of your system by dividing the magnitude of the output signal that corresponds to all ones, by the number of discrete voltage steps that the system is capable of providing. Do not count sign bits.
3. Divide the quantity from step 2 by the quantity from step 1 and multiply by 100 to get the accuracy expressed as a percentage.

You should realize that in step 1 you were concerned with the magnitude of the signal that you would be measuring, not with the maginitude of the signal that you were capable of measuring. The truncating and rounding procedure that the A/D converter performs to get the input signal to fall into predetermined voltage slots has the effect of causing the accuracy to vary as a function of the magnitude of the input signal (even though the resolution remains constant). For this reason, you should always be aware of the magnitude of the signal that you will be measuring; often the system you choose will have to be a compromise between accuracy and dynamic range.

Figure 3.28 shows a schematic diagram of a high-speed A/D converter for the Mod III, and Figure 3.29 shows a schematic diagram of a crystal-controlled time base oscillator, which we will be using to determine the sampling rate. IC1 is an analog multiplexer used to select one of eight possible input signals. Control of input signal selection is accomplished by latching a given bit pattern at the output pins of the quad D-type flip-flop (IC7). You should notice that one of the lines from the flip-flop is connected to the A/D converter. This is the control line (CONVERT*), discussed earlier in the overview of the AD571 A/D converter (IC2), which is used to signal that a conversion is to begin. Data lines D1, D2, and D3 then control the selection of the analog input signal and D0 controls the initiation of the conversion process. If you executed the following BASIC commands, you would convert the analog signal present an input #1 into a digital quantity.

```
100 OUT 236,16    (Initialize I/0)
110 OUT 1,0       (Initialize A/D)
120 OUT 1,3       (Start conversion)
130 OUT 1,2
```

IC12, IC13, IC14, and IC15 are operational amplifiers that are configured as unity gain, noninverting buffers. They are used to isolate an input signal from

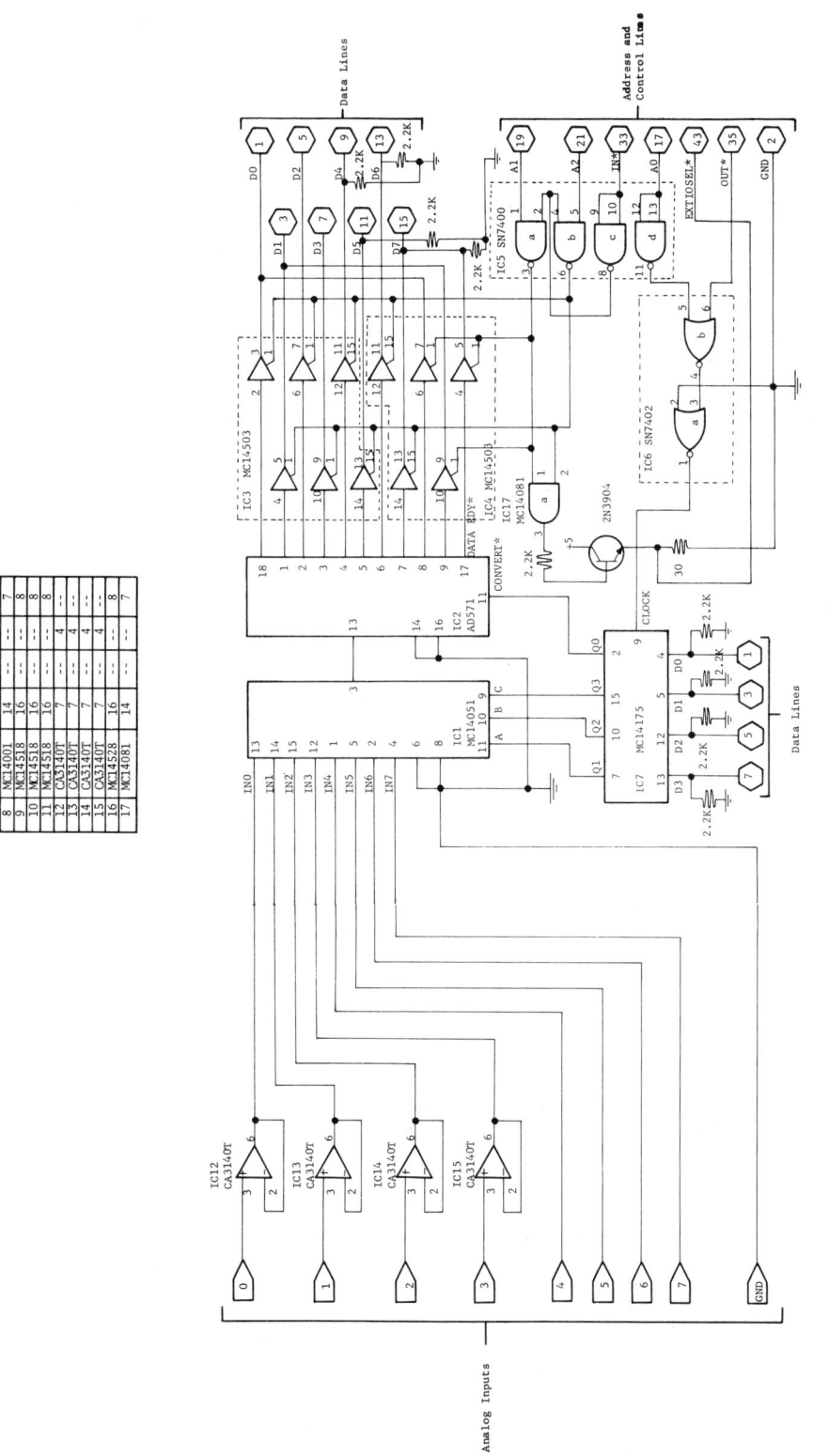

FIGURE 3-28 High speed A/D converter.

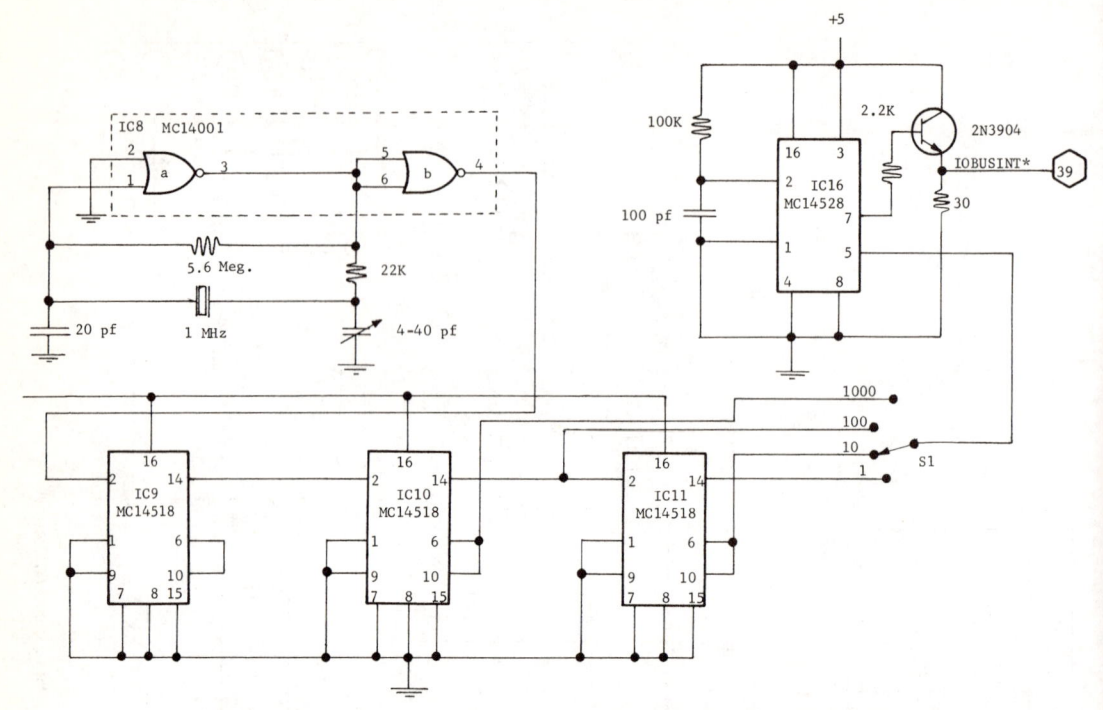

FIGURE 3-29 Crystal controlled time base for the high speed A/D converter.

the input of the AD571 to avoid problems associated with the relatively low input resistance of this device. Four unbuffered inputs are also provided for input signals that do not need isolation (that is, they have a low value of series output resistance), or that require an additional stage of amplification.

All the data and status lines to the Mod III have been isolated through the use of the MC14503 3-state buffers (IC3 and IC4). Since the Mod III is an 8-bit machine, the 10 bits from the AD571 are transferred to memory in a two-step operation. The DATA RDY* line and the 2 most significant bits are read into the machine through the use of an IN A, (02) machine language command. When the AD571 signals the Mod III that a conversion has been completed (by dropping DATA RDY* to 0V), the following sequence of operations should be performed:

1. The most significant 2 bits of data (appearing on D0 and D1 of the data bus) should be stored in memory.
2. The least significant 8 bits should be transferred into the computer through the use of an IN A, (04) machine language command and stored in memory.
3. The Mod III should then either process the data or return to gather more data.

IC8 and the 1-MHz crystal provide a stable pulse train that is used to determine the sampling frequency. IC9, IC10, and IC11 divide the 1-MHz pulse train by multiples of 10 so that sampling rates of 1, 10, 100, and 1,000 samples per second can be obtained. IC16 is a monostable multivibrator that is used to provide an inverted output pulse, the width being independent of the output frequency, to the Mod III I/O interrupt input. The 2N3904 transistor is configured as an emitter follower to provide the current drive requirements necessary to drive the interrupt line.

Once you have constructed the interface, connect it to the Mod III and perform the following tests to make sure that it is working correctly:

1. If you execute the following BASIC statements, pin #7 and pin #2 on IC7 should go to +5V. Pin #10 and pin #15 should remain at 0V.
    100 OUT 236,16
    110 OUT 1,3
2. If you execute the following BASIC statements, pin #2 on IC7 should go to 0V. Pin #7 should remain at +5V. Pin #10 and #15 should remain at 0V.
    100 OUT 236,16
    110 OUT 1,2
3. If you now apply an analog signal to input IN1, you should see that signal at the output (pin #3) of the multiplexer (IC1).

If you have an oscilloscope, you can perform the following tests and adjustments:

1. If you execute the following BASIC statements, you should see the DATA RDY* line periodically go from 0 to +5V.
    100 OUT 236,16
    110 OUT 1,2
    120 OUT 1,3
    130 OUT 1,2
    140 FOR I=1 to 100
    142 NEXT I
    150 GOTO 100
2. If you execute the following BASIC statements, you should see the EXTIOSEL* line periodically go from 0 to +5V.
    100 OUT 236,16
    110 X=INP(02)
    120 GOTO 100
3. Adjust the 4–40-pF trimmer capacitor in the crystal oscillator until the output of IC8 is equal to 1 MHz. The IOBUSINT* line should reflect the sampling frequency that you have selected.

The software portion of the high-speed A/D converter interface was handled in two parts:

Decimal Address	Contents	Hexidecimal Address
0 → 16384	Reserved for System Use	0 → 4000
17129 → 20479	User Memory for BASIC Program	42E9 → 4FFF
20480 → 28672	User Memory for Data Storage	5000 → 7000
28928 → 32767	User Memory for Machine Language Program	7100 → 7FFF

TABLE 3-2 Memory map for the high speed A/D converter.

1. A routine written in TRS-80 BASIC takes the binary representation of the analog data and converts it into a decimal number, which then can be either displayed or stored for future reference.
2. A machine language routine was written to control the AD571 and to provide high-speed transfer of the binary data into the Mod III.

Table 3.2 shows how the available memory is used. Figure 3.30 shows a flow chart for the machine language routine, and Listing 3.8 gives the actual program with comments. When the subroutine is entered, all necessary registers are saved to allow a successful return to the BASIC calling routine. The program then defines the data storage space and initializes the system I/O bus. The interrupt

FIGURE 3-30 Flow chart for the machine language routine for controlling the high speed A/D converter.

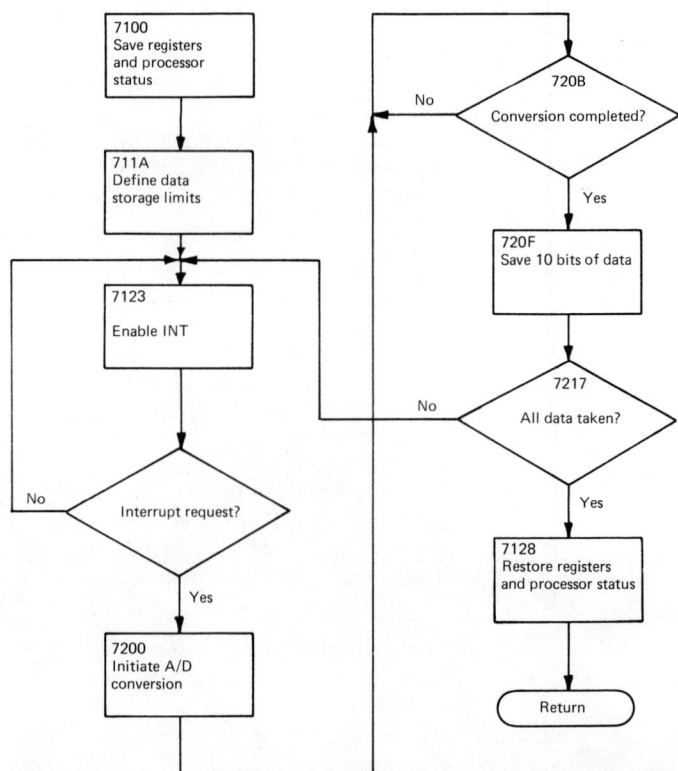

LISTING 3-8 Machine language program to control the AD571 analog-to-digital converter.

```
             00100 ;HIGH SPEED A/D CONVERTER, MOD III
             00110 ;R. HALLGREN, 6-20-81
7100         00120        ORG    7100H
7100 F3      00130 START  DI
7101 08      00140        EX     AF,AF'
7102 D9      00150        EXX
7103 3E10    00160        LD     A,10H
7105 D3EC    00170        OUT    (0ECH),A      ;INITIALIZE I/O
7107 3E00    00180        LD     A,00H
7109 D301    00190        OUT    (01H),A       ;INITIALIZE A/D
710B 3EC3    00200        LD     A,0C3H        ;LOAD INT VECTOR
710D 321240  00210        LD     (4012H),A
7110 3E00    00220        LD     A,00H
7112 321340  00230        LD     (4013H),A
7115 3E72    00240        LD     A,72H
7117 321440  00250        LD     (4014H),A
711A 010050  00260        LD     BC,5000H      ;BEGINNING OF DATA STORAGE
711D DBE0    00270        IN     A,(0E0H)      ;CLEAR RTCINT
711F 3E08    00280        LD     A,08H
7121 D3E0    00290        OUT    (0E0H),A      ;ENABLE I/O INT
7123 FB      00300 INT    EI
7124 00      00310        NOP
7125 C32371  00320        JP     INT
7128 3E18    00330 BACK   LD     A,18H         ;RESTORE SYSTEM INT VECTOR
712A 321340  00340        LD     (4013H),A
712D 3E30    00350        LD     A,30H
712F 321440  00360        LD     (4014H),A
7132 D9      00370        EXX
7133 08      00380        EX     AF,AF'
7134 33      00390        INC    SP
7135 33      00400        INC    SP
7136 C9      00410        RET                  ;RETURN TO BASIC PROGRAM
7200         00420        ORG    7200H         ;LOCATION OF INT VECTOR
7200 3E01    00430        LD     A,01H         ;INITIATE CONVERSION
7202 D301    00440        OUT    (01H),A
7204 3E00    00450        LD     A,00H
7206 D301    00460        OUT    (01H),A
7208 DB02    00470 TEST   IN     A,(02H)       ;SAMPLE CONVERSION STATUS
720A 17      00480        RLA                  ;ROTATE INTO CARRY BIT
720B DA0872  00490        JP     C,TEST
720E 1F      00500        RRA                  ;RESTORE DATA
720F E603    00510        AND    03H           ;SAVE L.S. TWO DIGITS
7211 02      00520        LD     (BC),A        ;STORE DATA
7212 03      00530        INC    BC
7213 DB04    00540        IN     A,(04H)       ;INPUT EIGHT L.S. DIGITS
7215 02      00550        LD     (BC),A        ;STORE DATA
7216 03      00560        INC    BC
7217 78      00570        LD     A,B
7218 FE70    00580        CP     70H
721A CA2871  00590        JP     Z,BACK
721D ED4D    00600 RETURN RETI
```

request line is then activated, and the program loops until an interrupt request is made. The request for an interrupt comes from the output of the crystal time base oscillator, the frequency depending on the position of switch S1. After receiving an interrupt request, the program initiates an A/D conversion and waits

FIGURE 3-31
Flow chart for the BASIC routine.

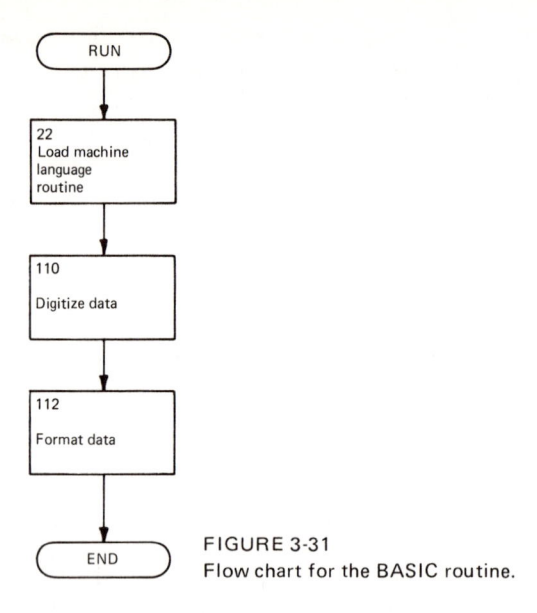

until the AD571 signals that the conversion is completed. The 10 data bits are then stored in memory and the program tests to see if the data storage is filled. If all the data storage has been filled, the program restores all the necessary registers and returns to the BASIC calling routine. If all the data storage has

LISTING 3-9 BASIC program which formats the output from the high speed A/D converter.

```
10 REM HIGH SPEED A/D ROUTINE DEMONSTRATION
12 REM R. HALLGREN, MOD III, 6-23-81
22 FOR I=1 TO 55:READ K:POKE (28927+I),K:NEXT I
24 FOR I=1 TO 31:READ K:POKE (29183+I),K:NEXT I
90 DIM X(500)
100 POKE 16526,0:POKE 16527,113
108 CLS:PRINT @524,"DATA BEING DIGITIZED"
110 X=USR(0)
112 CLS: PRINT @524,"DATA BEING FORMATTED"
120 FOR I=1 TO 1000 STEP 2
130 X1=PEEK(20479+I):X2=PEEK(20479+I+1)
132 IF X1>1 THEN GOTO 150
140 REM VOLTAGE IS NEGATIVE
142 X(I/2)=-((511-(256*X1+X2))/100)
144 GOTO 160
150 REM VOLTAGE IS POSITIVE
152 X(I/2)=(256*(X1-2)+X2)/100
160 NEXT I
199 END
10000 DATA 243,8,217,62,16,211,236,62,0,211,1,62,395,50,18,64,62,0,50,19,64,62,114
10001 DATA 50,20,64,1,0,80,219,224,62,8,211,224,251,0,195,35,113,62,24,50,19,64,62
10002 DATA 48,50,20,64,217,8,51,51,201,62,1,211,1,62,0,211,1,219,2,23,218,8,114,31,230
10003 DATA 3,2,3,219,4,2,3,120,254,112,202,40,113,237,77
```

not been filled, the program returns to activate the interrupt system and to take more data.

Figure 3.31 shows a flow chart for the BASIC program, and Listing 3.9 gives the actual program with comments. The BASIC routine first loads the machine language routine by using the READ and POKE statements. Then the machine language routine is called to obtain a block of digitized analog data. When the program returns from the machine language routine, the BASIC program creates a file that can be either stored or processed. You can examine the digitized data by printing $x(1), x(2), \ldots, x(500)$.

DIGITAL-TO-ANALOG CONVERSION

Digital-to-analog (D/A) convertors are devices that take a digital input, usually from the data bus of a computer, and convert it into an analog signal. While the analog signal is often thought of as being a continuous quantity, the output of the D/A converter will actually consist of a series of discrete and easily measurable voltages. Resolution, the voltage difference between steps, will depend on the number of bits that the D/A converter can handle.

The Analog Devices AD558 Dacport is an 8-bit digital-to-analog converter that includes a precision voltage reference, a microprocessor interface, a data latch, and an output amplifier all on a single monolithic chip. Thin-film silicon-chromium resistors are used in a current driven ladder to provide an analog voltage that is stable over a large temperature range. Figure 4.1 shows a functional block diagram of the AD558. The data latch is connected to the computer data bus, with data being accepted when both control inputs, CE* and CS*, are low. When either control input returns high, the 8-bit data word is latched and the analog output is unaffected by further activity on the data lines. For a maximum output voltage of 2.56V, the resolution of the converter will be equal to 0.01V; that is, a change in the least significant digit will result in 0.01-V change in the output voltage.

Figure 4.2 shows the schematic diagram for a D/A converter interface for the Mod III. Data is strobed into the converter by writing data to I/O port 1. The analog output will then remain stable until I/O port 1 is next addressed.

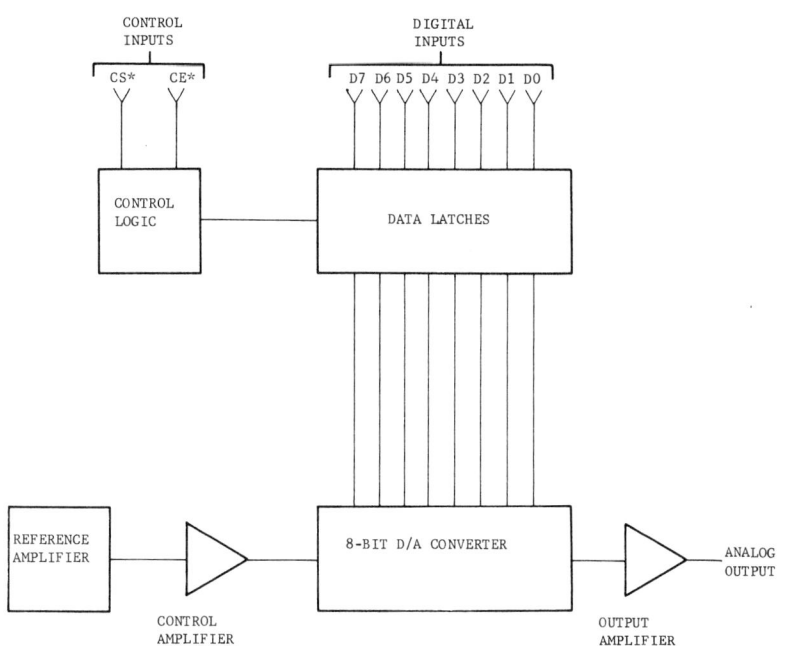

FIGURE 4-1 Functional block diagram of the AD558.

After you have finished building the interface, perform the following tests to make sure that it is working correctly:

1. If you execute the following **BASIC** statements, you should see the output of IC3 periodically go from 0 to +5V.
   ```
   100 OUT 236,16
   110 OUT 1,0
   120 GOTO 100
   ```
2. If you execute the following **BASIC** statements, you should see the analog output ramp from 0 to 2.55V.
   ```
   100 OUT 236,16
   110 FOR I=0 to 255
   120 OUT 1,I
   130 NEXT I
   199 END
   ```

Digital-to-analog converters are commonly used in digitally controlled power supplies for automated test equipment, digital generation of analog waveforms, and digital control of automatic process control systems. I am going to cover two examples of automatic test equipment that might be constructed to perform quality control testing in a manufacturing facility.

The first example involves cycling an incandescent lamp through a number of voltages to determine if the lamp intensity is acceptably high. The lamp might

Number	Type	+5	GND
IC1	AD558	11	12
IC2	MC14049	1	8
IC3	MC14075	14	7

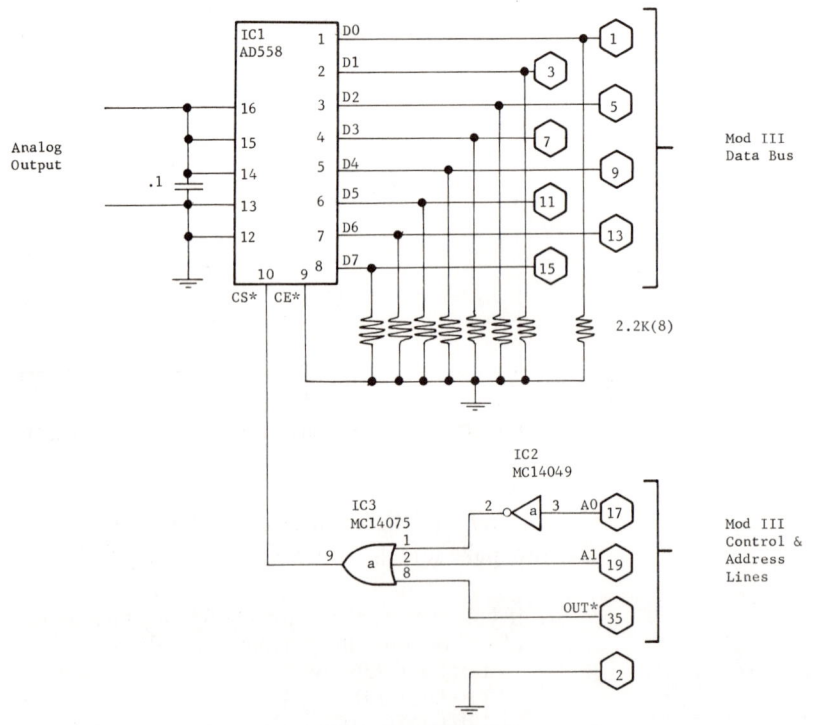

FIGURE 4-2 Interface schematic for the AD558 D/A converter.

be used in a simple colorimeter for a chemistry laboratory, and its intensity may need to be above a certain level to ensure reliable operation. Since checking each lamp could be very time-consuming, it would be desirable to have the computer automatically increase the lamp voltage and record the lamp intensity at each voltage. At the end of the test, the computer could then make a decision regarding the acceptability of the lamp. The output of the AD558 is already buffered, but by itself it cannot provide enough current to drive an incandescent lamp. What we will do is build a voltage-programmable power supply—a power supply whose output voltage is some multiple of the input voltage supplied by the D/A converter.

Figure 4.3 shows a block diagram of the proposed testing arrangement. The data bus from the Mod III will supply a binary number that will be con-

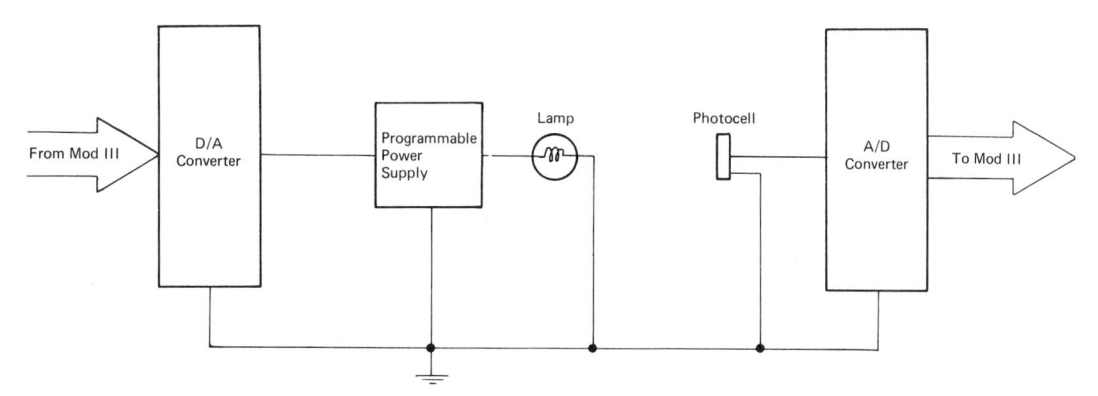

FIGURE 4-3 Block diagram of proposed testing arrangement.

verted by the D/A converter into an analog voltage. This voltage will then be used to control the lamp voltage. Lamp intensity will be monitored by a photocell connected to the high-speed A/D converter (discussed in Chapter 3). Figure 4.4 shows a schematic diagram of the programmable power supply. Figure 4.5 shows a flow chart for a TRS-80 BASIC program to cycle the lamp voltage from 0 to 2.0V. Listing 4.1 shows the actual program with comments.

The second example deals with testing the frequency response of a low-pass filter. We will use the D/A converter to directly control the output frequency of a B&K 3010 Function Generator (Dynascan Corporation, 6460 W. Cortland Street, Chicago, Illinois 60635). This instrument has an input jack that allows an external voltage to directly control its output frequency. Figure 4.6 shows a block diagram of the proposed testing arrangement. Again, the data bus from the Mod III will supply a binary number that will be converted

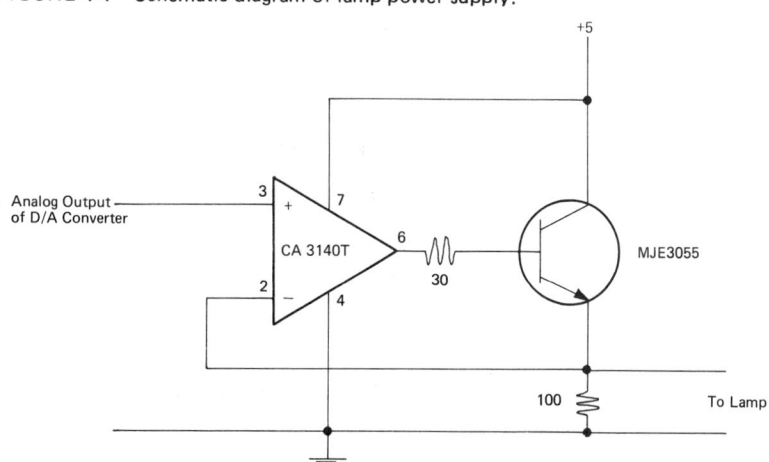

FIGURE 4-4 Schematic diagram of lamp power supply.

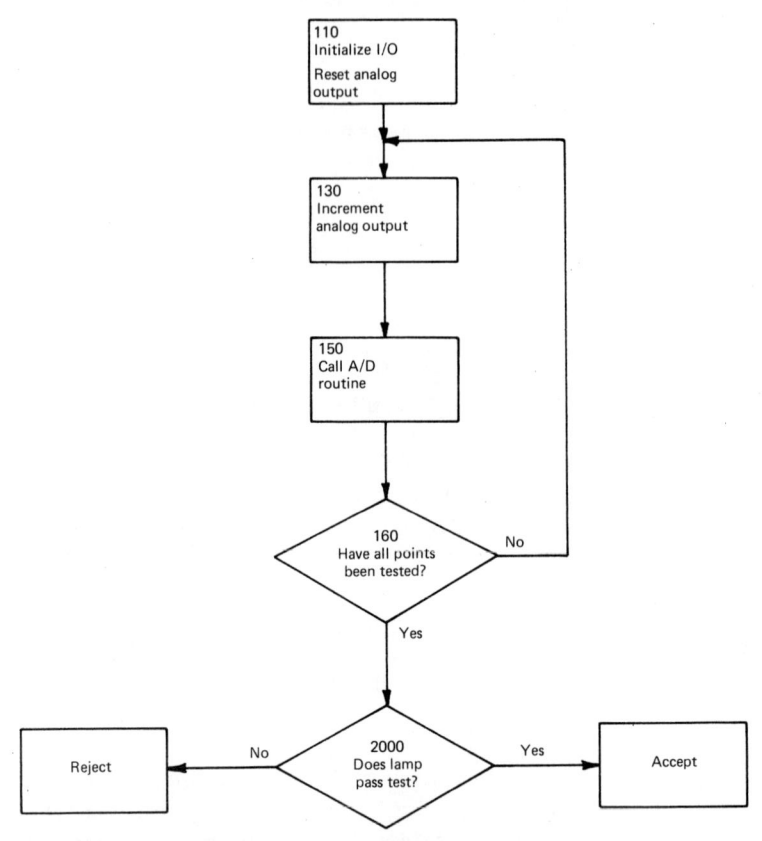

FIGURE 4-5 Flow chart of BASIC program for automatic testing of incandescent lamps.

LISTING 4-1 BASIC routine for lamp test example.

```
100 REM LAMP TEST ROUTINE
102 REM R. HALLGREN, 6-30-81
104 REM MOD III
110 OUT 236,16:OUT 1,0
120 FOR I=1 TO 10
130 OUT 1,20*I
140 FOR J=1 TO 500:NEXT J
150 GOSUB 1000
160 NEXT I
170 GOSUB 2000
199 END
1000 REM ANALOG-TO-DIGITAL SUBROUTINE
1999 RETURN
2000 REM LAMP PASS/NOT PASS DECISION
2999 RETURN
```

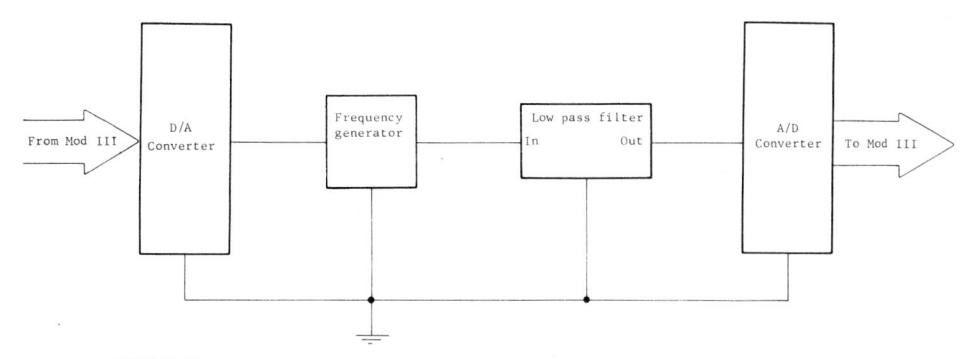

FIGURE 4-6 Block diagram for low pass filter testing arrangement.

by the D/A converter into an analog voltage. This voltage will then be used to control the frequency of the function generator. The output of the low-pass filter could be monitored by connecting it to the high-speed A/D converter, and the computer could determine if the 3-dB cutoff frequency is within acceptable limits.

For both examples, the goal was to reduce the amount of the personnel time required to perform a routine test operation. This was accomplished through the use of a computer-controlled test protocol.

5

UTILIZATION OF THE MOD III IN SERIAL APPLICATIONS

HIGH-RESOLUTION DIGITAL PLOTTING

Utilization of personal computers, such as the Mod III, in business and research applications has met with considerable success. Not only do they function as computational tools, but, when used in conjuction with peripheral devices, they can be used to perform complex functions at reduced expense. For example, the research laboratory often deals with complex, time-dependent waveforms. This type of data can be easily digitized (Chapter 3) and analyzed (Chapter 8), but a major problem arises when a permanent copy of the data is required. Printing a column of numbers does little to convey to the researcher the nature of the data, especially several months after the data are taken. Plotting with a terminal such as the DecWriter II is possible, but it lacks the necessary resolution for many applications. The Hiplot Digital Plotter, manufactured by Houston Instruments, gives the researcher a cost-effective means of obtaining quality digital plots. The plotter accepts an 8-1/2 x 11-inch sheet of paper and allows plotting within a 7 x 10-inch boundary. Reversable stepper motors are used to give bidirectional steps of either 200 or 100 steps per inch, amounting to a resolution of 0.005 or 0.01 inches per step, respectively. The plotter comes with a standard RS-232C serial interface, so interfacing it to the computer is a relatively straightforward task.

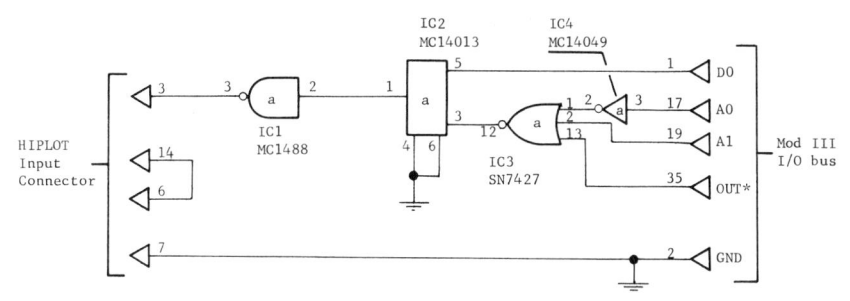

FIGURE 5-1 HIPLOT and Mod III interface connections.

To implement a TTL to RS232-C conversion, we have already discussed the serial data format (Chapter 2), and we examined the necessary hardware (Figure 2.9) and software (Listing 2.1). If you have not already built this circuit, you should do so now. Refer to Appendix C for power supply circuits that will provide the +12, −12, and +5V that you will need. Once you have constructed the interface, connect it to the plotter as shown in Figure 5.1, and perform the following tests to make sure that it is working correctly:

1. If you execute the following BASIC statements, the output of IC1 should go to +12V.
   100 OUT 236,16
   110 OUT 1,1
2. If you execute the following BASIC statements, the output of IC1 should go to −12V.
   100 OUT 236,16
   110 OUT 1,0
3. Load and execute the BASIC program shown in Listing 5.1. If everything is working correctly, the plotter pen should begin moving toward the right-hand side of the platen. If you execute the program and nothing happens, you should borrow an oscilloscope and check both the bit pattern and the bit spacing of the serial data. Figure 5.2 shows the bit pattern and spacing that should be obtained.

Being able to accomplish the transfer of information in a RS-232C format is only the first step towards using the plotter. The Hiplot consists of two stepper motors that control the x-y position of the plotter pen. Control of the pen position, along with all other plotter functions, is accomplished by sending specific control characters to the device. Figure 5.3 shows the axis system for the plotter pen, and Table 5.1 shows the character that produces an increment of the pen along the given vector. Also included are the characters that produce control functions such as "pen up." Since the plotter comes without any software, it is necessary to write subroutines to generate an axis system, to lable the axis, and to plot the data.

69

LISTING 5-1 Digital plotter demonstration program.

```
10 REM DIGITAL PLOTTER DEMO
12 REM MOD III
14 REM R. HALLGREN         5-18-81
20 FOR I=1 TO 52:READ K
22 POKE (32511+I),K
24 NEXT I
40 GOSUB 9000
50 FOR I=1 TO 100
52 GOSUB 9100
54 NEXT I
99 END
199 END
9000 REM INITIALIZE OUTPUT
9010 OUT 236,16
9020 POKE 16526,00:POKE 16527,127
9030 RETURN
9100 REM VECTOR GENERATOR
9130 REM "R"
9132 POKE 32575,114
9134 X=USR(0)
9136 RETURN
10000 DATA 243,00,00,58,63,127,22,09,55,63,50,63,127,218,23,127,62,01,211,01,210,27,127,62,00,211
10002 DATA 01,62,09,61,194,29,127,58,63,127,31,21,194,10,127,62,00,211,01,62,44,61,194,47,127,201
```

Listing 5.2 shows a program that provides some of these capabilities. Figure 5.4 shows a flow chart for the BASIC program. This program draws an x-y axis sytem, labels the system with numeric characters, and plots an ex-

LISTING 5-2 BASIC program for operation of the digital plotter.

```
10 REM DIGITAL PLOTTER
12 REM MOD III
14 REM R. HALLGREN         5-18-81
20 FOR I=1 TO 52:READ K
22 POKE (32511+I),K
24 NEXT I
100 REM MAIN PROGRAM
110 CLS
112 PRINT CHR$(23)
114 PRINT "POSITION PEN IN LOWER RIGHT"
116 PRINT "HAND CORNER."
118 PRINT "",""
120 PRINT "PRESS THE SPACE BAR TO"
122 PRINT "CONTINUE."
124 K$=INKEY$
126 IF K$<>" " THEN GOTO 124
128 CLS
130 PRINT CHR$(23)
132 PRINT "INPUT THE SCALE FACTOR(3<K<19)"
134 INPUT K
136 IF K<4 OR K>18 THEN GOTO 130
138 CLS
140 GOSUB 1000
150 GOSUB 2000
200 REM PLOT DEMONSTRATION
202 GOSUB 9210
```

```
210 FOR I=0 TO .5*K STEP .005
220 V=5*(1-EXP(-10*I/K))
222 L=INT(10*K*V)
224 IF L-Z=0 THEN GOTO 250:REM NO CHANGE IN POTENTIAL
226 IF L-Z<0 THEN GOTO 240:REM POTENTIAL IS DECREASING
228 FOR J=1 TO (L-Z):REM POTENTIAL IS INCREASING
230 GOSUB 9110:REM MOVE PEN IN +Y DIRECTION
232 NEXT J
234 GOTO 248
240 FOR J=1 TO (Z-L)
242 GOSUB 9150:NEXT J:MOVE PEN IN -Y DIRECTION
248 Z=L
250 GOSUB 9130:NEXT I:REM MOVE PEN IN +X DIRECTION
255 GOSUB 9200
299 END
999 END
1000 REM X-AXIS
1004 GOSUB 9000
1010 GOSUB 9200
1012 FOR I=1 TO 100+3*K:GOSUB 9110:NEXT I
1013 FOR I=1 TO K+90:GOSUB 9130:NEXT I
1014 GOSUB 9210
1016 FOR I=1 TO 100*K:GOSUB 9130:NEXT I
1020 GOSUB 1900
1030 GOSUB 9200
1032 FOR I=1 TO 3*K:GOSUB 9170:NEXT I
1033 GOSUB 8100
1034 GOSUB 9200:FOR I=1 TO 4*K:GOSUB 9130:NEXT I
1035 GOSUB 8360
1036 GOSUB 9200:FOR I=1 TO K:GOSUB 9170:NEXT I
1037 GOSUB 9200:FOR I=1 TO 8*K:GOSUB 9110:NEXT I
1040 GOSUB 9200
1041 FOR I=1 TO 10*K:GOSUB 9170:NEXT I:GOSUB 1900:GOSUB 9200
1042 FOR I=1 TO K:GOSUB 9170:NEXT I
1043 GOSUB 8330
1044 GOSUB 9200:FOR I=1 TO 8*K:GOSUB 9110:NEXT I
1050 GOSUB 9200
1052 FOR I=1 TO 9*K:GOSUB 9170:NEXT I
1054 GOSUB 1900
1055 GOSUB 9200:FOR I=1 TO K:GOSUB 9170:NEXT I
1056 GOSUB 8300
1057 GOSUB 9200:FOR I=1 TO 8*K:GOSUB 9110:NEXT I
1060 GOSUB 9200
1062 FOR I=1 TO 9*K:GOSUB 9170:NEXT I
1064 GOSUB 1900
1065 GOSUB 9200:FOR I=1 TO K:GOSUB 9170:NEXT I
1066 GOSUB 8280
1067 GOSUB 9200:FOR I=1 TO 8*K:GOSUB 9110:NEXT I
1070 GOSUB 9200
1072 FOR I=1 TO 9*K:GOSUB 9170:NEXT I
1074 GOSUB 1900
1075 GOSUB 9200:FOR I=1 TO K:GOSUB 9170:NEXT I
1076 GOSUB 8250
1077 GOSUB 9200:FOR I=1 TO 8*K:GOSUB 9110:NEXT I
1080 GOSUB 9200
1082 FOR I=1 TO 9*K:GOSUB 9170:NEXT I
```

LISTING 5-2 (continued)

```
1084 GOSUB 1900
1085 GOSUB 9200:FOR I=1 TO K:GOSUB 9170:NEXT I
1086 GOSUB 8220
1087 GOSUB 9200:FOR I=1 TO 8*K:GOSUB 9110:NEXT I
1090 GOSUB 9200
1092 FOR I=1 TO 9*K:GOSUB 9170:NEXT I
1094 GOSUB 1900
1095 GOSUB 9200:FOR I=1 TO K:GOSUB 9170:NEXT I
1096 GOSUB 8180
1097 GOSUB 9200:FOR I=1 TO 8*K:GOSUB 9110:NEXT I
1100 GOSUB 9200
1102 FOR I=1 TO 9*K:GOSUB 9170:NEXT I
1104 GOSUB 1900
1105 GOSUB 9200:FOR I=1 TO K:GOSUB 9170:NEXT I
1106 GOSUB 8150
1107 GOSUB 9200:FOR I=1 TO 8*K:GOSUB 9110:NEXT I
1110 GOSUB 9200
1112 FOR I=1 TO 9*K:GOSUB 9170:NEXT I
1114 GOSUB 1900
1115 GOSUB 9200:FOR I=1 TO K:GOSUB 9170:NEXT I
1116 GOSUB 8120
1117 GOSUB 9200:FOR I=1 TO 8*K:GOSUB 9110:NEXT I
1120 GOSUB 9200
1122 FOR I=1 TO 9*K:GOSUB 9170:NEXT I
1124 GOSUB 1900
1125 GOSUB 9200:FOR I=1 TO K:GOSUB 9170:NEXT I
1126 GOSUB 8100
1127 GOSUB 9200:FOR I=1 TO 8*K:GOSUB 9110:NEXT I
1130 GOSUB 9200:FOR I=1 TO 9*K:GOSUB 9170:NEXT I
1899 RETURN
1900 REM X-AXIS MARKINGS
1910 GOSUB 9200
1914 FOR I=1 TO 2*K:GOSUB 9110:NEXT I
1916 GOSUB 9210
1918 FOR I=1 TO 4*K:GOSUB 9150:NEXT I
1920 GOSUB 9200
1922 FOR I=1 TO 6*K:GOSUB 9150:NEXT I
1999 RETURN
2000 REM Y-AXIS
2014 GOSUB 9210
2016 FOR I=1 TO 70*K:GOSUB 9110:NEXT I
2020 GOSUB 2900
2030 GOSUB 8280
2035 GOSUB 9200:FOR I=1 TO 6*K:GOSUB 9130:NEXT I
2040 FOR I=1 TO 8*K:GOSUB 9150:NEXT I
2042 GOSUB 2900
2044 GOSUB 8250
2045 GOSUB 9200:FOR I=1 TO 6*K:GOSUB 9130:NEXT I
2050 FOR I=1 TO 8*K:GOSUB 9150:NEXT I
2052 GOSUB 2900
2054 GOSUB 8220
2055 GOSUB 9200:FOR I=1 TO 6*K:GOSUB 9130:NEXT I
2060 FOR I=1 TO 8*K:GOSUB 9150:NEXT I
2062 GOSUB 2900
2064 GOSUB 8180
2065 GOSUB 9200:FOR I=1 TO 6*K:GOSUB 9130:NEXT I
```

```
2070 FOR I=1 TO 8*K:GOSUB 9150:NEXT I
2072 GOSUB 2900
2074 GOSUB 8150
2075 GOSUB 9200:FOR I=1 TO 6*K:GOSUB 9130:NEXT I
2080 FOR I=1 TO 8*K:GOSUB 9150:NEXT I
2082 GOSUB 2900
2084 GOSUB 8120
2085 GOSUB 9200:FOR I=1 TO 6*K:GOSUB 9130:NEXT I
2090 FOR I=1 TO 8*K:GOSUB 9150:NEXT I
2092 GOSUB 2900
2094 GOSUB 8100
2095 GOSUB 9200:FOR I=1 TO 6*K:GOSUB 9130:NEXT I
2100 FOR I=1 TO 8*K:GOSUB 9150:NEXT I
2899 RETURN
2900 REM Y-AXIS MARKINGS
2910 GOSUB 9200
2914 FOR I=1 TO 2*K:GOSUB 9130:NEXT I
2916 GOSUB 9210
2918 FOR I=1 TO 4*K:GOSUB 9170:NEXT I
2920 GOSUB 9200
2922 FOR I=1 TO 4*K:GOSUB 9170:NEXT I
2924 FOR I=1 TO 2*K:GOSUB 9150:NEXT I
2999 RETURN
8000 REM NUMERIC SUBROUTINES
8100 REM "1"
8101 GOSUB 9210
8102 FOR I=1 TO 2*K:GOSUB 9130:NEXT I
8104 FOR I=1 TO K:GOSUB 9170:NEXT I
8106 FOR I=1 TO 4*K:GOSUB 9110:NEXT I
8108 FOR I=1 TO K:GOSUB 9160:NEXT I
8110 GOSUB 9200:FOR I=1 TO K:GOSUB 9120:NEXT I:FOR I=1 TO 4*K:GOSUB 9150:NEXT I:
FOR I=1 TO K:GOSUB 9170:NEXT I
8112 RETURN
8120 REM "2"
8122 FOR I=1 TO 4*K:GOSUB 9110:NEXT I
8123 GOSUB 9210
8124 FOR I=1 TO 2*K:GOSUB 9130:NEXT I
8126 FOR I=1 TO 2*K:GOSUB 9150:NEXT I
8128 FOR I=1 TO 2*K:GOSUB 9170:NEXT I
8130 FOR I=1 TO 2*K:GOSUB 9150:NEXT I
8132 FOR I=1 TO 2*K:GOSUB 9130:NEXT I
8134 GOSUB 9200
8136 FOR I=1 TO 2*K:GOSUB 9170:NEXT I
8138 RETURN
8150 REM "3"
8152 GOSUB 9200
8154 FOR I=1 TO 2*K:GOSUB 9110:NEXT I
8156 GOSUB 9210
8158 FOR I=1 TO 2*K:GOSUB 9130:NEXT I
8160 GOSUB 9200
8162 FOR I=1 TO 2*K:GOSUB 9170:NEXT I
8164 FOR I=1 TO 2*K:GOSUB 9110:NEXT I
8166 GOSUB 9210
8168 FOR I=1 TO 2*K:GOSUB 9130:NEXT I
8170 FOR I=1 TO 4*K:GOSUB 9150:NEXT I
8172 FOR I=1 TO 2*K:GOSUB 9170:NEXT I
```

LISTING 5-2 (continued)

```
8174 RETURN
8180 REM "4"
8182 GOSUB 9200
8184 FOR I=1 TO 4*K:GOSUB 9110:NEXT I
8186 GOSUB 9210
8188 FOR I=1 TO 2*K:GOSUB 9150:NEXT I
8190 FOR I=1 TO 2*K:GOSUB 9130:NEXT I
8192 GOSUB 9200
8194 FOR I=1 TO 2*K:GOSUB 9110:NEXT I
8196 GOSUB 9210
8198 FOR I=1 TO 4*K:GOSUB 9150:NEXT I
8200 GOSUB 9200
8210 FOR I=1 TO 2*K:GOSUB 9170:NEXT I
8212 RETURN
8220 REM "5"
8222 GOSUB 9200
8224 FOR I=1 TO 4*K:GOSUB 9110:NEXT I
8226 FOR I=1 TO 2*K:GOSUB 9130:NEXT I
8228 GOSUB 9210
8230 FOR I=1 TO 2*K:GOSUB 9170:NEXT I
8232 FOR I=1 TO 2*K:GOSUB 9150:NEXT I
8234 FOR I=1 TO 2*K:GOSUB 9130:NEXT I
8236 FOR I=1 TO 2*K:GOSUB 9150:NEXT I
8238 FOR I=1 TO 2*K:GOSUB 9170:NEXT I
8240 RETURN
8250 REM "6"
8252 GOSUB 9200
8254 FOR I=1 TO 2*K:GOSUB 9110:NEXT I
8256 GOSUB 9210
8258 FOR I=1 TO 2*K:GOSUB 9130:NEXT I
8260 FOR I=1 TO 2*K:GOSUB 9150:NEXT I
8262 FOR I=1 TO 2*K:GOSUB 9170:NEXT I
8264 FOR I=1 TO 4*K:GOSUB 9110:NEXT I
8266 GOSUB 9200
8268 FOR I=1 TO 4*K:GOSUB 9150:NEXT I
8270 RETURN
8280 REM "7"
8282 GOSUB 9200
8284 FOR I=1 TO 4*K:GOSUB 9110:NEXT I
8286 GOSUB 9210
8288 FOR I=1 TO 2*K:GOSUB 9130:NEXT I
8290 FOR I=1 TO 4*K:GOSUB 9150:NEXT I
8292 GOSUB 9200
8294 FOR I=1 TO 2*K:GOSUB 9170:NEXT I
8296 RETURN
8300 REM "8"
8302 GOSUB 9210
8304 FOR I=1 TO 4*K:GOSUB 9110:NEXT I
8306 FOR I=1 TO 2*K:GOSUB 9130:NEXT I
8308 FOR I=1 TO 4*K:GOSUB 9150:NEXT I
8310 FOR I=1 TO 2*K:GOSUB 9170:NEXT I
8312 GOSUB 9200
8314 FOR I=1 TO 2*K:GOSUB 9110:NEXT I
8316 GOSUB 9210
8318 FOR I=1 TO 2*K:GOSUB 9130:NEXT I
8320 GOSUB 9200
```

```
8322 FOR I=1 TO 2*K:GOSUB 9170:NEXT I
8324 FOR I=1 TO 2*K:GOSUB 9150:NEXT I
8326 RETURN
8330 REM "9"
8332 GOSUB 9200
8334 FOR I=1 TO 2*K:GOSUB 9110:NEXT I
8336 FOR I=1 TO 2*K:GOSUB 9130:NEXT I
8338 GOSUB 9210
8340 FOR I=1 TO 2*K:GOSUB 9170:NEXT I
8342 FOR I=1 TO 2*K:GOSUB 9110:NEXT I
8344 FOR I=1 TO 2*K:GOSUB 9130:NEXT I
8346 FOR I=1 TO 4*K:GOSUB 9150:NEXT I
8348 GOSUB 9200
8350 FOR I=1 TO 2*K:GOSUB 9170:NEXT I
8352 RETURN
8360 REM "0"
8362 GOSUB 9210
8364 FOR I=1 TO 4*K:GOSUB 9110:NEXT I
8366 FOR I=1 TO 2*K:GOSUB 9130:NEXT I
8368 FOR I=1 TO 4*K:GOSUB 9150:NEXT I
8370 FOR I=1 TO 2*K:GOSUB 9170:NEXT I
8372 RETURN
9000 REM INITIALIZE OUTPUT
9010 OUT 236,16
9020 POKE 16526,00:POKE 16527,127
9030 RETURN
9100 REM VECTOR GENERATOR
9110 REM "p"
9112 POKE 32575,112
9114 X=USR(0)
9116 RETURN
9120 REM "q"
9122 POKE 32575,113
9124 X=USR(0)
9126 RETURN
9130 REM "r"
9132 POKE 32575,114
9134 X=USR(0)
9136 RETURN
9140 REM "s"
9142 POKE 32575,115
9144 X=USR(0)
9146 RETURN
9150 REM "t"
9152 POKE 32575,116
9154 X=USR(0)
9156 RETURN
9160 REM "u"
9162 POKE 32575,117
9164 X=USR(0)
9166 RETURN
9170 REM "v"
9172 POKE 32575,118
9174 X=USR(0)
9176 RETURN
9180 REM "w"
```

LISTING 5-2 (continued)
```
9182 POKE 32575,119
9184 X=USR(0)
9186 RETURN
9200 REM PEN UP(y)
9202 POKE 32575,121
9204 X=USR(0)
9206 RETURN
9210 REM PEN DOWN(z)
9212 POKE 32575,122
9214 X=USR(0)
9216 RETURN
10000 DATA 243,00,00,58,63,127,22,09,55,63,50,63,127,218,23,127,62,01,211,01,210
,27,127,62,00,211
10002 DATA 01,62,09,61,194,29,127,58,63,127,31,21,194,10,127,62,00,211,01,62,44,
61,194,47,127,201
```

Command	Character	BASIC Address
+Y	p	9110
+X,+Y	q	9120
+X	r	9130
+X,-Y	s	9140
-Y	t	9150
-X,-Y	u	9160
-X	v	9170
-X,+Y	w	9180
Pen up	y	9200
Pen down	z	9210

TABLE 5-1   HIPLOT command characters.

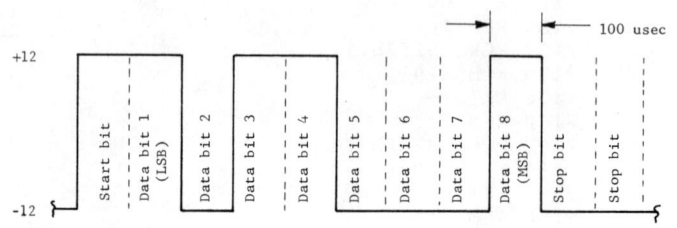

FIGURE 5-2   Bit pattern and spacing of RS232-C output from the demonstration program.

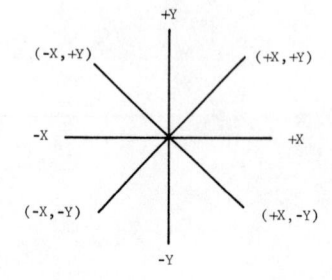

FIGURE 5-3   HIPLOT vector notations.

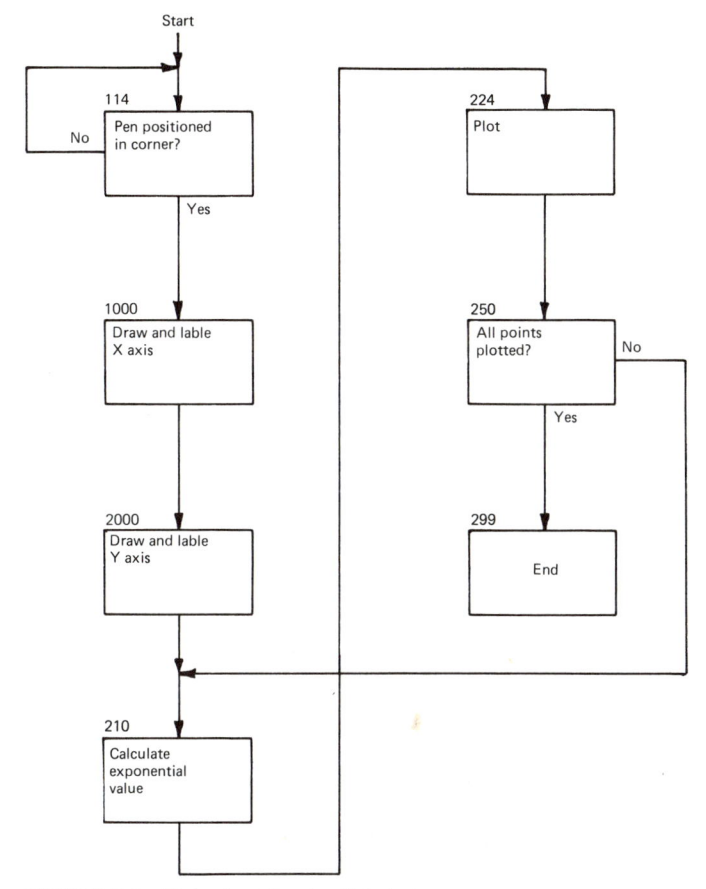

FIGURE 5-4 Flow chart for the digital plotter program.

ponential increase in voltage as a function of time. Figure 5.5 shows a series of plots taken for increasing values of the time constant. The software was written so that the entire plot could be scaled to different dimensions. Figure 5.6 shows the maximum range of plot size. It should be obvious to the reader that the program will most likely have to be modified to meet the requirements of his specific application. The program shown in Listing 5.2 was written in a very general sense to make it easier for the reader to follow. As a result of this fact, a significant increase in plotting speed can be realized by reducing the number of subroutine calls and by keeping the software as compact as possible.

VIDEO TERMINAL

There are going to be times when you will want to use your Mod III as a video terminal to connect into a large, host computer network. Networks that provide a message retrieval system have been around for quite a while, and we are

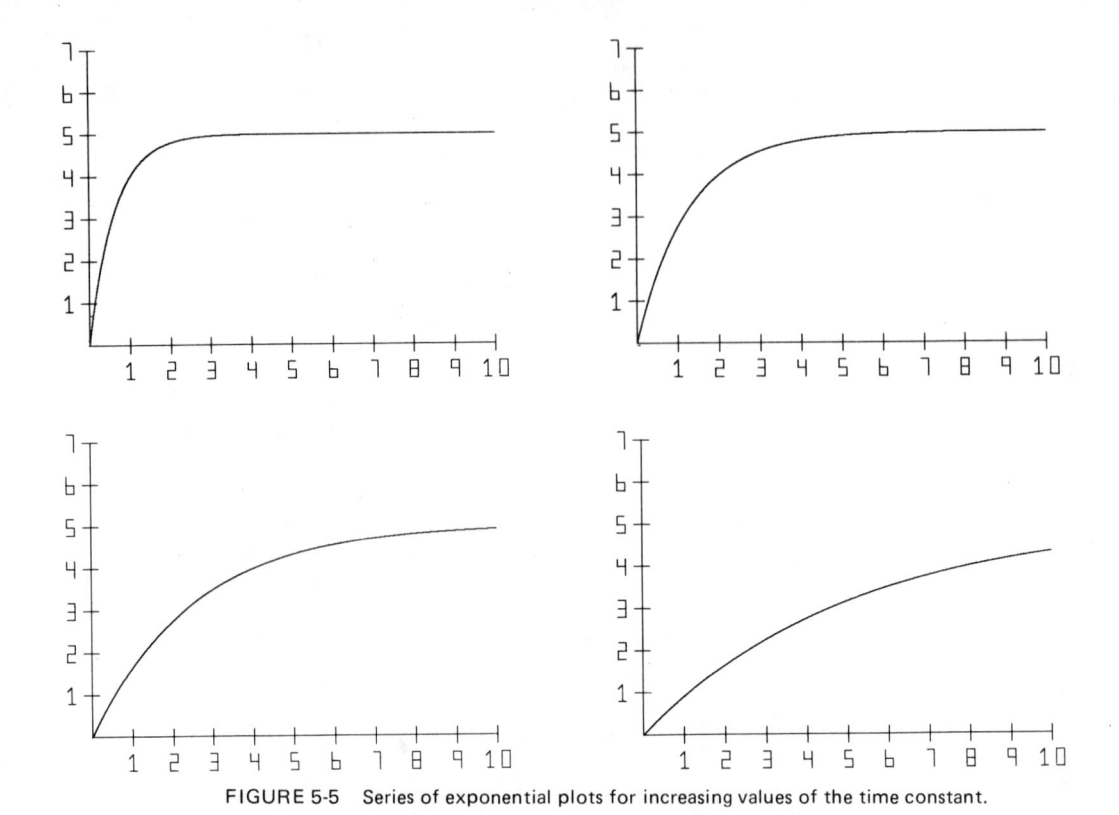

FIGURE 5-5 Series of exponential plots for increasing values of the time constant.

now beginning to see a proliferation of information services that provide local, national, and international news, weather, sports, and investment-related topics. In the future, you will probably be able to access information on suppliers dealing with banking, car rental, classified ads, and reservation services. Individuals usually access one of these networks through the use of a modem connected between a video terminal and their telephone. A *modem* is a device that performs two basic functions (Figure 5.7):

1. It accepts digital input from a computer and converts the pulses into analog-frequency signals for transmission over the telephone lines.
2. It converts analog-frequency signals from the telephone into digital signals, which the computer can process.

Modems that transmit information at 300 bps are readily available through a multitude of suppliers for under $200. The Mod III can be used as a video terminal by building a bidirectional serial interface and writing some software. You could accomplish the same thing by buying a commercial serial interface board, but you can save a few dollars by building your own. You should realize that my

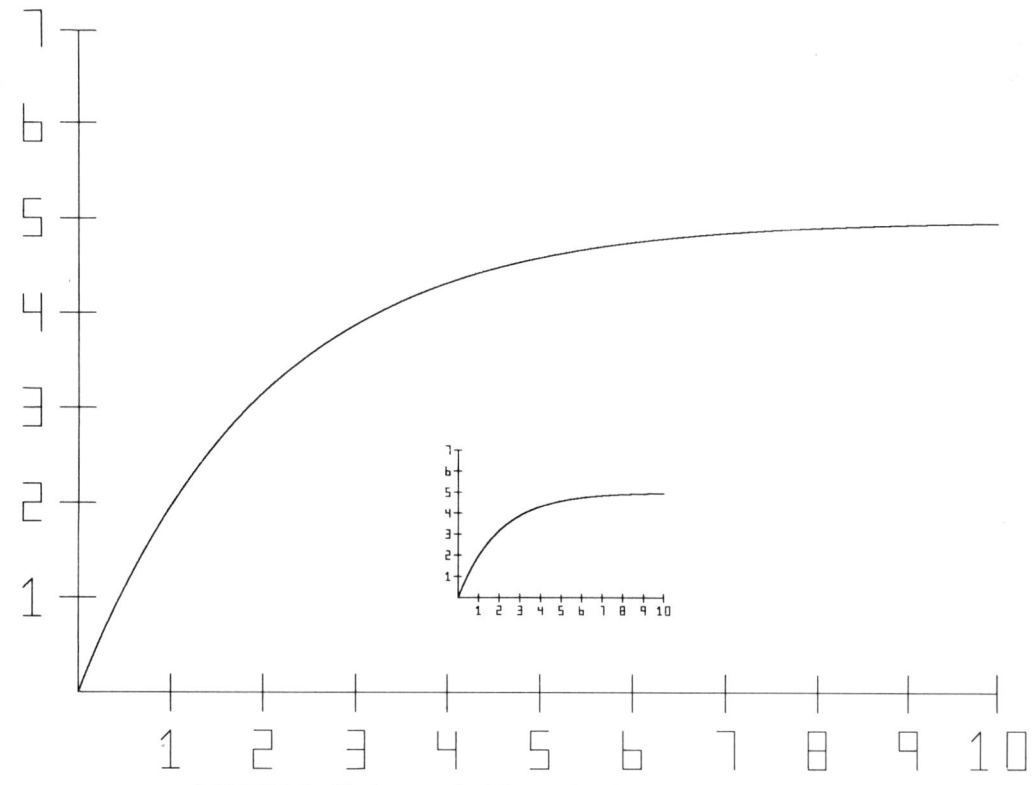

FIGURE 5-6 Maximum and minimum plot dimensions.

approach minimizes hardware and maximizes software, thus saving money at the expense of versatility. Figure 5.8 shows the hardware that will be needed, and the connections that will have to be made to the Mod III and to the modem. You should recognize the circuits as ones that were developed and described in Chapter 2. Once you have constructed the interface and made the interconnections, perform the following test to make sure that everything is working correctly:

1. If you execute the following BASIC statements, the output of IC1 should go to +12V.
   100 OUT 236,16
   110 OUT 1,1
2. If you execute the following BASIC statements, the output of IC1 should go to −12V.
   100 OUT 236,16
   110 OUT 1,0
3. If you execute the following BASIC statements, the number displayed on the video monitor should change from a 1 to a 0 when you ground the serial input line.

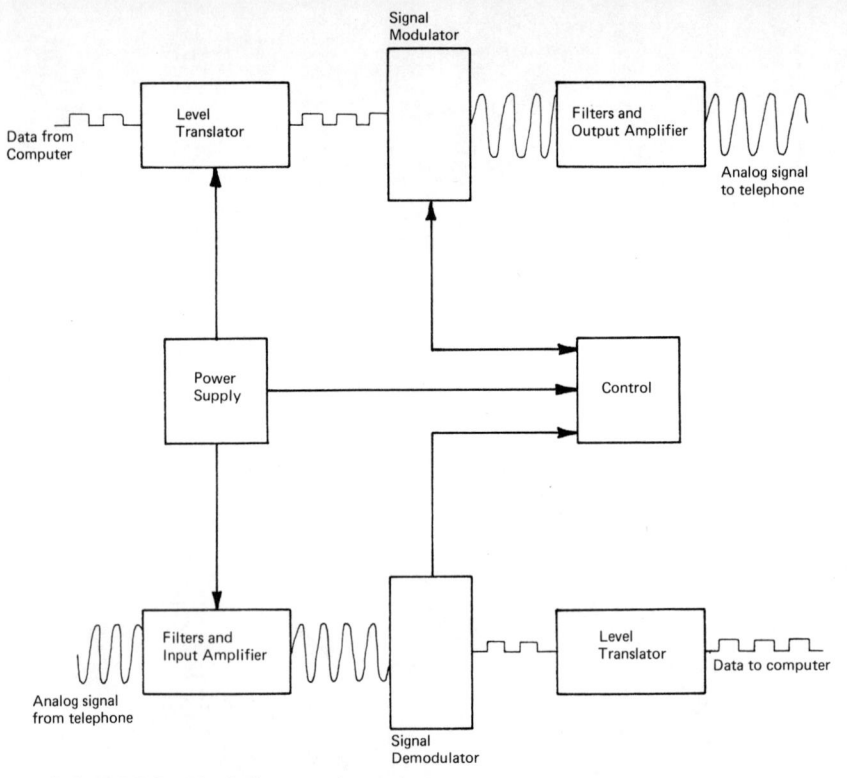

FIGURE 5-7 Block diagram of a modem.

FIGURE 5-8 Video terminal interface circuit and system connections.

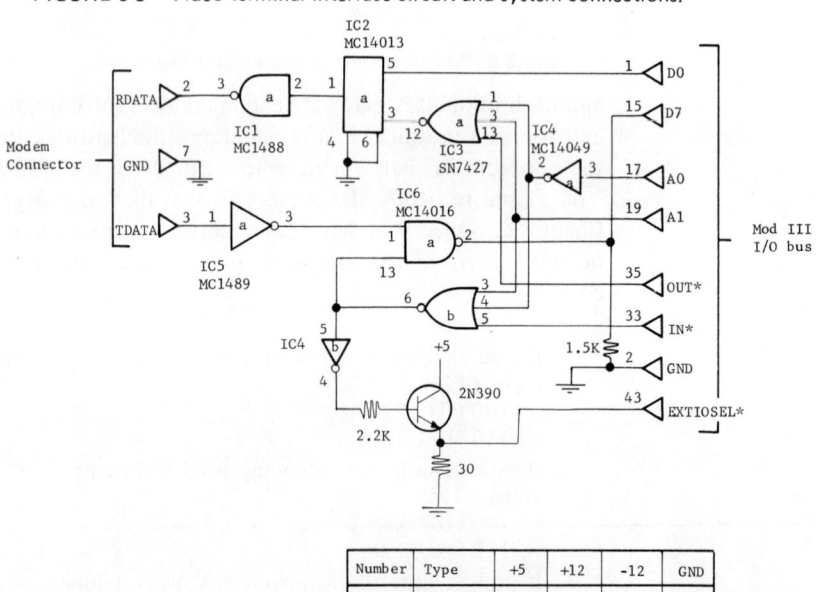

Number	Type	+5	+12	-12	GND
IC1	MC1488	--	14	1	7
IC2	MC14013	14	--	--	7
IC3	SN7427	14	--	--	7
IC4	MC14049	1	--	--	8
IC5	MC1489	14	--	--	7
IC6	MC14016	14	--	--	7

Utilization of the Mod III in Serial Applications

```
100 OUT 236,16
110 K=INP (1)
120 IF K <128 THEN PRINT "0"
130 IF K >128 THEN PRINT "1"
140 GOTO 100
```

Listing 5.3 shows the machine language program that allows the Mod III to transmit and receive serial data at 300 bps (see Figure 5.9 for the program flow chart). Listing 5.4 shows the program converted over to a series of BASIC statements.

LISTING 5-3   Machine language program for the bidirectional serial interface.

```
                    00100           ;VIDEO TERMINAL
                    00110           ;R. HALLGREN   5-25-81
7F00                00120           ORG     7F00H
7F4F                00130 TEMP      EQU     7F4FH       ;CHARACTER STORAGE
7F00 F3             00140           DI                  ;DISABLE INT
7F01 3E10           00150           LD      A,10H
7F03 D3EC           00160           OUT     (0ECH),A
7F05 CD8D02         00170 RS        CALL    28DH
7F08 C2977F         00180           JP      NZ,BRK
7F0B CD2B00         00190           CALL    2BH         ;GET KEYBOARD CHARACTER
7F0E FE00           00200           CP      00H         ;CHECK FOR CHARACTER
7F10 CA507F         00210           JP      Z,RECV
7F13 1609           00220 SEND      LD      D,09H       ;1 START BIT, 8 DATA BITS
7F15 37             00230           SCF
7F16 3F             00240           CCF                 ;CLEAR CARRY (START BIT)
7F17 324F7F         00250 DATA      LD      (TEMP),A    ;SAVE DATA
7F1A DA277F         00260           JP      C,MARK      ;IF CARRY, SEND MARK
7F1D 3E01           00270           LD      A,01H
7F1F D301           00280           OUT     (01H),A     ;SEND SPACE
7F21 D48A7F         00290           CALL    NC,DELAY    ;JUMP IF SPACE SENT
7F24 C32E7F         00300           JP      NEWD
7F27 3E00           00310 MARK      LD      A,00H
7F29 D301           00320           OUT     (01H),A     ;SEND A MARK
7F2B CD8A7F         00330           CALL    DELAY
7F2E 3A4F7F         00340 NEWD      LD      A,(TEMP)    ;GET DATA
7F31 1F             00350           RRA                 ;LSD INTO CARRY
7F32 15             00360           DEC     D
7F33 C2177F         00370           JP      NZ,DATA     ;JUMP IF ALL BITS NOT SENT
7F36 3E00           00380 STPBIT    LD      A,00H
7F38 D301           00390           OUT     (01H),A     ;SEND MARK
7F3A CD8A7F         00400           CALL    DELAY
7F3D C3507F         00410           JP      RECV
7F50                00420           ORG     7F50H
7F50 0600           00430 RECV      LD      B,00H
7F52 1608           00440           LD      D,08H       ;8 DATA BITS
7F54 DB01           00450 SAMP      IN      A,(01H)     ;SAMPLE INPUT
7F56 17             00460           RLA                 ;ROTATE BIT INTO CARRY
7F57 DA057F         00470           JP      C,RS
7F5A 3EE6           00480           LD      A,0E6H
7F5C 3D             00490           DEC     A
7F5D C25C7F         00500           JP      NZ,$-1
7F60 CD8A7F         00510 AGAIN     CALL    DELAY
7F63 DB01           00520           IN      A,(01H)
```

LISTING 5-3 (continued)

```
7F65  E680      00530         AND    80H        ;SAVE MSB
7F67  B0        00540         OR     B          ;ADD NEW BIT TO DATA
7F68  47        00550         LD     B,A
7F69  CB08      00560         RRC    B          ;ROTATE BITS
7F6B  15        00570         DEC    D
7F6C  C2607F    00580         JP     NZ,AGAIN
7F6F  CB10      00590         RL     B
7F71  78        00600         LD     A,B        ;TRANSFER DATA INTO ACC.
7F72  E67F      00610         AND    7FH
7F74  47        00620         LD     B,A
7F75  FE40      00630         CP     40H
7F77  CA507F    00640         JP     Z,RECV
7F7A  78        00650         LD     A,B
7F7B  FE0D      00660         CP     0DH
7F7D  CA507F    00670         JP     Z,RECV
7F80  78        00680 CR      LD     A,B
7F81  CD3300    00690         CALL   33H
7F84  CD8A7F    00700         CALL   DELAY
7F87  C3057F    00710         JP     RS
7F8A  0E02      00720 DELAY   LD     C,02H
7F8C  3EE6      00730 DEL     LD     A,0E6H
7F8E  3D        00740         DEC    A
7F8F  C28E7F    00750         JP     NZ,$-1
7F92  0D        00760         DEC    C
7F93  C28C7F    00770         JP     NZ,DEL
7F96  C9        00780         RET
7F97  3E1B      00790 BRK     LD     A,1BH
7F99  C3137F    00800         JP     SEND
```

I will describe the start-up procedure that I use for interacting with the university computer system. Since operating systems will differ from location to location, this should be used as an example only.

1. Load and execute the BASIC program.
2. Dial up the computer facility, listen for the carrier tone, and insert the handset into the modem. (This step assumes that you have not purchased a direct-connect modem.)
3. Press the ENTER key. If the host does not respond, press the ENTER key again.
4. Once the host responds, sign on in the normal way.
5. Limit the right-hand margin to 61 characters to prevent losing data. Double the delay time before printing is resumed after a line feed. Failing to do so can result in the Mod III becoming "confused" and refusing to print characters on the CRT. If this happens, you can restart the program by executing a SYSTEM command and responding with /32512 ENTER.
6. To abort an operation, press the BREAK key.

FIGURE 5-9 Video terminal program flow chart.

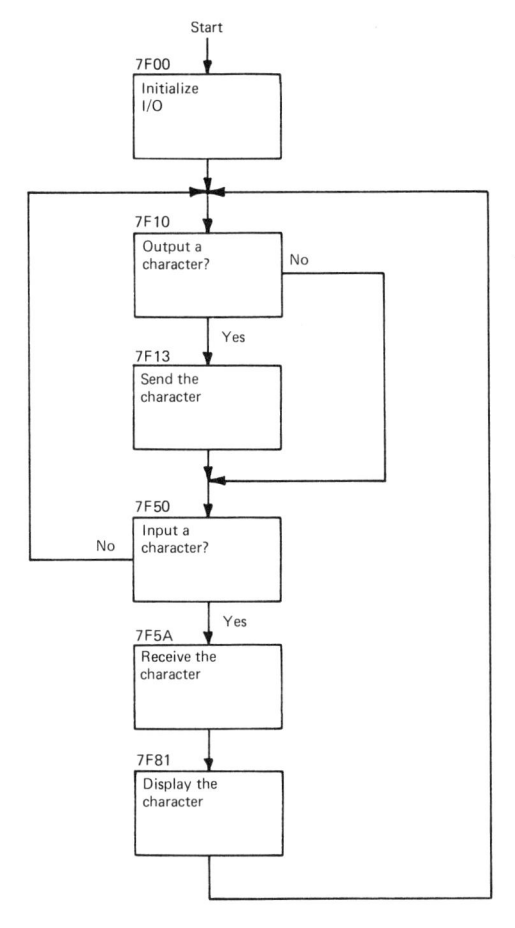

LISTING 5-4   Listing 5-3 converted to BASIC program.
```
100 REM MOD III VIDEO TERMINAL
110 REM R. HALLGREN
112 REM 5-27-81
120 FOR I=32512 TO 32667:READ K:POKE I,K:NEXT I
122 CLS
124 PRINT "Dial up the host system and press the ENTER key"
125 PRINT "",""
126 PRINT "If the Mod III should become confused, re-enter the program by:":PRINT "","",""
127 PRINT "         1. Press RESET":PRINT ""
128 PRINT "         2. Answer with L and ENTER":PRINT ""
129 PRINT "         3. Enter SYSTEM":PRINT ""
130 PRINT "         4. Enter /32512":PRINT ""
140 PRINT " Remember to limit the right margin to 61 characters and to"
142 PRINT "double the delay that comes after a line feed."
150 POKE 16526,0:POKE 16527,127
152 X=USR(0)
199 END
10000  DATA 243,62,16,211,236,205,141,2,194,151,127,205,43,0,254,0,202,80,127,22,9
10010  DATA 55,63,50,79,127,218,39,127,62,1,211,1,212,138,127,195,46,127,62,0,211,1,205
10015  DATA 138,127,58,79,127,31,21,194,23,127,62,0,211,1,205,138,127,195,80,127
10017  DATA 0,0,0,0,0,0,0,0,0,0,0,0,0,0,0,6,0,22
10020  DATA 8,219,1,23,218,5,127,62,230,61,194,92,127,205,138,127,219,1,230,128,176,71
10022  DATA 203,8,21,194,96,127,203,16,120,230,127,71,254,64,202,80,127,120,254,13,202,80,127
10030  DATA 120,205,51,0,205,138,127,195,5,127,14,2,62,230,61,194,142,127,13,194,140
10032  DATA 127,201,62,27,195,19,127
```

6

BIOFEEDBACK

Have you ever thought about the number of complex operations that your body is required to perform in the course of a "normal" day's activity? While we often take for granted our ability to perform complex, coordinated muscular activity, it results from years of trial-and-error training. An infant has very little muscular control over its body and develops greater control by constantly practicing. Most of us have observed a young child learning how to walk: repeatedly standing, taking a few steps, and falling down.

The human brain is composed of billions of specialized cells called neurons. Neurons are designed to transmit information between peripheral sensory receptors and the brain, to analyze this information, and to transmit commands, if necessary, back to muscles. For example, when you touch an object, sensory receptors in the skin send to the brain coded information related to the temperature of the object. The brain then processes the information and decides the course of action to be taken. Coded information is then sent to the muscles in the hand and arm. The possible result is that the hand may be jerked back from a very hot object, or left in place if the object is cool.

The body is equipped with many similar neuromuscular pathways that never get developed because there is no common use for them. Yet it is no big trick to learn how to wiggle your ears; you just spend some time in front of a mirror teaching yourself which nerves are connected to that particular set of muscles. The normal process of leaning requires that "feedback" accompany the behavior pattern being established—that is, you normally expect to see, hear, or feel the results of a particular action. For example, it would be difficult, if not impossible, to learn how to play the violin if you were deaf; the normal learning experience requires that auditory "feedback" accompany the manipulation of the bow.

Many functions of the body, such as heart rate and skin temperature, which have long been thought to be under exclusive control of the autonomic nervous system, have been found to be controllable. Training involuntary muscles is normally not possible, because we lack a natural feedback path to tell us how we are affecting the system. However, with the aid of sensitive electronic equipment, physiological changes that a person is normally incapable of sensing can be altered and controlled. Thus, the term *biofeedback* is used when a biological process is measured, and the results of the measurement are fed back to the individual. Through a training experience, the individual can learn to control phenomena such as skin temperature and heart rate.

SKIN TEMPERATURE

Heat is produced in the human body by muscular exercise, the assimilation of food, and all the processes that contribute to the basal metabolic rate. Heat is lost to the surroundings through radiation, conduction, and vaporization of water in the nasal passages and from the skin. Man, and vertebrates in general, have multiple mechanisms for regulating heat loss so that the body remains at an almost constant temperature under normal conditions. One of the primary mechanisms for heat regulation is through the control of skin temperature. Skin temperature is controlled by regulating the amount of blood that is allowed to flow to the skin. Cold hands and feet, a common phenomenon, result from peripheral vasoconstriction under the control of the contraction of the smooth muscles lining peripheral blood vessels, thus reducing blood circulation and skin temperature at the extremities and conserving heat.

Peripheral skin temperature is influenced by a number of factors:

1. Stress causes fingertip temperature to drop several degrees below room temperature.
2. A variety of drugs, including tobacco, have an influence on vasoconstriction.
3. Vigorous activity increases peripheral circulation, while inactivity decreases circulation.

We will be using the low-speed A/D converter that we developed in Chapter 3, along with an analog circuit, to interface a thermistor to the Model III. Figure

Number	Type	+5	-5	GND
IC1	AD580	1	--	3
IC2	CA3140T	7	4	--

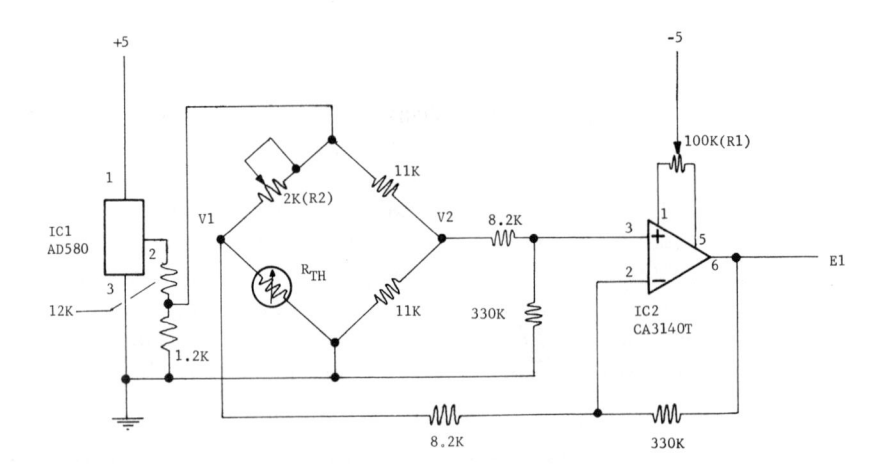

R_{TH} is a Yellow Springs Instrument YSI 409A Attachable Surface Temperature Probe. Obtain information from the Scientific Division, Yellow Springs Instrument Co., Inc. Yellow Springs, Ohio 45387.

FIGURE 6-1 Schematic diagram of the analog circuitry for the biofeedback temperature monitor.

6.1 shows the schematic diagram of the analog circuitry. This design uses a *thermistor*, a device whose resistance is a function of its temperature, in one leg of a bridge circuit. Bridge circuits allow us to detect small changes in resistance by measuring imbalances in the bridge with a differential amplifier.

Mechanically, thermistors are nearly ideal components. They are usually small in size and rugged, and they demonstrate the reliability and extended life common to semiconductor products. By using appopriate values of resistance in the bridge circuit, small changes in temperature can be made to produce large changes in the output voltage. Since the output voltage is amplified by a differential amplifier (Appendix B), there will be little problem with noise being introduced into the measurements.

In Figure 6.1, IC1 is a voltage regulator that provides a stable reference voltage to the bridge circuitry. The output voltage from IC1 has been reduced to minimize temperature variations that might occur as a result of self-heating in the thermistor. Such variations, which would appear as a slow drifting of the output signal, are undesirable. IC2 is a high-grain, differential amplifier that is used to measure the difference between voltages V1 and V2.

Once you have built the analog circuit, you should make the following adjustments and voltage checks:

1. The voltage at pin #2 on IC1 should be equal to +2.5V.
2. Short the points labeled V1 and V2 together and adjust R1 until the voltage at E1 is equal to 0V. This ensures that the output of the differential amplifier will be equal to 0 when the inputs are equipotential.
3. Remove the short from the points labeled V1 and V2, hold the thermistor in your mouth for one minute, and adjust R2 (the temperature calibration adjustment) until the output voltage E1, is equal to +1.07V. You should realize that we are going to be interested in relative changes in temperature and not in absolute values of temperature, so calibration is not going to be performed precisely.
4. Connect the output, E1, to the input of the A/D converter. Load and execute BASIC program 1 (Listing 3.6). The video display should indicate that you are measuring a voltage that increases when you hold the thermistor between your fingertips and decreases when you let go of it.
5. Load and execute BASIC program 2 (Listing 6.1 and Figure 6.2). You should see temperature plotted as each sample is taken. The plot should move toward the top of the screen for increases in temperature and move toward the bottom of the screen for decreases in temperature. Figure 6.3 shows a photograph of the graphic display that results from first putting the thermistor into, and then taking the thermistor out of, my mouth. Notice how the temperature of the thermistor goes below the room temperature as a result of evaporation.

LISTING 6-1 BASIC program for biofeedback skin temperature experiments.

```
10 REM LOWSPEED A/D CONVERTER #2
12 REM R. HALLGREN    4-15-81
20 DIM K(100)
22 FOR I=31248 TO 31344:READ K:POKE I,K:NEXT I
24 GOSUB 1000
30 REM CONVERT ONE SAMPLE
31 CLS:Q=0:GOSUB 5000
32 POKE 16919,1
34 FOR I=1 TO 20
40 L=PEEK(16919)
41 IF L=0 THEN L=61
42 IF L<Q+P THEN GOTO 40
43 IF L=61 THEN L=0
44 Q=L
50 POKE 16526,16:POKE 16527,122
60 X=USR(0)
70 X1=PEEK(31232):X2=PEEK(31233):X3=PEEK(31234):X4=PEEK(31235)
71 W4=X4
72 IF X4>7 THEN X4=0
```

LISTING 6-1 (continued)

```
73 IF X4=0 THEN GOTO 80
74 X4=1
80 X$=STR$(X4)+STR$(X3)+STR$(X2)+STR$(X1)
82 K(I)=-VAL(X$)/1000
83 IF X4=0 THEN W4=W4-8
84 IF W4>3 THEN K(I)=-K(I)
88 GOSUB 5110
90 NEXT I
92 GOTO 30
99 END
1000 REM INTRODUCTION
1010 CLS
1030 PRINT "THIS IS A DEMONSTRATION PROGRAM FOR CONTROLLING SKIN"
1031 PRINT "TEMPERATURE USING BIOFEEDBACK IN CONFUNCTION WITH THE LOW"
1032 PRINT "SPEED A/D CONVERTER AND THE DATA PLOT ROUTINE."
1040 PRINT "",""
1050 PRINT "THE PLOT ROUTINE EXPECTS THE INPUT VOLTAGE TO BE POSITIVE."
1070 PRINT "",""
1102 PRINT "YOU CAN HAVE A DATA POINT PLOTTED EVERY"
1103 PRINT "     1. SECOND"
1104 PRINT "     2. 5 SECONDS"
1105 PRINT "     3. 10 SECONDS"
1106 PRINT "     4. 30 SECONDS"
1107 PRINT "     5. MINUTE"
1108 PRINT "",""
1110 PRINT "PRESS THE KEY CORRESPONDING TO YOUR CHOICE"
1120 K$=INKEY$
1130 IF K$="1" THEN P=1:RETURN
1132 IF K$="2" THEN P=5:RETURN
1133 IF K$="3" THEN P=10:RETURN
1134 IF K$="4" THEN P=30:RETURN
1135 IF K$="5" THEN P=60:RETURN
1139 GOTO 1120
1140 RETURN
2000 DATA 8,217,62,16,211,236,211,02,219,01,23,210,24,122,219,3
2010 DATA 50,04,122,230,128,254,128,194,30,122,58,04,122,230,15
2020 DATA 50,3,122,219,3,50,4,122,230,64,254,64,194,50,122,58,4,122
2030 DATA 230,15,50,2,122,219,3,50,4,122,230,32,254,32,194,70,122,58,4,122
2040 DATA 230,15,50,1,122,219,3,50,4,122,230,16,254,16,194,90,122
2050 DATA 58,4,122,230,15,50,0,122,8,217,201
5000 REM DATA PLOT ROUTINE
5008 CLS:J=0
5010 PRINT @993,"TIME ( X";P;")";CHR$(28)
5015 PRINT @512,"TEMP(F)";CHR$(28)
5020 PRINT @907,"0";CHR$(28):PRINT @912,"2";CHR$(28):PRINT @917,"4";CHR$(28)
5021 PRINT @922,"6";CHR$(28):PRINT @927,"8";CHR$(28):PRINT @932,"10";CHR$(28)
5022 PRINT @947,"16";CHR$(28):PRINT @952,"18";CHR$(28):PRINT @957,"20";CHR$(28)
5024 PRINT @937,"12";CHR$(28):PRINT @942,"14";CHR$(28)
5030 FOR I=1 TO 53:PRINT @(842+I),CHR$(176);CHR$(28):NEXT I
5100 REM SCALE PLOT
5101 FOR I=0 TO 13
5102 PRINT @(11+64*I),CHR$(191);CHR$(28)
5103 NEXT I
5104 FOR I=0 TO 7
5105 PRINT @(2+64*I),112-4*I;CHR$(28)
5106 NEXT I
```

```
5107 FOR I=9 TO 13
5108 PRINT @(2+64*I),112-4*I;CHR$(28):NEXT I
5109 RETURN
5110 REM DATA PLOT
5111 J=0:M=1.4:DM=.1
5114 IF K(I)=0 THEN GOTO 5192
5116 IF K(I)<0 THEN GOTO 5192
5122 Y=M-J*(DM/3)
5130 IF Y<K(I) THEN Y=J:GOTO 5180
5140 J=J+1
5142 IF J>40 THEN GOTO 5180
5144 GOTO 5122
5180 X=(23+5*I)
5182 IF Y<0 THEN Y=0
5184 SET (X,Y)
5192 RETURN
```

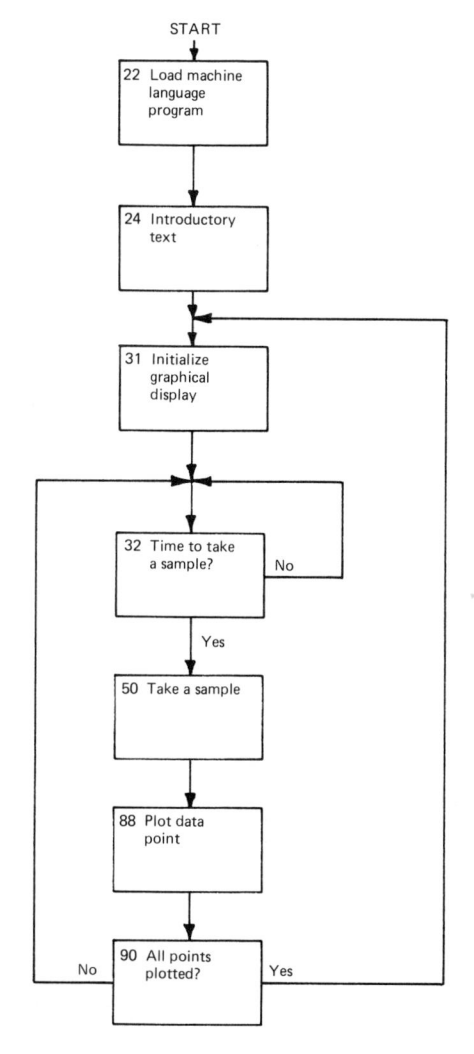

FIGURE 6-2
Flow chart of the BASIC program.

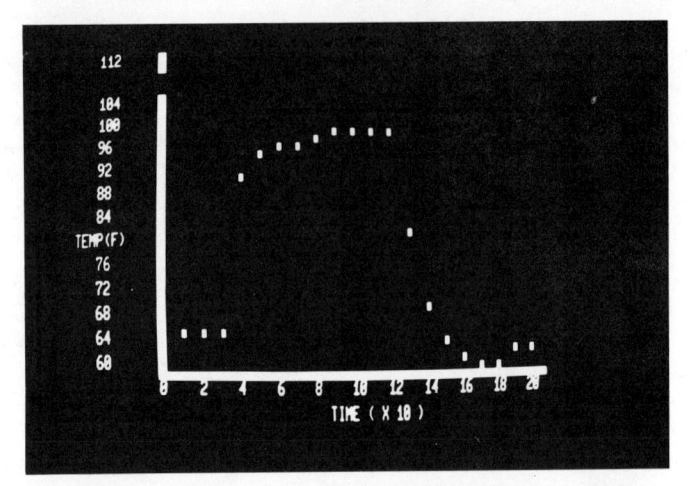

FIGURE 6-3 Graphic display resulting from placing the thermistor in the author's mouth and then removing it.

Figure 6.4 shows a diagrammatic representation of the experimental set-up. You should tape the thermistor to the index finger on your dominant hand (the hand you write with). You will "see" temperature changes that are too small for you to detect, but that are easily detected by the thermistor. The graphic display on the CRT will serve as the feedback link to your central nervous system.

FIGURE 6-4 Diagramatic representation of temperature feedback. The electronic measuring system informs the subject of temperature changes so small that they are not sensed normally.

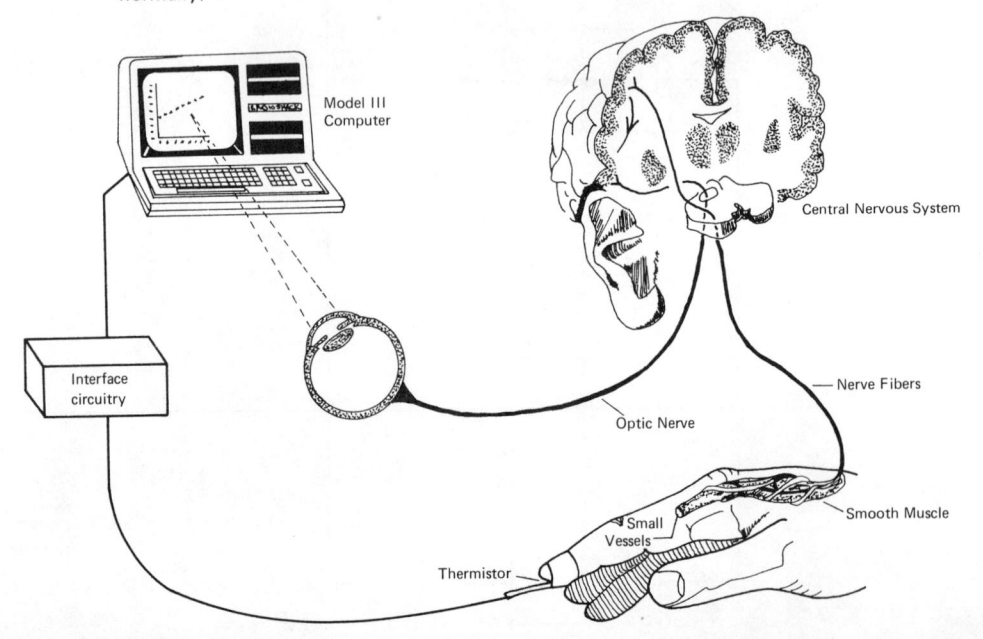

First seat yourself in a comfortable chair and, once you are relaxed, imagine that your hand has been placed in hot water. With some practice you should be able to precisely control an increase or decrease in temperature. Within a few minutes you should be able to raise or lower your temperature one or two degrees merely by "telling" yourself to raise or lower your finger temperature. After some practice you should be able to increase that variation to ten degrees.

You may want to monitor your temperature while watching a television program. Or try taping the thermistor to another part of your body, such as your face, to see how vasoconstriction effects skin temperature in different locations.

HEART RATE

Heart rate changes as a function of many factors. Some emotions, such as anger and excitement, cause an increase in heart rate. Other emotions, such as fear and grief, cause a decrease in heart rate. The body has several regulatory mechanisms to monitor the concentration of carbon dioxide in the blood and the distension of blood vessels, as well as to adjust heart rate to maintain cardiovascular system parameters within acceptable limits. We normally do not think of regulating our heart rate, primarily because there is not an obvious pathway for feedback. However, we can use an electronic measuring system to allow us to monitor our heart rate and to allow us to investigate normal responses to such things as breathing and relaxation.

We can conveniently get an indirect measurement of heart rate by using a system called *photoplethysmography*. Light can easily be transmitted through capillary beds existing in the ear lobe or the fingertip. As arterial pulsations cause the blood volume in the capillary bed to increase and decrease, the amount of scattered, absorbed, and reflected light changes. This phenomena can be used to give us a signal that varies as a function of heart rate. Such a system is sensitive to motion, and therefore performs best when the subject is sitting quietly.

Figure 6.5 shows a diagrammatic representation of the experimental setup. We will be using the capillary bed in your fingertip to monitor pulsations in blood volume due to contractions of the cardiac muscle. A pulse detector and an analog circuit will be used to detect, filter, and amplify the pulses so that they can be measured by the low-speed A/D converter. The computer will then count the pulses and present your heart rate in the form of a graphical display.

Figure 6.6 shows a schematic diagram of the analog circuitry that we will be using to interface the pulse detector to the low-speed A/D converter. You should notice that it is a modification of the circuit that we used for measuring skin temperature. In this case we use a *photocell*, a device whose resistance changes as a function of the intensity of light falling upon its surface, to detect changes

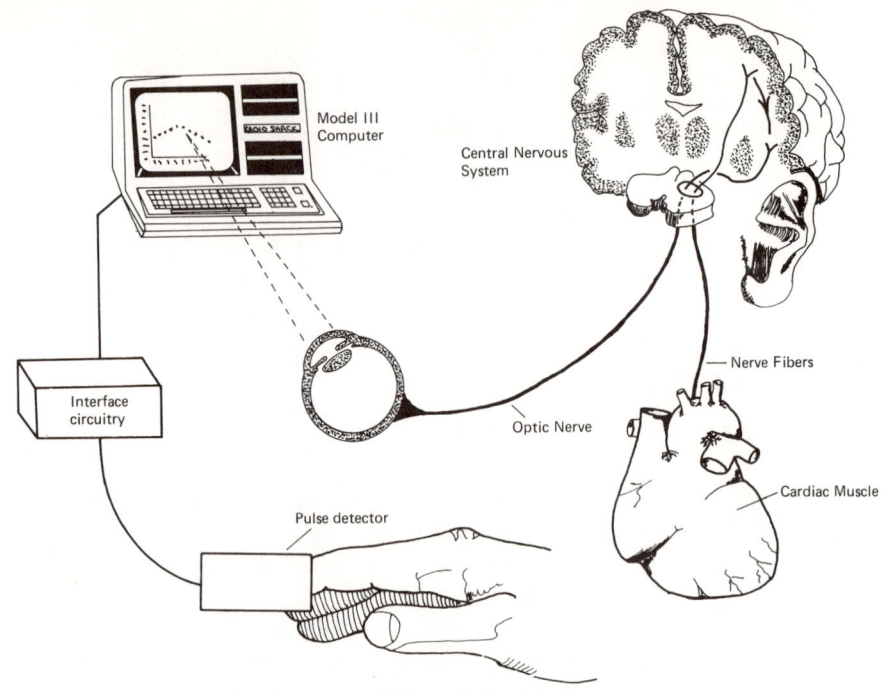

FIGURE 6-5   Diagramatic representation of heart rate feedback. The electronic measuring system informs the subject of changes too small to be sensed normally.

FIGURE 6-6   Schematic diagram of the analog circuitry for biofeedback heart rate monitor.

Number	Type	+5	-5	GND
IC1	AD580	1	---	3
IC2	CA3140T	7	4	---

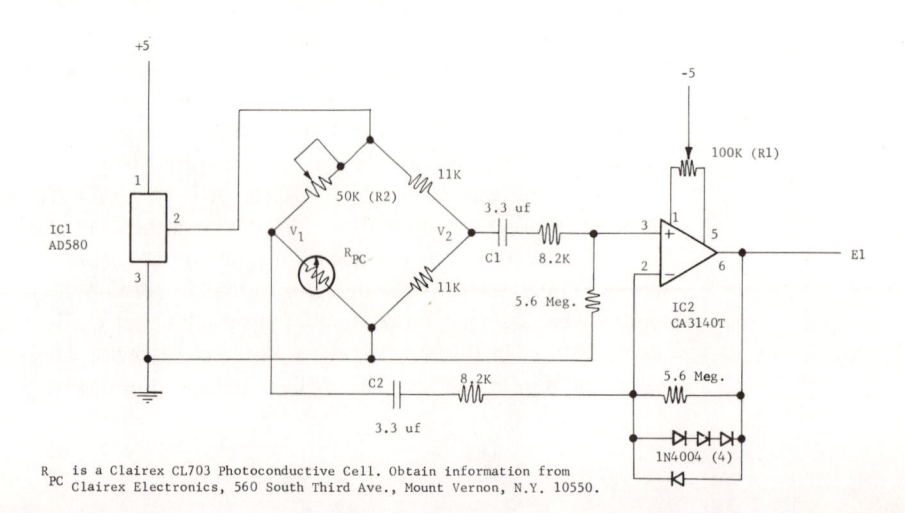

R_{PC} is a Clairex CL703 Photoconductive Cell. Obtain information from Clairex Electronics, 560 South Third Ave., Mount Vernon, N.Y. 10550.

in light passing through the capiliary bed in the finger. When the photocell is put into a bridge circuit, small changes in resistance that occur due to small changes in light intensity can be made to produce large changes in output voltage.

In Figure 6.6, IC1 is a voltage regulator that provides a stable reference voltage to the bridge circuitry. Since we are counting pulses and not really measuring a value of resistance, we do not have to be overly concerned about output voltage drift due to the internal heating of the photocell. Consequently, we do not have to reduce the output of the regulator, and we can thus obtain increased sensitivity from the output of the bridge. IC2 is a high-gain, differential amplifier that is used to measure the difference between voltages V1 and V2. Capacitors C1 and C2 block the dc component of the signal. Diodes are included in the feedback loop of the amplifier to limit the output voltage, increasing the sharpness of the voltage change that occurs when the heart beats.

You should first concern yourself with the construction of the pulse detector. Figure 6.7a shows a drawing indicating the position of the photocell relative to the light source. The distance between the photocell and the light source will depend on the size of your fingers. To keep this distance to a minimum, you should make the hole just large enough to fit the smallest finger on your hand; usually the little finger. To get enough intensity from the lamp you will need a 3-V dc supply that can provide about 250 mA. You can use two D-cell batteries connected in series, or you can build a 5-V supply from Appendix C and use a 10-Ω, 1-W resistor in series with the lamp. I have shown the latter. To simplify construction as much as possible, I mounted the photocell and the lamp on a small block of wood.

Once you have built the pulse detector and the analog circuit, you should make the following adjustments and voltage checks:

1. The voltage at pin #2 on IC1 should be equal to 2V.
2. Short the points labeled V1 and V2 together and adjust R1 until the voltage at E1 is equal to 0V.
3. Remove the short from the points labeled V1 and V2, and connect the output E1 to the input of the A/D converter. Load and execute BASIC program 3 (Listing 6.2). With the lamp disconnected to its power supply, the flashing should stop.

FIGURE 6-7a Position of the photocell relative to the lamp.

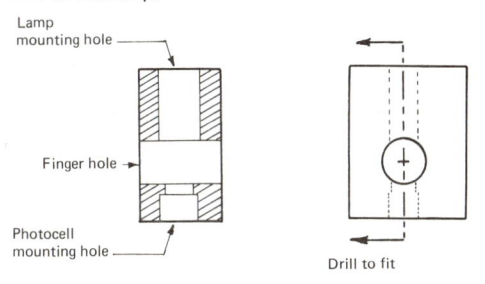

LISTING 6-2 BASIC program for biofeedback heart rate system set-up.

```
10 REM BIOFEEDBACK; HEART RATE
20 REM R. HALLGREN
22 FOR I=31248 TO 31308:READ K:POKE I,K:NEXT I
24 GOSUB 1000
1000 REM DEMONSTRATION
1010 CLS
1020 PRINT "THIS PROGRAM WILL RESPOND TO THE PULSE DETECTOR OUTPUT"
1022 PRINT "",""
1024 PRINT "YOU WILL START THE TEST WITH THE LAMP TURNED OFF"
1026 PRINT "",""
1028 PRINT "AFTER DETERMINING THAT THE INTERFACE CIRCUIT IS PERFORMING OK,"
1030 PRINT "YOU WILL TURN THE LAMP ON AND DETERMINE IF THE SOFTWARE IS OK"
1032 PRINT "","",""
1040 PRINT "PRESS THE SPACE BAR TO CONTINUE"
1042 K$=INKEY$
1044 IF K$<>" " THEN GOTO 1042
1100 POKE 16526,16:POKE 16527,122
1110 X=USR(0)
1112 CLS:PRINT CHR$(23)
1114 PRINT @346,"THROB"
1120 FOR I=1 TO 100:NEXT I
1130 GOTO 1110
2000 DATA 8,217,62,16,211,236,211,02,219,01,23,210,24,122,219,03
2010 DATA 50,04,122,230,128,254,128,194,30,122,58,04,122,230,04
2020 DATA 254,00,194,18,122,219,03,50,04,122,230,64,254,64,194,52,122,58,04,122,230,15
2030 DATA 254,02,250,18,122,08,217,201
```

4. Due to the simplicity of the design, you are going to have to develop some skill in positioning your finger in the pulse detector to ensure consistant operation. We learned in the previous section that cold hands are a good indication of poor circulation. Poor circulation means that blood flow is reduced; consequently, the signals from the pulse detector will be small, resulting in erratic operation. If your hands are cold, hold them under warm water for a few minutes. Now, insert your little finger into the pulse detector. Figure 6.7b shows the relative position of the finger with respect to the photocell. As you insert your finger, you should see the display flash in response to the motion of your finger. After you have settled

FIGURE 6-7b Position of the finger relative to the photocell.

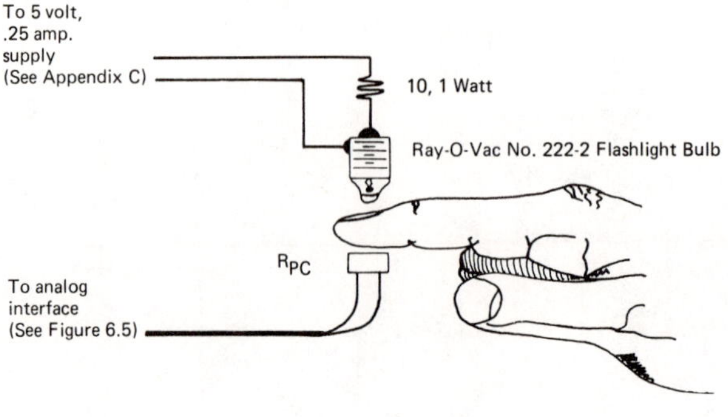

down, you should see the graphics display start to periodically pulse in response to the beat of your heart. Your finger should rest lightly upon the face of the photocell. Too much pressure will stop circulation and cause the display to skip beats.

5. Load and execute BASIC program 4 (Listing 6.3, Listing 6.4, and Figure 6.8). The program should flash in response to each heart beat, and it should display a graphical representation of pulse rate in beats per minute. Figure 6.9a shows a graphical display of the author's resting heart rate. Figure 6.9b shows the change in heart rate that occurred after a period of light exercise.

LISTING 6-3 BASIC program for biofeedback heart rate experiments.

```
10 REM BIOFEEDBACK; HEART RATE
12 DIM V(30)
14 V(1)=76:V(2)=76
20 REM R. HALLGREN
22 FOR I=31248 TO 31308:READ K:POKE I,K:NEXT I
24 GOSUB 1000
31 CLS:GOSUB 5000
34 FOR I=3 TO 22
36 Q=0
50 REM AVERAGE HEART RATE
52 POKE 16919,0
54 L=PEEK(16919)
56 IF L>P THEN GOTO 200
60 GOSUB 1100
70 Q=Q+1
72 GOTO 54
200 REM PLOT AVERAGE
204 V(I)=(V(I-1)+V(I-2)+(60/P)*Q)/3
220 GOSUB 5110
230 NEXT I
240 GOTO 31
1000 REM INTRODUCTION
1010 CLS
1030 PRINT "THIS IS A DEMONSTRATION PROGRAM FOR CONTROLLING HEART RATE"
1032 PRINT "USING BIOFEEDBACK IN CONJUNCTION WITH THE LOW SPEED A/D"
1034 PRINT "CONVERTER AND A DATA PLOT ROUTINE."
1036 PRINT "","",""
1050 PRINT "YOU CAN HAVE YOUR AVERAGE HEART RATE PLOTTED EVERY"
1054 PRINT "          1. 5 SECONDS"
1056 PRINT "          2. 10 SECONDS"
1057 PRINT "          3. 20 SECONDS"
1058 PRINT "          4. 30 SECONDS"
1070 PRINT "","",""
1072 PRINT "PRESS THE KEY CORRESPONDING TO YOUR CHOICE"
1080 K$=INKEY$
1083 IF K$="1" THEN P=5:RETURN
1084 IF K$="2" THEN P=10:RETURN
1085 IF K$="43 THEN P=20:RETURN
1086 IF K$="4" THEN P=30:RETURN
1090 GOTO 1080
1100 REM SAMPLE PULSE DETECTOR
```

LISTING 6-3 (continued)

```
1105 POKE 16526,16:POKE 16527,122
1110 X=USR(0)
1120 FOR R=1 TO 50:NEXT R
1130 RETURN
2000 DATA 8,217,62,16,211,236,211,02,219,01,23,210,24,122,219,03
2010 DATA 50,04,122,230,128,254,128,194,30,122,58,04,122,230,04
2020 DATA 254,00,194,18,122,219,03,50,04,122,230,64,254,64,194,52,122,58
2022 DATA 4,122,230,15
2030 DATA 254,02,250,18,122,08,217,201
5000 REM GRAPHIC DISPLAY
5010 CLS:J=0
5012 PRINT @993,"TIME ( X";P;")";CHR$(28)
5015 PRINT @512,"HEART";CHR$(28)
5016 PRINT @576,"RATE";CHR$(28)
5020 PRINT @907,"0";CHR$(28):PRINT @912,"2";CHR$(28):PRINT @917,"4";CHR$(28)
5021 PRINT @922,"6";CHR$(28):PRINT @927,"8";CHR$(28):PRINT @932,"10";CHR$(28)
5022 PRINT @947,"16";CHR$(28):PRINT @952,"18";CHR$(28):PRINT @957,"20";CHR$(28)
5024 PRINT @937,"12";CHR$(28):PRINT @942,"14";CHR$(28)
5030 FOR I=1 TO 53:PRINT @(842+I),CHR$(176);CHR$(28):NEXT I
5100 REM SCALE PLOT
5101 FOR I=0 TO 13
5102 PRINT @(11+64*I),CHR$(191);CHR$(28)
5103 NEXT I
5104 FOR I=0 TO 7
5105 PRINT @(2+64*I),120-6*I;CHR$(28)
5106 NEXT I
5107 FOR I=10 TO 13
5108 PRINT @(2+64*I),120-6*I;CHR$(28):NEXT I
5109 RETURN
5110 REM DATA PLOT
5111 J=0:M=120:DM=6
5114 IF V(I)=0 THEN GOTO 5192
5116 IF V(I)<0 THEN GOTO 5192
5122 Y=M-J*(DM/3)
5130 IF Y<V(I) THEN Y=J:GOTO 5180
5140 J=J+1
5142 IF J>40 THEN Y=J:GOTO 5180
5144 GOTO 5122
5180 X=(13+5*I)
5182 IF Y<0 THEN Y=0
5184 SET (X,Y)
5192 RETURN
```

LISTING 6-4 Machine language routine contained within the BASIC program.

```
                 00100 ;BIOFEEDBACK, HEART RATE
                 00110 ;CALL FROM BASIC PROGRAM
                 00120 ;R. HALLGREN
      7A04       00130 TEMP   EQU   7A04H        ;TEMPERARY DATA STORAGE
      7A10       00140        ORG   7A10H        ;INTERRUPT ENTRY POINT
      7A10 08    00150 CONVRT EX    AF,AF'
      7A11 D9    00160        EXX
      7A12 3E10  00170 CON    LD    A,10H
      7A14 D3EC  00180        OUT   (0ECH),A     ;INITIALIZE I/O PORTS
      7A16 D302  00190        OUT   (02H),A      ;START CONVERSION
      7A18 DB01  00200 SAMP   IN    A,(01H)      ;SAMPLE STATUS LINE
      7A1A 17    00210        RLA
      7A1B D2187A 00220       JP    NC,SAMP
      7A1E DB03  00230 INPT1  IN    A,(03H)      ;SAMPLE DATA LINES
      7A20 32047A 00240       LD    (TEMP),A     ;STORE DATA
      7A23 E680  00250        AND   80H
```

```
7A25  FE80       00260          CP    80H
7A27  C21E7A     00270          JP    NZ,INPT1
7A2A  3A047A     00280          LD    A,(TEMP)
7A2D  E604       00290          AND   04H                  ;PEEL OFF DIGIT CODE
7A2F  FE00       00300          CP    00H
7A31  C2127A     00310          JP    NZ,CON
7A34  DB03       00320  INPT2   IN    A,(03H)
7A36  32047A     00330          LD    (TEMP),A
7A39  E640       00340          AND   40H
7A3B  FE40       00350          CP    40H
7A3D  C2347A     00360          JP    NZ,INPT2
7A40  3A047A     00370          LD    A,(TEMP)
7A43  E60F       00380          AND   0FH
7A45  FE02       00390          CP    02H
7A47  FA127A     00400          JP    M,CON
7A4A  08         00410          EX    AF,AF'
7A4B  D9         00420          EXX
7A4C  C9         00430          RET
```

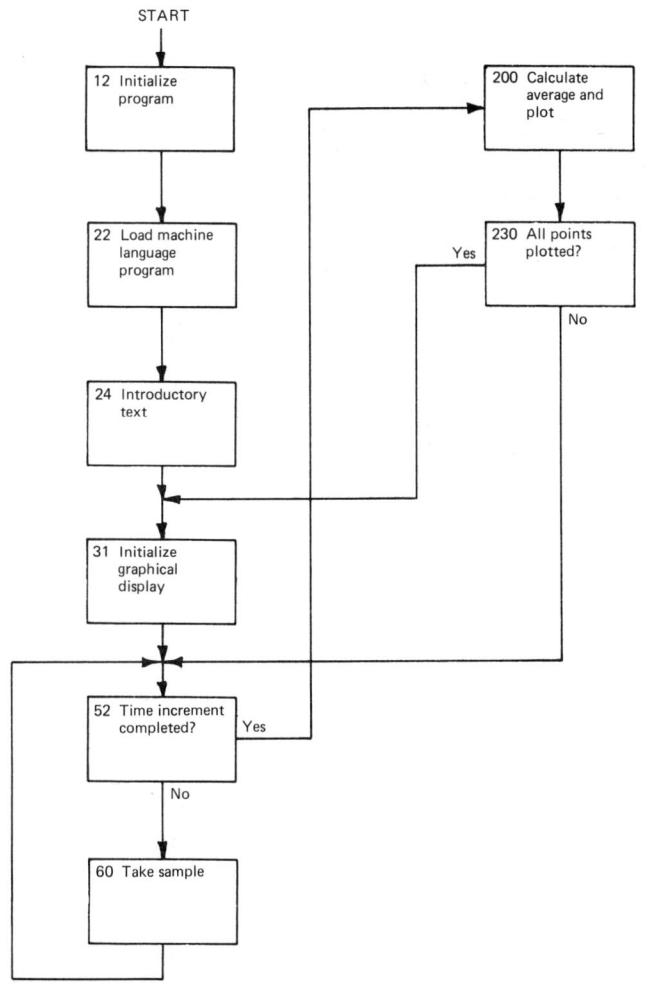

FIGURE 6-8
Flow chart for the BASIC program.

97

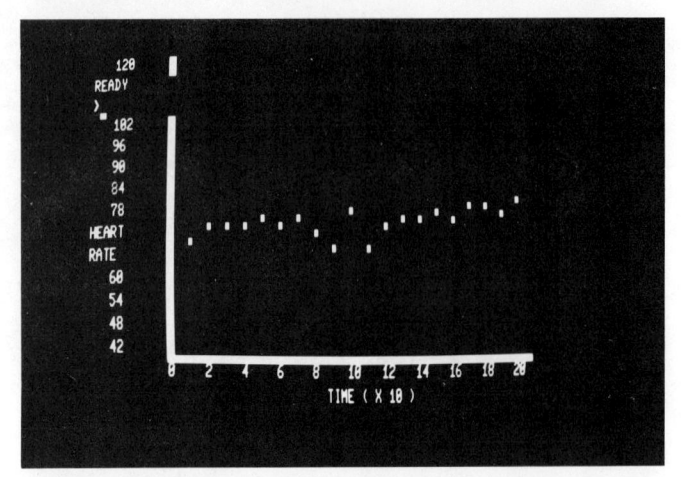

FIGURE 6-9a Graphical display of resting level heart rate.

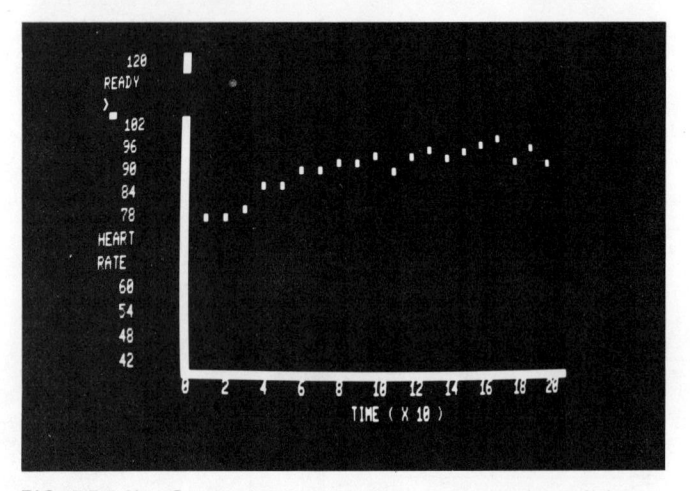

FIGURE 6-9b Graphical display of heart rate change due to light exercise.

Once you have confirmed that the system is working correctly, insert your finger into the pulse detector, and we will learn some things about your cardiovascular system. Remember that the detector is motion-sensitive, so you should assume a quiet sitting position with your arm and hand supported on a surface.

The first thing that you will notice is that your heart rate is a function of respiration. When you inhale, your heart rate decreases. Also if you hold your breath for several seconds, you should expect to see a decrease followed by an increase in heart rate. The graphical display on the CRT will be used as the feedback path to your central nervous system.

You can also alter your heart rate by practicing progressive relaxation exercises. The idea behind these exercises is to learn how to relax by learning to sense the difference between tension and relaxation. Start by assuming a comfortable position. Starting with the feet, alternately tense and relax your muscles. Suppose you have tensed the muscles in your left leg. When you relax that group of muscles, you should feel the leg become limp and heavy. As you progress through this relaxation process, your heart rate should decrease, indicating a state of relaxation.

You may want to monitor your heart rate while watching your favorite television program. Sporting events or mystery shows are good candidates for causing your heart rate to significantly increase and decrease. Monitor your pulse rate while you drink a cup of coffee or as you smoke a cigarette. For the more daring individual, you might want to monitor your heart rate as you balance your checkbook at the end of the month.

7

CONTROLLING A VIDEO PLAYBACK DEVICE

"One picture is worth a thousand words." This phrase illustrates the importance of the visual representation of material in the learning process. Educators have been able to effectively utilize snapshots, slides, film strips, and motion pictures to allow students to visualize objects and physical phenomena without some of the problems associated with actually bringing the students in contact with them. While these media serve the purpose, their effectiveness is limited by the facts that the viewing speed is fixed, the content of the material is fixed, and there is no simple means of allowing individual students to interact with the viewing device.

In an attempt to increase the student's interaction with teaching systems, slide/audio cassette systems have been developed. For many years, these systems have been used successfully as a low-cost supplement to textbook instruction at all educational levels. Using individual viewing screens and headphones, the student can view and review such things as sequential anatomical dissections, while listening to a detailed description of what they are seeing.

Television has expanded upon slide/audio tape systems by making possible the low-cost presentation of prepared lecture material, and by permitting live demonstrations of such things as surgical procedures to large audiences. The introduction of the videotape recorder has increased the impact of television by allowing lecture and demonstration materials to be recorded and then played back any number of times. Recently, less expensive videocassette players have made it possible for students to individually view and review prerecorded lecture material. The intimacy of videocassette presentations is surpassed only by the live, classroom lecture where the important ingredient of student-teacher interaction is present.

The availability of low-cost personal computing systems have provided another (and more sophisticated) tool for educators. *Computer-assisted instruction (CAI)* is a term used for a system in which the computer carries on a predetermined instructional strategy, while permitting conversational interaction with the student. Computers, with their high-speed computational ability, can be used in real-time simulations of complex, physical systems. When interfaced with a graphic display, they can also be very effective in assisting students in their understanding of these systems.

While the use of the small personal computer in an educational environment is not a new concept, the use of a personal computer to interactively control a videocassette player is. Videotaped material is abundant and readily available. Often the student will not need (or desire) to review a complete lecture, but will be concerned only with a specific segment. In such a case, the computer can be used to provide a menu from which the student can choose the desired segment. The computer is then responsible for finding the starting point of the desired segment, initiating the PLAY command, and stopping the presentation when the end of the segment is reached. The interaction of the computer and the video device can also be used as a teaching machine where the computer is used to control the presentation of videotaped lectures. At appropriate times, the lecture could be interrupted and questions asked of the viewer. Depending on the response, the viewer would be either allowed to continue, supplied with remedial material, or just returned to the start of the most recently viewed segment. This immediate feedback is an important part of the system concept and is a particularly strong feature of computer-assisted instruction. Theoretically, this system should have the following advantages over conventional methods of instruction, such as a group lecture:

1. Students can proceed through material at a rate consistent with their ability.
2. Correct responses to questions allow additional material to be presented. Incorrect responses cause material to be repeated, or supplementary material to be presented.
3. Material presentation can be organized so that special guidance can be given to correct deficiences in individual educational backgrounds.
4. Teaching material can be organized for an optimal sequence of presentation.
5. The student is obliged to play an active part in the learning process.

Betamax Connector Pin	Signal	Source/Destination
CN1-20	BEGINNING OF TAPE*	Status signal from Betamax
CN1-7	CASSETTE IN*	Status signal from Betamax
CN1-11	REWIND*	Command signal to Betamax
CN1-8	STOP*	Command signal to Betamax
CN1-13	PLAY*	Command signal to Betamax
CN1-12	FAST FORWARD*	Command signal to Betamax
CN1-15	COUNT*	Timing signal from Betamax

TABLE 7-1 Betamax status and control signals available through the pins that connect the recorder to the RM-300 Auto Search control unit.

The design of the Sony Betamax SL0-320 videocassette recorder makes interfacing it to the MOD III computer a relatively easy task. Table 7.1 shows the control, status, and timing lines that are avilable from the interface connector on the back of the Betamax. During the recording process, a timing signal is recorded onto the video tape. This timing signal, available on pin #15 of the Auto Search control unit interface connector, can be sampled by the computer and used to index the tape to any relative location. Two status signals are available at the interface connector: one signal (CASSETTE IN*) indicates when the videocassette has been inserted into the player, and the other signal (BEGINNING OF TAPE*) indicates when the videocassette tape has been fully rewound. These signals were not used in the system that is being described, but they certainly could be used if a modification of the system concept makes it desirable. Four control lines (STOP*, PLAY*, FAST FORWARD*, and REWIND*) are also available at the interface connector, and they are used to indicate to the Betamax the desired mode of operation.

Figure 7.1 shows the Betamax-to-MOD-III interface in schematic form. The left side of the schematic shows connections made to the Betamax through the RM-300 Auto Search control unit connector, while the right side of the schematic shows the connections made to the MOD III through the I/O bus connector. Line #15 (COUNT*) from the Betamax carries the timing signal formatted onto the videotape. This signal is divided by a factor of 60 by the combined action of integrated circuits IC1 (SN7490) and IC2 (SN7492). IC3 (MC14512) is an 8-channel data selector used to connect the divided timing signal to the Mod III data line D7. Increased channel sampling capability was incorporated so that the two status lines from the Betamax, or other user-defined status lines, could be sampled if so desired. Data line D7 was chosen because its state is easily tested by rotating its contents into the carry bit. Integrated circuit IC7 (MC14514) is a 4- to 16-line decoder latch used to selectively turn on one of the four transistors, thus causing the Betamax to enter either the PLAY, the REWIND, the FAST FORWARD, or the STOP mode.

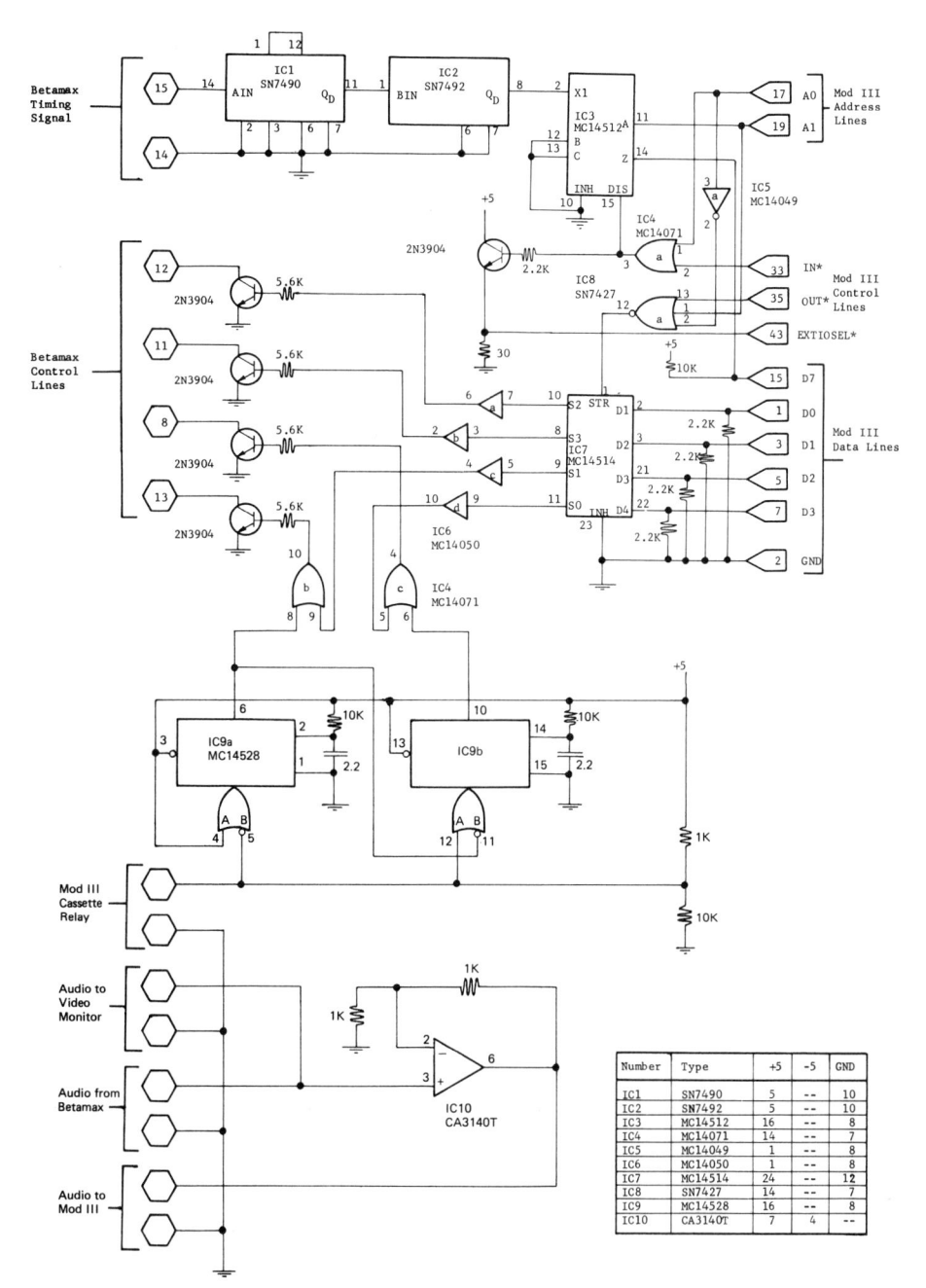

FIGURE 7-1 Betamax/Mod III interface schematic. Radio Shack TRS-80 video interface. It will interface between the TRS-80 Model III and a Sony Betamax-brand video tape player. Reproduction of this circuit diagram is by written permission of Tandy Corporation.

103

Control Signal	BASIC Command	Machine Language Command

REWIND*	OUT 236,16
	OUT 01,03
		LD A,10H
		OUT (0ECH),A
		LD A,03H
		OUT (01H),A

STOP*	OUT 236,16
	OUT 01,00
		LD A,10H
		OUT (0ECH),A
		LD A,00H
		OUT (01H),A

PLAY*	OUT 236,16
	OUT 01,01
		LD A,10H
		OUT (0ECH),A
		LD A,01H
		OUT (01H),A

FAST FORWARD*	OUT 236,16
	OUT 01,02
		LD A,10H
		OUT (0ECH),A
		LD A,02H
		OUT (01H),A

TABLE 7-2 Software commands, in both BASIC and Z80 machine language, necessary to activate the Betamax control lines.

Table 7.2 shows the function that will be accessed for a given BASIC statement or a given machine language command.

Provision was made for storing the computer program on a beginning segment of the video tape. To record the program on the video tape, you should amplify the program output of the computer going to the cassette recorder during a CSAVE operation by a factor of 11. Figure 7.2 shows a simple circuit for doing this (refer to Appendix B for a description of the circuit). For the program to be recorded, you will have to provide both the program signal and a video signal. IC12 (MC14528) is a dual monostable multivibrator configured so that it switches the Betamax into the PLAY mode when CLOAD is entered from

FIGURE 7-2 Operational amplifier circuit for recording Mod III cassette output onto the video tape.

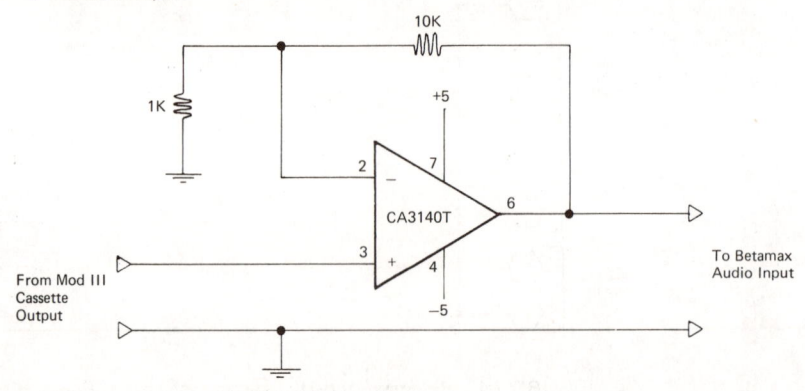

the Mod III keyboard, and switches it into the STOP mode when the program has been loaded. IC11 (CA3140T) buffers the audio output from the Betamax to the Mod III cassette audio input during the program load operation.

Once you have completed constructing the interface, you should perform the following tests to make sure that it is working correctly:

1. For each of the Betamax control functions listed in Table 7.2, execute the two BASIC commands associated with the control function. The Betamax should respond in an appropriate manner.
2. Load the Mod III with the test program that is shown in Listing 7.1. Using a prerecorded video tape placed in the cassette player, execute the program. The program should exercise the following player functions:
    a. FAST FORWARD
    b. PLAY
    c. STOP
    d. REWIND
    e. STOP
3. If everything functions correctly up to this point, try storing the test program on the beginning segment of a blank video cassette. Remember to connect the audio cables from the Mod III to the Betamax and back again. Remember also to provide some type of video signal to the Betamax during the recording process. If you now rewind the tape and enter CLOAD, you should see the Betamax begin to play, and the curser should begin to flash, indicating that a normal load is taking place.

LISTING 7-1   Betamax/Mod III test program.

```
10 REM TEST PROGRAM FOR THE BETAMAX/MOD III INTERFACE
12 REM R. HALLGREN, 6-8-81
52 GOSUB 12000
54 CLS
56 POKE 32515,0:POKE 32516,0
1000 REM EXERCISE BETAMAX CONTROL FUNCTIONS
1010 SR=100:SP=150
1011 CLS
1012 GOSUB 10000
1014 FOR I=1 TO 2000:NEXT I
1020 SR=100:SP=100
1022 GOSUB 10000
1999 END
10000 REM BETAMAX CONTROLLER
10002 R1=0:R2=0:P1=0:P2=0
10010 X=PEEK(32515)+256*PEEK(32516)
10020 R1=SR
10021 R1=R1-256
10022 IF R1=0 THEN GOTO 10030
10023 IF R1>0 THEN GOTO 10032
10024 IF R1<0 THEN GOTO 10035
```

LISTING 7-1 (continued)

```
10030 R2=R2+1:GOTO 10090
10032 R2=R2+1:GOTO 10021
10035 R1=R1+256
10050 P1=SP
10051 P1=P1-256
10052 IF P1=0 THEN GOTO 10080
10053 IF P1>0 THEN GOTO 10082
10054 IF P1<0 THEN GOTO 10085
10080 P2=P2+1:GOTO 10090
10082 P2=P2+1:GOTO 10051
10085 P1=P1+256
10090 IF X<SR THEN GOTO 10100
10092 IF X>SR THEN GOTO 10200
10094 IF X=SR THEN GOTO 10300
10100 REM FAST FORWARD
10110 POKE 32517,R1:POKE 32518,R2
10112 POKE -1,2
10114 POKE 16526,00:POKE 16527,123
10115 X=USR(0)
10116 POKE -1,0
10118 GOTO 10300
10200 REM REWIND
10202 R3=0:R4=0
10210 R3=SR+2
10211 R3=R3-256
10212 IF R3=0 THEN GOTO 10220
10213 IF R3>0 THEN GOTO 10230
10214 IF R3<0 THEN GOTO 10240
10220 R4=R4+1:GOTO 10250
10230 R4=R4+1:GOTO 10211
10240 R3=R3+256
10250 POKE 32517,R3:POKE 32518,R4
10252 POKE -1,3
10254 POKE 16526,96:POKE 16527,123
10256 X=USR(0)
10257 POKE -1,0
10258 POKE 32515,R1:POKE 32516,R2
10300 REM PLAY
10310 POKE 32517,P1:POKE 32518,P2
10320 POKE -1,1
10322 POKE 16526,00:POKE 16527,123
10324 X=USR(0)
10400 REM STOP
10412 POKE -1,0:POKE -1,14:RETURN
10999 RETURN
12000 REM MACHINE LANGUAGE ROUTINE
12010 POKE 31488,245:POKE 31489,58:POKE 31490,02:POKE 31491,128:POKE 31492,23:
      POKE 31493,218:POKE 31494,01:POKE 31495,123:POKE 31496,58
12012 POKE 31497,02:POKE 31498,128:POKE 31499,23:POKE 31500,210:POKE 31501,08:
      POKE 31502,123:POKE 31503,33:POKE 31504,03:POKE 31505,127:POKE 31506,52:
      POKE 31507,194
12014 POKE 31508,26:POKE 31509,123:POKE 31510,33:POKE 31511,04:POKE 31512,127:
      POKE 31513,52:POKE 31514,33:POKE 31515,05:POKE 31516,127:POKE 31518,03:POKE
      31519,127:POKE 31517,58
12016 POKE 31520,190:POKE 31521,194:POKE 31522,01:POKE 31523,123:POKE 31524,33:
      POKE 31525,06:POKE 31526,127:POKE 31527,58:POKE 31528,04:POKE 31529,127
```

```
12018 POKE 31530,190:POKE 31531,194:POKE 31532,01:POKE 31533,123:POKE 31534,241:
      POKE 31535,201
12020 POKE 31584,245:POKE 31585,58:POKE 31586,02:POKE 31587,128:POKE 31588,23:
      POKE 31589,218:POKE 31590,97:POKE 31591,123:POKE 31592,58:POKE 31593,02:
      POKE 31594,128:POKE 31595,23
12022 POKE 31596,210:POKE 31597,104:POKE 31598,123:POKE 31599,63:POKE 31600,58:
      POKE 31601,03:POKE 31602,127:POKE 31603,222:POKE 31604,01:POKE 31605,50:
      POKE 31606,03:POKE 31607,127:POKE 31608,58
12024 POKE 31609,04:POKE 31610,127:POKE 31611,222:POKE 31612,00:POKE 31613,50:
      POKE 31614,04:POKE 31615,127:POKE 31616,33:POKE 31617,05:POKE 31618,127:
      POKE 31619,58:POKE 31620,03:POKE 31622,190:POKE 31621,127
12026 POKE 31623,194:POKE 31624,97:POKE 31625,123:POKE 31626,33:POKE 31627,06:
      POKE 31628,127:POKE 31629,58:POKE 31630,04:POKE 31631,127:POKE 31632,190:
      POKE 31633,194:POKE 31634,97:POKE 31635,123
12028 POKE 31636,241:POKE 31637,201
12999 RETURN
```

The software portion of the controller was written in two parts:

1. Two machine language routines were written to count the pulses coming from the timing track stored on the video tape, and to determine when the desired destination on the video tape had been reached. One routine is used when the tape is moving backward.
2. A routine was written in TRS-80 BASIC to lead the desired tape destination, and to control the operational mode of the cassette player.

Figure 7.3 shows a flow chart of the machine language routine used when the tape is moving forward, and Listing 7.2 shows the actual program with comments. Figure 7.4 shows a flow chart of the machine language routine used when the tape is moving backward, and Listing 7.3 shows the actual program with comments. Upon entering either routine, the processor status and the accumulator are pushed onto the stack. The line containing the pulses from the timing track on the video tape is then sampled until it has been determined that the tape has moved a distance equal to one pulse width. A register containing two, 8-bit words is then either incremented or decremented depending on whether the tape is being moved forward or in reverse. The contents of this register is then compared to the contents of a register containing the two 8-bit words representing the destination. If the two registers are equal, the tape has reached its destination and the computer returns to the BASIC routine. If the two registers are not equal, the program goes back to wait for the next timing pulse.

Figure 7.5 shows a flow chart of a BASIC routine used for demonstration purposes, and Listing 7.4 shows the actual program with comments. At an initial decision point at line 232, students decide whether they needs to watch the whole program or just selected parts. After viewing a segment of instructional material, the student is asked a series of questions designed to test retention and comprehension of the material viewed. If retention and/or comprehension is below a specified level, the video tape is rewound to the segment starting point and the material is presented again to the student. Once comprehension and retention are demonstrated, the student is allowed to continue on to new material.

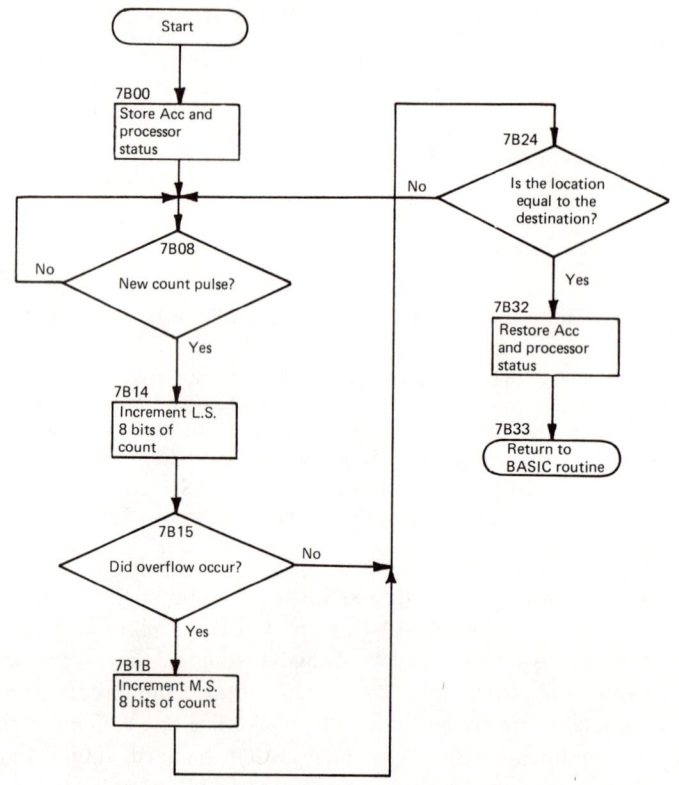

FIGURE 7-3 Flow chart of the machine language routine for incrementing and comparing the videotape location count.

LISTING 7-2 Machine language program for incrementing and comparing the videotape location count.

```
                  00100  ;INCREMENT AND COMPARE LOCATION COUNT
                  00110  ;MOD III, DEMO, R.HALLGREN, 6-8-81
7B00              00120         ORG     7B00H
7B00 08           00130         EX      AF,AF'        ;SAVE ACC & PROCESSOR STATUS
7B01 3E10         00140  RESTR: LD      A,10H
7B03 D30E         00150         OUT     (0EH),A       ;INITIALIZE I/O
7B05 DB02         00160         IN      A,(02H)       ;SAMPLE COUNT
7B07 17           00170         RLA                   ;ROTATE INTO CARRY
7B08 DA017B       00180         JP      C,RESTR
```

```
7B0B  DB02      00190 AGAIN   IN    A,(02H)
7B0D  17        00200         RLA
7B0E  D20B7B    00210         JP    NC,AGAIN       ;JUMP IF PULSE NOT CHANGED
7B11  2A037F    00220         LD    HL,(7F03H)     ;LOAD COUNT LOCATION
7B14  34        00230         INC   (HL)           ;INCREMENT
7B15  C21C7B    00240         JP    NZ,AHEAD       ;JUMP IF NO OVERFLOW
7B18  2A047F    00250         LD    HL,(7F04H)     ;LOAD COUNT LOCATION
7B1B  34        00260         INC   (HL)
7B1C  2A057F    00270 AHEAD   LD    HL,(7F05H)     ;LOAD DESTINATION LOCATION
7B1F  3A037F    00280         LD    A,(7F03H)
7B22  EDA9      00290         CPD                  ;COMPARE LOCATION WITH DEST
7B24  C2017B    00300         JP    NZ,RESTR       ;JUMP IF NOT EQUAL
7B27  21067F    00310         LD    HL,7F06H
7B2A  3A047F    00320         LD    A,(7F04H)
7B2D  EDA9      00330         CPD                  ;COMPARE LOCATION WITH DEST
7B2F  C2017B    00340         JP    NZ,RESTR       ;JUMP IF NOT EQUAL
7B32  08        00350         EX    AF,AF'         ;RESTORE ACC & PROCESSOR STATUS
7B33  C9        00360         RET                  ;RETURN TO BASIC ROUTINE
```

FIGURE 7-4 Flow chart of the machine language routine for decrementing and comparing the videotape location count.

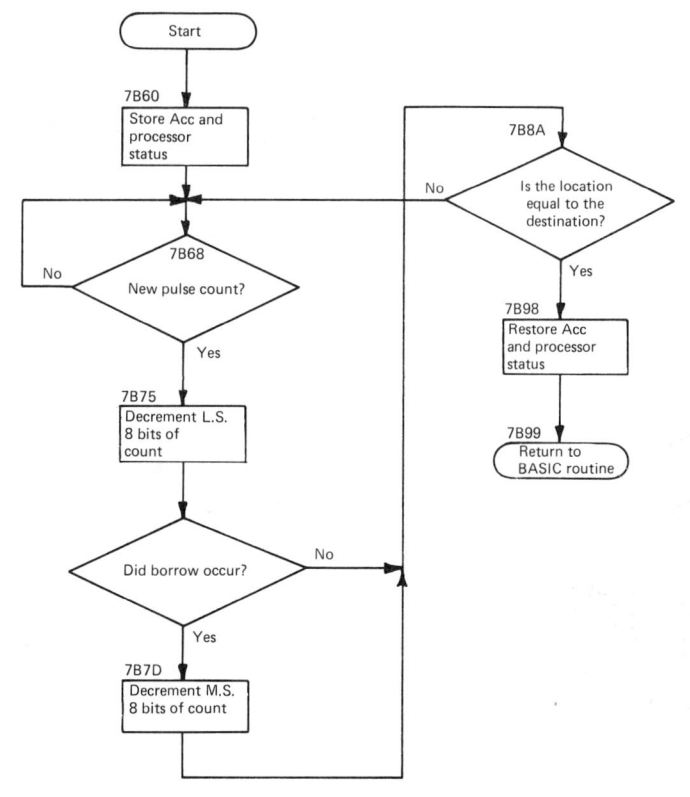

LISTING 7-3 Machine language program for decrementing and comparing the videotape location count.

```
                00370   ;DECREMENT AND COMPARE LOCATION COUNT
                00380   ;MOD III, DEMO, R. HALLGREN, 6-8-81
7B60            00390           ORG     7B60H
7B60 08         00400           EX      AF,AF'          ;SAVE ACC & PROCESSOR STATUS
7B61 3E10       00410   REST    LD      A,10H
7B63 D30E       00420           OUT     (0EH),A         ;INITIALIZE I/O
7B65 DB02       00430           IN      A,(02H)         ;SAMPLE COUNT
7B67 17         00440           RLA
7B68 DA617B     00450           JP      C,REST          ;ROTATE INTO CARRY
7B6B DB02       00460   AGANE   IN      A,(02H)
7B6D 17         00470           RLA
7B6E D26B7B     00480           JP      NC,AGANE
7B71 37         00490           SCF                     ;SET CARRY
7B72 3A037F     00500           LD      A,(7F03H)       ;LOAD COUNT
7B75 D601       00510           SUB     01H             ;SUBTRACT ONE(DECREMENT)
7B77 32037F     00520           LD      (7F03H),A
7B7A 3A047F     00530           LD      A,(7F04H)       ;LOAD COUNT
7B7D D600       00540           SUB     00H             ;SUBTRACT ONE IF BORROW OCCURRED
7B7F 32047F     00550           LD      (7F04H),A
7B82 2A057F     00560           LD      HL,(7F05H)      ;LOAD DESTINATION LOCATION
7B85 3A037F     00570           LD      A,(7F03H)
7B88 EDA9       00580           CPD                     ;COMPARE LOCATION WITH DEST
7B8A C2617B     00590           JP      NZ,REST         ;JUMP IF NOT EQUAL
7B8D 2A067F     00600           LD      HL,(7F06H)
7B90 3A047F     00610           LD      A,(7F04H)
7B93 EDA9       00620           CPD                     ;COMPARE LOCATION WITH DEST
7B95 C2617B     00630           JP      NZ,REST
7B98 08         00640           EX      AF,AF'          ;RESTORE ACC & PROCESSOR STATUS
7B99 C9         00650           RET                     ;RETURN TO BASIC ROUTINE
```

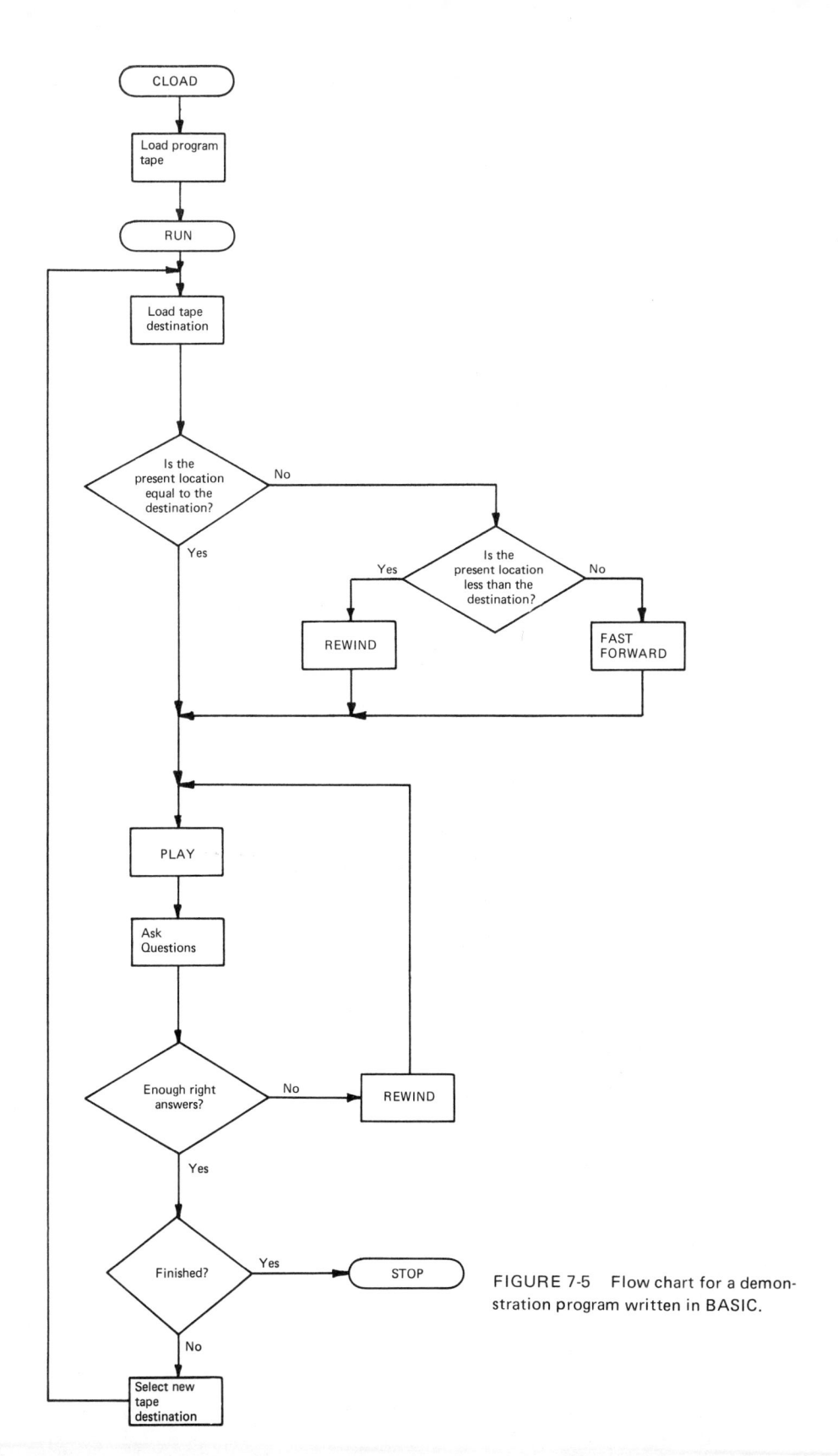

FIGURE 7-5 Flow chart for a demonstration program written in BASIC.

LISTING 7-4   Betamax/Mod III demonstration routine: Hypercalcemia.

```
52 GOSUB 12000
54 CLS
56 POKE 32515,0:POKE 32516,0
58 SR=24:SP=25
60 GOSUB 10000
100 REM PROGRAM START
101 GOSUB 12000
102 CLS
103 POKE 32515,0:POKE 32516,0
104 PRINT CHR$(23)
200 REM WHOLE PROGRAM OR PARTS?
204 PRINT "******************************"
205 PRINT "*                            *"
206 PRINT "* THE FOLLOWING IS A         *"
207 PRINT "*                            *"
208 PRINT "* DEMONSTRATION OF THE USE OF *"
210 PRINT "*                            *"
212 PRINT "* A VIDEO TAPE RECORDER IN AN *"
214 PRINT "* INTERACTIVE COMPUTER       *"
216 PRINT "* APPLICATION.               *"
222 PRINT "*                            *"
224 PRINT "******************************"
230 FOR I=0 TO 1000:NEXT I
232 CLS:PRINT CHR$(23)
233 PRINT "******************************"
234 PRINT "*                            *"
236 PRINT "* WOULD YOU LIKE TO VIEW THE *"
238 PRINT "*                            *"
239 PRINT "* WHOLE TAPE?                *"
240 PRINT "*                            *"
242 PRINT "* PRESS Y FOR YES            *"
244 PRINT "*                            *"
246 PRINT "* OR N FOR NO.               *"
247 PRINT "*                            *"
248 PRINT "******************************"
250 A$=INKEY$
252 IF A$="Y" THEN GOTO 1000
253 IF A$="N" THEN GOTO 2000
254 IF A$="*" THEN GOTO 100
258 IF A$="" THEN GOTO 250
260 GOTO 232
999 FOR I=0 TO 400:NEXT I:RETURN
1000 REM WHOLE TAPE  DEMONSTRATION
1010 SR=10:SP=100
1011 CLS
1012 GOSUB 10000
1014 GOSUB 2200
1020 SR=100:SP=130
1021 CLS
1022  GOSUB 10000
1024 GOSUB 3100
1030 SR=130:SP=195
1031 CLS
1032 GOSUB 10000
1034 GOSUB 4100
1036 CLS
1040 SR=195:SP=257
```

```
1042 GOSUB 10000
1044 GOSUB 5100
1050 SR=257:SP=322
1051 CLS
1052 GOSUB 10000
1054 GOSUB 6100
1060 SR=322:SP=450
1061 CLS
1062 GOSUB 10000
1064 GOSUB 7100
1070 SR=450:SP=850
1071 CLS
1072 GOSUB 10000
1074 GOSUB 8100
1080 SR=850:SP=1135
1081 CLS
1082 GOSUB 10000
1084 GOSUB 9100
1090 GOTO 232
1999 END
2000 REM SELECTED TAPE PRESENTATION
2002 CLS
2003 POKE -1,14:PRINT CHR$(23)
2010 PRINT "******************************"
2012 PRINT "*        CHOSE A TOPIC       *"
2014 PRINT "* 1. CALCIUM REGULATION      *"
2016 PRINT "* 2. HYPERCALCEMIA SYMPTOMS  *"
2018 PRINT "* 3. CAUSES OF HYPERCALCEMIA *"
2020 PRINT "* 4. TESTING FOR HYPERCALCEMIA*"
2022 PRINT "* 5. RANGE OF NORMAL VALUES  *"
2024 PRINT "* 6. CORRECTION FACTORS      *"
2026 PRINT "* 7. CASE HISTORY--MILD CASE *"
2028 PRINT "* 8. CASE HISTORY--SEVERE CASE*"
2030 PRINT "*                            *"
2032 PRINT "* PRESS THE KEY CORRESPONDING *"
2034 PRINT "* TO YOUR CHOICE.            *"
2036 PRINT "*                            *"
2038 PRINT "******************************"
2040 A$=INKEY$
2042 IF A$="1" THEN GOSUB 2100:GOTO 2000
2044 IF A$="2" THEN GOSUB 3000:GOTO 2000
2046 IF A$="3" THEN GOSUB 4000:GOTO 2000
2048 IF A$="4" THEN GOSUB 5000:GOTO 2000
2050 IF A$="5" THEN GOSUB 6000:GOTO 2000
2052 IF A$="6" THEN GOSUB 7000:GOTO 2000
2054 IF A$="7" THEN GOSUB 8000:GOTO 2000
2056 IF A$="8" THEN GOSUB 9000:GOTO 2000
2057 IF A$="*" THEN GOTO 100
2058 IF A$="" THEN GOTO 2040
2060 GOTO 2000
2100 REM CALCIUM REGULATION
2110 SR=10:SP=100
2112 GOSUB 10000
2200 REM FIRST QUESTION
2201 R=0:CLS
2202 POKE -1,14:PRINT CHR$(23)
```

LISTING 7-4 (continued)

```
2203 PRINT "******************************"
2204 PRINT "*                              *"
2206 PRINT "* HYPERCALCEMIA IS BEING       *"
2208 PRINT "* DIAGNOSED MORE BECAUSE OF    *"
2212 PRINT "* 1. INCREASED STRESS IN OUR   *"
2214 PRINT "*    DAILY LIVES               *"
2218 PRINT "* 2. INCREASED ABILITY TO      *"
2220 PRINT "*    TEST CALCIUM LEVELS       *"
2224 PRINT "* 3. INCREASED SUGAR IN  OUR   *"
2228 PRINT "*    DIET                      *"
2230 PRINT "*                              *"
2232 PRINT "* PRESS THE KEY CORRESPONDING  *"
2234 PRINT "* TO YOUR CHOICE.              *"
2238 PRINT "******************************"
2240 A$=INKEY$
2242 IF  A$="2" THEN GOTO 2250
2243 IF A$="" THEN GOTO 2240
2244 IF A$="*" THEN GOTO 100
2245 PRINT "INCORRECT"
2246 GOTO 2255
2250 PRINT "CORRECT"
2254 R=R+1
2255 GOSUB 999
2300 REM SECOND QUESTION
2346 IF R<1 THEN GOTO 2382
2350 CLS:POKE -1,14:PRINT CHR$(23)
2352 PRINT "YOU HAVE SCORED WELL ENOUGH TO"
2353 PRINT ""
2354 PRINT "PROCEED ON TO NEW MATERIAL."
2355 GOSUB 999
2360 RETURN
2382 CLS:POKE -1,14:PRINT CHR$(23)
2384 PRINT "YOU HAVE NOT SCORED WELL ENOUGH"
2385 PRINT ""
2386 PRINT " TO PROCEED ON TO NEW MATERIAL!"
2387 PRINT ""
2388 PRINT "PAY CLOSE ATTENTION TO THE"
2390 PRINT "LECTURE MATERIAL."
2392 GOSUB 999
2394 GOTO 2100
3000 REM SYMPTOMS
3010 SR=100:SP=130
3012 GOSUB 10000
3100 REM FIRST QUESTION
3102 R=0
3104 CLS:POKE -1,14:PRINT CHR$(23)
3110 PRINT "******************************"
3112 PRINT "*                              *"
3114 PRINT "* PATIENTS HAVING MILD         *"
3116 PRINT "*                              *"
3118 PRINT "* HYPERCALCEMIA CAN BE         *"
3120 PRINT "*                              *"
3122 PRINT "* DESCRIBED   AS BEING ------- *"
3124 PRINT "*                              *"
3126 PRINT "******************************"
3128 PRINT "":PRINT ""
3130 INPUT A$
```

```
3132 IF A$="ASYMPTOMATIC" THEN GOTO 3150
3134 IF A$="*" THEN GOTO 100
3140 PRINT "INCORRECT"
3142 GOTO 3154
3150 PRINT "CORRECT":R=R+1
3154 GOSUB 999
3200 REM SECOND QUESTION
3202 CLS:POKE -11,14:PRINT CHR$(23)
3210 PRINT "******************************"
3212 PRINT "*                            *"
3214 PRINT "* LIST TWO SYMPTOMS OF HYPER- *"
3216 PRINT "* CALCEMIA WHICH ARE         *"
3218 PRINT "* ASSOCIATED WITH DEHYDRATION *"
3220 PRINT "* AND IMPAIRED RENAL FUNCTION *"
3222 PRINT "*                            *"
3224 PRINT "******************************"
3230 INPUT "1. ";A1$
3232 GOSUB 3300
3234 INPUT "2. ";A2$
3236 GOSUB 3320
3237 GOSUB 999
3238 IF R<2 THEN GOTO 3252
3240 CLS:POKE -1,14:PRINT CHR$(23)
3242 PRINT "YOU HAVE SCORED WELL ENOUGH"
3243 PRINT ""
3244 PRINT "TO CONTINUE ON TO NEW MATERIAL"
3246 FOR I=0 TO 200:NEXT I
3247 RETURN
3252 CLS:POKE -1,14:PRINT CHR$(23)
3254 PRINT "YOU HAVE NOT SCORED WELL ENOUGH"
3255 PRINT ""
3256 PRINT "TOO CONTINUE ON TO NEW MATERIAL"
3257 PRINT ""
3258 PRINT "PAY CLOSE ATTENTION TO THE"
3259 PRINT ""
3260 PRINT "LECTURE MATERIAL"
3268 FOR I=0 TO 200:NEXT I
3270 GOTO 3000
3300 B1$="VOMITING":B2$="POLYURIA"
3310  IF A1$=B1$ THEN GOTO 3360
3312 IF A1$=B2$ THEN GOTO 3360
3313 IF A1$="*" THEN GOTO 100
3314 GOTO 3350
3320 IF A2$=B1$ THEN GOTO 3360
3322 IF A2$=B2$ THEN GOTO 3360
3324 IF A2$="*" THEN GOTO 100
3350 PRINT "INCORRECT"
3354 RETURN
3360 PRINT "CORRECT":R=R+1
3366 RETURN
4000 REM CAUSES FOR HYPERCALCEMIA
4010 SR=130:SP=195
4012 GOSUB 10000
4100 REM FIRST QUESTION
4102 CLS:POKE -1,14:PRINT CHR$(23)
4104 R=0
```

LISTING 7-4 (continued)

```
4110 PRINT "*******************************"
4112 PRINT "*                              *"
4114 PRINT "* THE MOST IMPORTANT           *"
4116 PRINT "* PATHOGENTIC MECHANISM OF     *"
4118 PRINT "* HYPERCALCEMIA EFFECTING      *"
4120 PRINT "* BONE IS:                     *"
4121 PRINT "*                              *"
4122 PRINT "* 1. INCREASED ABSORPTION      *"
4123 PRINT "* 2. INCREASED RESOBRPTION     *"
4124 PRINT "* 3. DECREASED ABS*RPTION      *"
4126 PRINT "*                              *"
4128 PRINT "* PRESS THE KEY CORRESPONDING  *"
4130 PRINT "* TO YOUR CHOICE.              *"
4134 PRINT "*******************************"
4136 A$=INKEY$
4137 IF A$="" THEN GOTO 4136
4138 IF A$="2" THEN GOTO 4150
4139 IF A$="*" THEN GOTO 100
4146 PRINT "INCORRECT"
4148 GOTO 4155
4150 PRINT "CORRECT":R=R+1
4155 GOSUB 999
4200 REM SECOND QUESTION
4202 CLS:POKE -1,14:PRINT CHR$(23)
4210 PRINT "*******************************"
4212 PRINT "*                              *"
4214 PRINT "* INCREASED BONE RESORPTION    *"
4216 PRINT "* RESULTS FROM THREE CAUSES,   *"
4218 PRINT "* LIST TWO OF THEM.            *"
4220 PRINT "*                              *"
4222 PRINT "*******************************"
4230 INPUT "1. ";A1$
4231 GOSUB 4280
4232 INPUT "2. ":A2$
4233 GOSUB 4286
4234 GOSUB 999
4236 GOTO 4300
4280 B1$="HYPERTHYROIDISM":B2$="METASTATIC CANCER":B3$="BONE-RESORBING HORMONE"
4281 IF A1$="*" THEN GOTO 100
4282 IF A1$=B1$ THEN GOTO 4295
4283 IF A1$=B2$ THEN GOTO 4295
4284 IF A1$=B3$ THEN GOTO 4295
4285 GOTO 4290
4286 IF A2$="*" THEN GOTO 100
4287 IF A2$=B1$ THEN GOTO 4295
4288 IF A2$=B2$ THEN GOTO 4295
4289 IF A2$=B3$ THEN GOTO 4295
4290 PRINT "INCORRECT"
4291 RETURN
4295 PRINT "CORRECT":R=R+1
4298 RETURN
4300 REM THIRD QUESTION
4302 CLS:POKE -1,14:PRINT CHR$(23)
4310 PRINT "*******************************"
4312 PRINT "*                              *"
4314 PRINT "* INCREASED GASTROINTESTINAL   *"
4316 PRINT "* ABSORPTION OF CALCIUM IS     *"
```

```
4318 PRINT "* DUE TO:                      *"
4320 PRINT "*                              *"
4322 PRINT "* 1. VITAMIN D INTOXICATION    *"
4324 PRINT "* 2. THYROTOXICOSIS            *"
4326 PRINT "* 3. PAGET'S DISEASE           *"
4328 PRINT "*                              *"
4330 PRINT "********************************"
4332 PRINT ""
4334 PRINT "PRESS THE KEY CORRESPONDING"
4336 PRINT "TO YOUR CHOICE."
4338 A$=INKEY$
4339 IF A$="" THEN GOTO 4338
4340 IF A$="*" THEN GOTO 100
4342 IF A$="1" THEN GOTO 4348
4344 PRINT "INCORRECT":GOTO 4350
4348 PRINT "CORRECT":R=R+1
4350 GOSUB 999
4351 IF R>2 THEN GOTO 4400
4352 CLS:POKE -1,14:PRINT CHR$(23)
4354 PRINT "YOU HAVE NOT SCORED WELL ENOUGH"
4356 PRINT ""
4358 PRINT "TO CONTINUE ON TO NEW MATERIAL"
4360 PRINT ""
4362 PRINT "PAY CLOSE ATTENTION TO THE"
4364 PRINT ""
4366 PRINT "LECTURE MATERIAL"
4368 GOSUB 999
4370 GOTO 4000
4400 CLS:POKE -1,14:PRINT CHR$(23)
4402 PRINT "YOU HAVE SCORED WELL ENOUGH TO"
4403 PRINT ""
4404 PRINT "CONTINUE ON TO NEW MATERIAL."
4405 FOR I=0 TO 200:NEXT I
4406 RETURN
5000 REM TESTING FOR HYPERCALCEMIA
5010 SR=195:SP=257
5012 GOSUB 10000
5100 REM FIRST QUESTION
5102 CLS:POKE -1,14:PRINT CHR$(23)
5103 R=0
5110 PRINT "********************************"
5112 PRINT "*                              *"
5114 PRINT "* A METHOD CURRENTLY USED TO   *"
5116 PRINT "* MEASURE TOTAL SERUM CALCIUM  *"
5118 PRINT "* CONCENTRATION IS:            *"
5120 PRINT "*                              *"
5222 PRINT "* 1. AUTOMATIC TITRATION       *"
5224 PRINT "* 2. ELECTROPHORESIS           *"
5226 PRINT "* 3. DIALYSIS                  *"
5228 PRINT "*                              *"
5230 PRINT "* PRESS THE KEY CORRESPONDING  *"
5232 PRINT "* TO YOUR CHOICE.              *"
5234 PRINT "*                              *"
5236 PRINT "********************************"
5238 A$=INKEY$
5239 IF A$="" THEN GOTO 5238
5240 IF A$="*" THEN GOTO 100
```

LISTING 7-4 (continued)

```
5241 IF A$="1" THEN GOTO 5262
5242 PRINT "INCORRECT":GOTO 5264
5262 PRINT "CORRECT":R=R+1
5264 FOR I=0 TO 200:NEXT I
5266 IF R=1 THEN GOTO 5280
5268 CLS:POKE -1,14:PRINT CHR$(23)
5269 PRINT "YOU HAVE NOT SCORED WELL ENOUGH"
5270 PRINT ""
5271 PRINT "TO CONTINUE ON TO NEW MATERIAL"
5272 PRINT ""
5273 PRINT "PAY CLOSE ATTENTION TO THE"
5274 PRINT ""
5275 PRINT "LECTURE MATERIAL."
5276 GOSUB 999
5278 GOTO 5000
5280 CLS:POKE -1,14:PRINT CHR$(23)
5282 PRINT "YOU HAVE SCORED WELL ENOUGH TO"
5283 PRINT ""
5284 PRINT "CONTINUE ON TO NEW MATERIAL."
5285 GOSUB 999
5286 RETURN
6000 REM RANGE OF NORMAL CALCIUM VALUES
6010 SR=257:SP=322
6012 GOSUB 10000
6100 REM FIRST QUESTION
6102 R=0
6104 CLS:POKE -1,14:PRINT CHR$(23)
6110 PRINT "******************************"
6112 PRINT "*                            *"
6114 PRINT "*  THE NORMAL SERUM CALCIUM  *"
6116 PRINT "*  CONCENTRATION RANGES FROM:*"
6118 PRINT "*                            *"
6120 PRINT "* 1. 88-104 MG/100ML         *"
6122 PRINT "* 2. 8.8-10.4 MG/100ML       *"
6124 PRINT "* 3. .88-1.04 MG/100ML       *"
6126 PRINT "*                            *"
6128 PRINT "* PRESS THE KEY CORRESPONDING*"
6130 PRINT "* TO YOUR CHOICE.            *"
6132 PRINT "*                            *"
6134 PRINT "******************************"
6140 A$=INKEY$
6142 IF A$="" THEN GOTO 6140
6144 IF A$="*" THEN GOTO 100
6145 IF A$="1" THEN GOTO 6150
6147 PRINT "INCORRECT":GOTO 6155
6150 PRINT "CORRECT":R=R+1
6155 GOSUB 999
6156 IF R=1 THEN GOTO 6170
6160 CLS:POKE -1,14:PRINT CHR$(23)
6161 PRINT "YOU HAVE NOT SCORED WELL ENOUGH":PRINT ""
6162 PRINT "TO CONINUE ON TO NEW MATERIAL!":PRINT ""
6164 PRINT "PAY CLOSE ATTENTION TO THE":PRINT ""
6166 PRINT "LECTURE MATERIAL."
6168 GOSUB 999
6169 GOTO 6000
6170 CLS:POKE -1,14:PRINT CHR$(23)
6172 PRINT "YOU HAVE SCORED WELL ENOUGH TO"
```

```
6173 PRINT ""
6174 PRINT "CONTINUE ON TO NEW MATERIAL."
6176 GOSUB 999
6178 RETURN
7000 REM CORRECTION FACTORS
7010 SR=322:SP=450
7012 GOSUB 10000
7100 REM FIRST QUESTION
7102 CLS:POKE -1,14:PRINT CHR$(23)
7104 R=0
7110 PRINT "*******************************"
7112 PRINT "* IF CALCIUM=10.2 MG/100ML    *"
7114 PRINT "*    ALBUMIN=3.5 MG/100ML     *"
7116 PRINT "* NORMAL ALBUMIN=4.5 MG/100ML *"
7118 PRINT "*                             *"
7120 PRINT "* WHAT WILL THE CORRECTED     *"
7122 PRINT "* CALCIUM CONCENTRATION EQUAL?*"
7124 PRINT "*                             *"
7126 PRINT "* 1.     11 MG/100ML          *"
7128 PRINT "* 2.     9.6 MG/100ML         *"
7130 PRINT "* 3.     13.8 MG/100ML        *"
7132 PRINT "*                             *"
7134 PRINT "* PRESS THE KEY CORRESPONDING *"
7136 PRINT "* TO YOUR CHOICE.             *"
7138 PRINT "*******************************"
7151 A$=INKEY$
7152 IF A$="" THEN GOTO 7151
7154 IF A$="*" THEN GOTO 100
7155 IF A$="1" THEN GOTO 7160
7156 PRINT "INCORRECT":GOTO 7165
7160 PRINT "CORRECT":R=R+1
7165 GOSUB 999
7170 IF R=1 THEN GOTO 7190
7172 CLS:POKE -1,14:PRINT CHR$(23)
7173 PRINT "YOU HAVE NOT SCORED WELL ENOUGH TO":PRINT ""
7177 PRINT "CONTINUE ON TO NEW MATERIAL!":PRINT ""
7178 PRINT "PAY CLOSE ATTENTION TO THE":PRINT ""
7180 PRINT "LECTURE MATERIAL."
7182 GOSUB 999
7184 GOTO 7000
7190 CLS:POKE -1,14:PRINT CHR$(23)
7191 PRINT "YOU HAVE SCORED WELL ENOUGH TO":PRINT ""
7193 PRINT "CONTINUE ON TO NEW MATERIAL."
7194 GOSUB 999
7196 RETURN
8000 REM CASE HISTORY(MILD)
8010 SR=450:SP=850
8012 GOSUB 10000
8100 REM FIRST QUESTION
8102 RETURN
9000 REM CASE HISTORY(SEVERE)
9010 SR=850:SP=1135
9012 GOSUB 10000
9100 REM FIRST QUESTION
9102 RETURN
9999 END
10000 REM BETAMAX CONTROLLER
```

LISTING 7-4 (continued)

```
10002 R1=0:R2=0:P1=0:P2=0
10010 X=PEEK(32515)+256*PEEK(32516)
10020 R1=SR
10021 R1=R1-256
10022 IF R1=0 THEN GOTO 10030
10023 IF R1>0 THEN GOTO 10032
10024 IF R1<0 THEN GOTO 10035
10030 R2=R2+1:GOTO 10090
10032 R2=R2+1:GOTO 10021
10035 R1=R1+256
10050 P1=SP
10051 P1=P1-256
10052 IF P1=0 THEN GOTO 10080
10053 IF P1>0 THEN GOTO 10082
10054 IF P1<0 THEN GOTO 10085
10080 P2=P2+1:GOTO 10090
10082 P2=P2+1:GOTO 10051
10085 P1=P1+256
10090 IF X<SR THEN GOTO 10100
10092 IF X>SR THEN GOTO 10200
10094 IF X=SR THEN GOTO 10300
10100 REM FAST FORWARD
10110 POKE 32517,R1:POKE 32518,R2
10112 POKE -1,2
10114 POKE 16526,00:POKE 16527,123
10115 X=USR(0)
10116 POKE -1,0
10118 GOTO 10300
10200 REM REWIND
10202 R3=0:R4=0
10210 R3=SR+2
10211 R3=R3-256
10212 IF R3=0 THEN GOTO 10220
10213 IF R3>0 THEN GOTO 10230
10214 IF R3<0 THEN GOTO 10240
10220 R4=R4+1:GOTO 10250
10230 R4=R4+1:GOTO 10211
10240 R3=R3+256
10250 POKE 32517,R3:POKE 32518,R4
10252 POKE -1,3
10254 POKE 16526,96:POKE 16527,123
10256 X=USR(0)
10257 POKE -1,0
10258 POKE 32515,R1:POKE 32516,R2
10300 REM PLAY
10310 POKE 32517,P1:POKE 32518,P2
10320 POKE -1,1
10322 POKE 16526,00:POKE 16527,123
10324 X=USR(0)
10400 REM STOP
10412 POKE -1,0:POKE -1,14:RETURN
10999 RETURN
12000 REM MACHINE LANGUAGE ROUTINE
```

120

```
12010 POKE 31488,245:POKE 31489,58:POKE 31490,02:POKE 31491,128:POKE 31492,23:
      POKE 31493,218:POKE 31494,01:POKE 31495,123:POKE 31496,58
12012 POKE 31497,02:POKE 31498,128:POKE 31499,23:POKE 31500,210:POKE 31501,08:
      POKE 31502,123:POKE 31503,33:POKE 31504,03:POKE 31505,127:POKE 31506,52:
      POKE 31507,194
12014 POKE 31508,26:POKE 31509,123:POKE 31510,33:POKE 31511,04:POKE 31512,127:
      POKE 31513,52:POKE 31514,33:POKE 31515,05:POKE 31516,127:POKE 31518,03:POKE
      31519,127:POKE 31517,58
12016 POKE 31520,190:POKE 31521,194:POKE 31522,01:POKE 31523,123:POKE 31524,33:
      POKE 31525,06:POKE 31526,127:POKE 31527,58:POKE 31528,04:POKE 31529,127
12018 POKE 31530,190:POKE 31531,194:POKE 31532,01:POKE 31533,123:POKE 31534,241:
      POKE 31535,201
12020 POKE 31584,245:POKE 31585,58:POKE 31586,02:POKE 31587,128:POKE 31588,23:
      POKE 31589,218:POKE 31590,97:POKE 31591,123:POKE 31592,58:POKE 31593,02:
      POKE 31594,128:POKE 31595,23
12022 POKE 31596,210:POKE 31597,104:POKE 31598,123:POKE 31599,63:POKE 31600,58:
      POKE 31601,03:POKE 31602,127:POKE 31603,222:POKE 31604,01:POKE 31605,50:
      POKE 31606,03:POKE 31607,127:POKE 31608,58
12024 POKE 31609,04:POKE 31610,127:POKE 31611,222:POKE 31612,00:POKE 31613,50:
      POKE 31614,04:POKE 31615,127:POKE 31616,33:POKE 31617,05:POKE 31618,127:
      POKE 31619,58:POKE 31620,03:POKE 31622,190:POKE 31621,127
12026 POKE 31623,194:POKE 31624,97:POKE 31625,123:POKE 31626,33:POKE 31627,06:
      POKE 31628,127:POKE 31629,58:POKE 31630,04:POKE 31631,127:POKE 31632,190:
      POKE 31633,194:POKE 31634,97:POKE 31635,123
12028 POKE 31636,241:POKE 31637,201
12999 RETURN
```

8

DATA ANALYSIS TECHNIQUES

CURVE FITTING

The observation of naturally occurring phenomena is often the basic approach of a scientific researcher. Data (the dependent variable) are recorded as a function of some *independent variable* (a parameter that is not a function of the phenomena being observed), and the researcher then draws conclusions based on the relationship between the two variables. The first step that usually occurs after the data have been gathered is to ask the question: What mathematical formula best describes the relationship between the two variables?

Linear Regression

The simplest relationship that two variables could have would be a *linear relationship,* in which the dependent and independent variables would increase or decrease with a one-to-one relationship. When a linear relationship occurs, the dependent variable can be expressed as a function of the independent variable by an equation having the following form:

$$y = a \times x + b \tag{8.1}$$
$$\text{where } a \text{ and } b = \text{constants}$$

The following program will find the values for *a* and *b* that will give the closest agreement between experimental data and equation 8.1. The technique that will be used is called *linear regression* by the method of least squares.

Listing 8.1 shows the program with comments. The program expects to receive *x* and *y* pairs of data. When all the values have been entered, the program computes the coeffecients for equation 8.1 and calculates a coefficient of determination to give a relative indication of the goodness of fit. Once the equation has been generated, you may predict values of *y* for given values of *x*.

LISTING 8-1   BASIC linear regression routine.

```
100 REM LINEAR REGRESSION
102 REM R. HALLGREN   3-5-81
110 CLS
120 PRINT CHR$(23)
130 PRINT "*******************************"
132 PRINT "*                              *"
134 PRINT "* YOU WILL INPUT THE PAIRED    *"
138 PRINT "* VALUES OF DATA THAT YOU      *"
142 PRINT "* HAVE GATHERED.               *"
144 PRINT "*                              *"
146 PRINT "* WHEN ALL DATA PAIRS HAVE     *"
150 PRINT "* BEEN ENTERED, PRESS * TO     *"
154 PRINT "* CALCULATE THE REGRESSION     *"
158 PRINT "* COEFFICIENTS.                *"
159 PRINT "*                              *"
160 PRINT "* PRESS THE SPACE BAR          *"
162 PRINT "* TO CONTINUE.                 *"
164 PRINT "*******************************"
180 K$=INKEY$
182 IF K$<>" " THEN GOTO 180
200 REM INPUT DATA PAIRS
210 J=0:K=0:L=0:M=0:R2=0
212 N=1
230 CLS
232 PRINT CHR$(23)
240 PRINT "DATA PAIR #";N
242 INPUT "X VALUE";X(N)
244 INPUT "Y VALUE";Y(N)
246 N=N+1
250 PRINT "":PRINT "":PRINT ""
252 PRINT "PRESS * TO CALCULATE"
253 PRINT "COEFFICIENTS."
254 PRINT ""
256 PRINT "PRESS THE SPACE BAR TO ENTER"
258 PRINT "MORE DATA PAIRS."
260 K$=INKEY$
262 IF K$="*" THEN GOTO 300
264 IF K$<>" " THEN GOTO 260
268 GOTO 230
300 REM CALCULATE REGRESSION COEFFICIENTS
302 N=N-1
310 FOR I=1 TO N
312 J=J+X(I)
314 K=K+Y(I)
```

LISTING 8-1 (continued)

```
316 L=L+(X(I))[2
318 M=M+(Y(I))[2
320 R2=R2+(X(I))*(Y(I))
330 NEXT I
340 A=(N*R2-K*J)/(N*L-J[2)
342 B=(K-A*J)/N
350 CLS
353 PRINT CHR$(23)
354 PRINT "Y=";A;"* X +";B
400 REM COMPUTE COEFFICIENT OF DETERMINATION
410 J=A*(R2-J*K/N)
412 M=M-K[2/N
414 K=M-J
416 R2=J/M
420 PRINT "":PRINT ""
424 PRINT "COEFFICIENT OF DETERMINATION = ";R2
430 PRINT "":PRINT ""
432 PRINT "DO YOU NEED TO PREDICT VALUES"
434 PRINT "OF Y FOR GIVEN VALUES OF X?"
440 PRINT ""
442 PRINT "PRESS Y OR N"
444 K$=INKEY$
446 IF K$="N" THEN END
448 IF K$<>"Y" THEN GOTO 444
450 REM CALCULATE Y FROM VALUES OF X
452 CLS
454 PRINT CHR$(23)
456 INPUT "X=";X
458 PRINT "Y=";A*X+B
460 GOTO 430
```

Example. A forgetful electrical engineering professor wakes up one morning and thinks that he might have a fever. A search through his medical cabinet produces an oral thermometer, but it slips through his fingers and falls to the floor, breaking into a thousand pieces. Disgusted with himself, he suddenly realizes that he has an outdoor thermometer that is calibrated in degrees Fahrenheit. But it is much to big to fit into his mouth. He remembers that the skin temperature, biofeedback project that he built has a themistor probe, but that it is not calibrated. He suspects that the probe is linear and that the relationship between the output voltage from the interface and temperature might be equal to equation 8.2. He knows that if he could get a few data points, he could run the linear regression program and solve for the coefficients of the following equation.

$$T = a \times V + b$$
where T = temperature in degrees Fahrenheit (8.2)
V = voltage

He places both the thermometer and the thermistor probe into a sink of warm water and records the following data points:

V	1.055	1.044	1.014	0.984	0.974	0.943
T	104	103	100	97	96	93

Can you find the values for *a* and *b*? What is the coefficient of determination? If the professor's temperature is equal to 1.006V, should he be worried?

Exponential Regression

Another common relationship between data pairs is described by an *exponential curve*, in which the dependent variable can be expressed as a function of the independent variable by an equation having the following form:

$$y = A e^{bx} \qquad (8.3)$$

The following program will find values for *a* and *b* that will give the closest agreement between the experimental data and equation 8.3. The technique that will be used is called *exponential regression* by the method of least squares.

Listing 8.2 shows the program with comments. The program expects to receive *x* and *y* pairs of data. When all the values have been entered, the program computes the coefficients for equation 8.3 and calculates a coefficient of determination to give a relative indication of the goodness of fit. Once the equation has been determined, you may predict values of *y* for given values of *x*.

LISTING 8-2   BASIC exponential regression routine.

```
100 REM EXPONENTIAL REGRESSION
102 REM R. HALLGREN   3-5-81
110 CLS
120 PRINT CHR$(23)
130 PRINT "*******************************"
132 PRINT "*                             *"
134 PRINT "* YOU WILL INPUT THE PAIRED   *"
138 PRINT "* VALUES OF DATA THAT YOU     *"
142 PRINT "* HAVE GATHERED.              *"
144 PRINT "*                             *"
146 PRINT "* WHEN ALL DATA PAIRS HAVE    *"
150 PRINT "* BEEN ENTERED, PRESS * TO    *"
154 PRINT "* CALCULATE THE REGRESSION    *"
158 PRINT "* COEFFICIENTS.               *"
159 PRINT "*                             *"
160 PRINT "* PRESS THE SPACE BAR         *"
162 PRINT "* TO CONTINUE.                *"
164 PRINT "*******************************"
180 K$=INKEY$
182 IF K$<>" " THEN GOTO 180
```

LISTING 8-2 (continued)

```
200 REM INPUT DATA PAIRS
210 J=0:K=0:L=0:M=0:R2=0
212 N=1
230 CLS
232 PRINT CHR$(23)
240 PRINT "DATA PAIR #";N
242 INPUT "X VALUE";X(N)
244 INPUT "Y VALUE";Y(N)
246 N=N+1
250 PRINT "":PRINT "":PRINT ""
252 PRINT "PRESS * TO CALCULATE"
253 PRINT "COEFFICIENTS."
254 PRINT ""
256 PRINT "PRESS THE SPACE BAR TO ENTER"
258 PRINT "MORE DATA PAIRS."
260 K$=INKEY$
262 IF K$="*" THEN GOTO 300
264 IF K$<>" " THEN GOTO 260
268 GOTO 230
300 REM CALCULATE REGRESSION COEFFICIENTS
302 N=N-1
310 FOR I=1 TO N
311 Y(I)=LOG(Y(I))
312 J=J+X(I)
314 K=K+Y(I)
316 L=L+(X(I))[2
318 M=M+(Y(I))[2
320 R2=R2+(X(I))*(Y(I))
330 NEXT I
340 B=(N*R2-K*J)/(N*L-J[2)
342 A=(K-B*J)/N
350 CLS
353 PRINT CHR$(23)
354 PRINT "B=";B
356 PRINT "A=";EXP(A)
400 REM COMPUTE COEFFICIENT OF DETERMINATION
410 J=B*(R2-J*K/N)
412 M=M-K[2/N
414 K=M-J
416 R2=J/M
420 PRINT "":PRINT ""
424 PRINT "COEFFICIENT OF DETERMINATION = ";R2
430 PRINT "":PRINT ""
432 PRINT "DO YOU NEED TO PREDICT VALUES"
434 PRINT "OF V FOR GIVEN VALUES OF T?"
440 PRINT ""
442 PRINT "PRESS Y OR N"
444 K$=INKEY$
446 IF K$="N" THEN END
448 IF K$<>"Y" THEN GOTO 444
450 REM CALCULATE Y FROM VALUES OF X
452 CLS
454 PRINT CHR$(23)
456 INPUT "T=";X
458 PRINT "V=";EXP(A)*EXP(B*X)
460 GOTO 430
```

Data Analysis 127

Example. Realizing a bargain when he sees one, Fred bought several large capacitors at the local flea market for a very low price. Unfortunately, these capacitors were unmarked. Fred knows that a capacitor, being charged through a series resistor from a fixed voltage source, will increase exponentially in voltage as time increases. Knowing the value of the series resistor, and by measuring the voltage across the resistor as a function of time, he should be able to use the exponential regression program to determine the value of the capacitance. Using his high school electronics text, Fred determines that the voltage across the series resistor will be equal to the following equation:

$$V = Ee^{\frac{-t}{RC}}$$

where V = resistor voltage (V)
E = battery voltage (V) = 5
R = resistance (Ω) = 1000
C = capacitance (F)
t = time (s)

(8.4)

Getting out the high-speed A/D converter that he built in Chapter 3, Fred gets ready to prove to his wife that the capacitors really were a bargain. Fred sets the sampling rate at 1 sample per second and obtains the following set of data points:

t	0	1	2	3	4	5
V	5	1.9	0.7	0.25	0.109	0.042

Find the values for A and b in equation 8.3 and calculate the capacitance of Fred's capacitor. If he needs 10 F for his plasma discharge generator, will he be able to use this particular capacitor?

Fast Fourier Analysis

The sounds that your ears receive are comprised of many individual frequencies summed together to form a complex waveform that gives the sound its characteristic quality. It is possible to take an arbitrary continuous signal, expressed in the time domain, and break it up into a series of individual frequencies. The magnitude of this spectrum at different frequencies is a measure of the frequency content that comprises the original signal. The concept of spectrum finds many practical applications in many varied disciplines including waveform analysis of music, frequency content of muscle voltages, vibrational characteristics of mechanical systems, and the like. Figure 8.1 shows a plot, in the time domain, of a complex analog waveform. It would be very difficult to come to any conclusions regarding the spectral content of the signal just by visually analyzing it. Figure

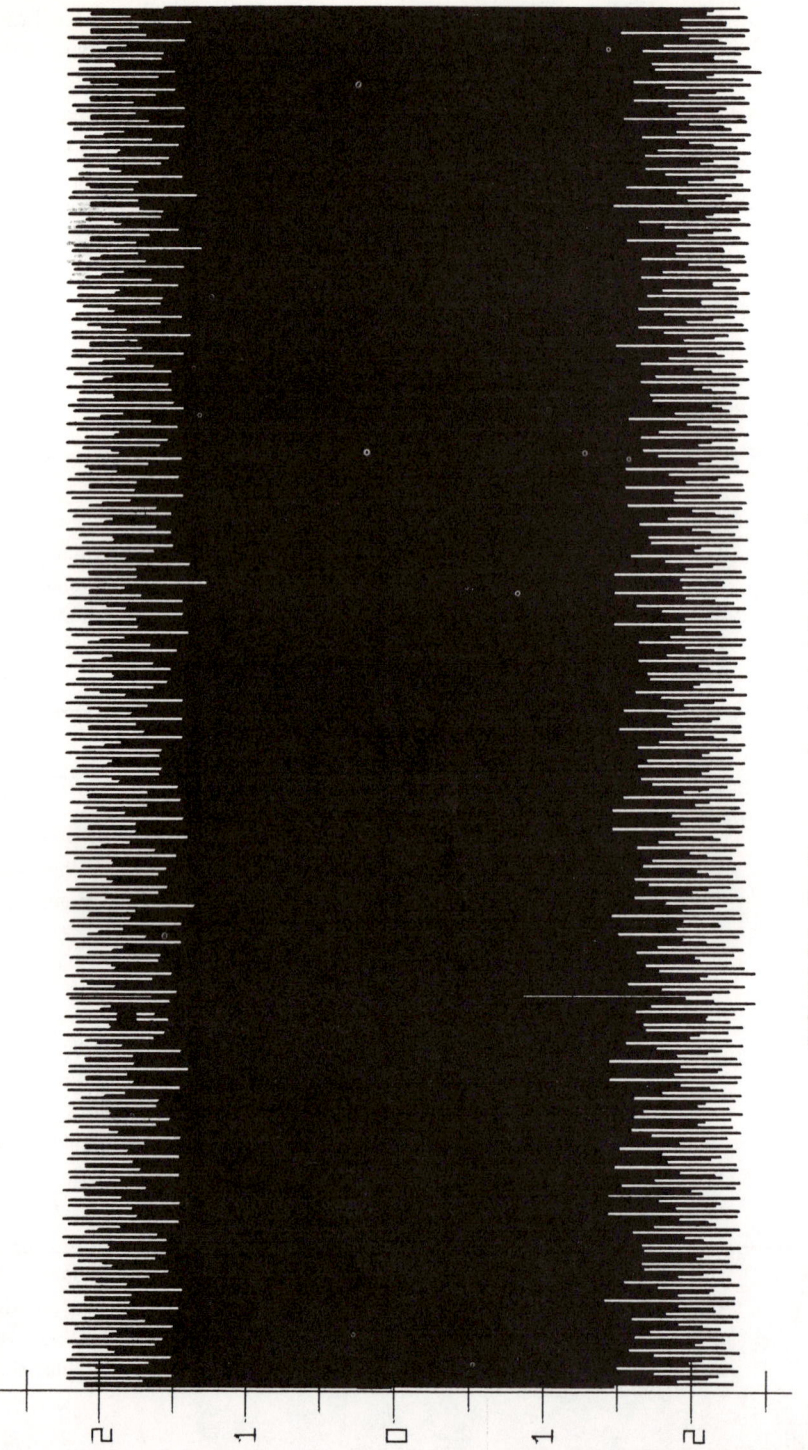

FIGURE 8-1 Continuous, analog signal plotted in the time domain.

FIGURE 8-2 Signal from Figure 8-1 analyzed by the fast Fourier transform and plotted as a function of frequency.

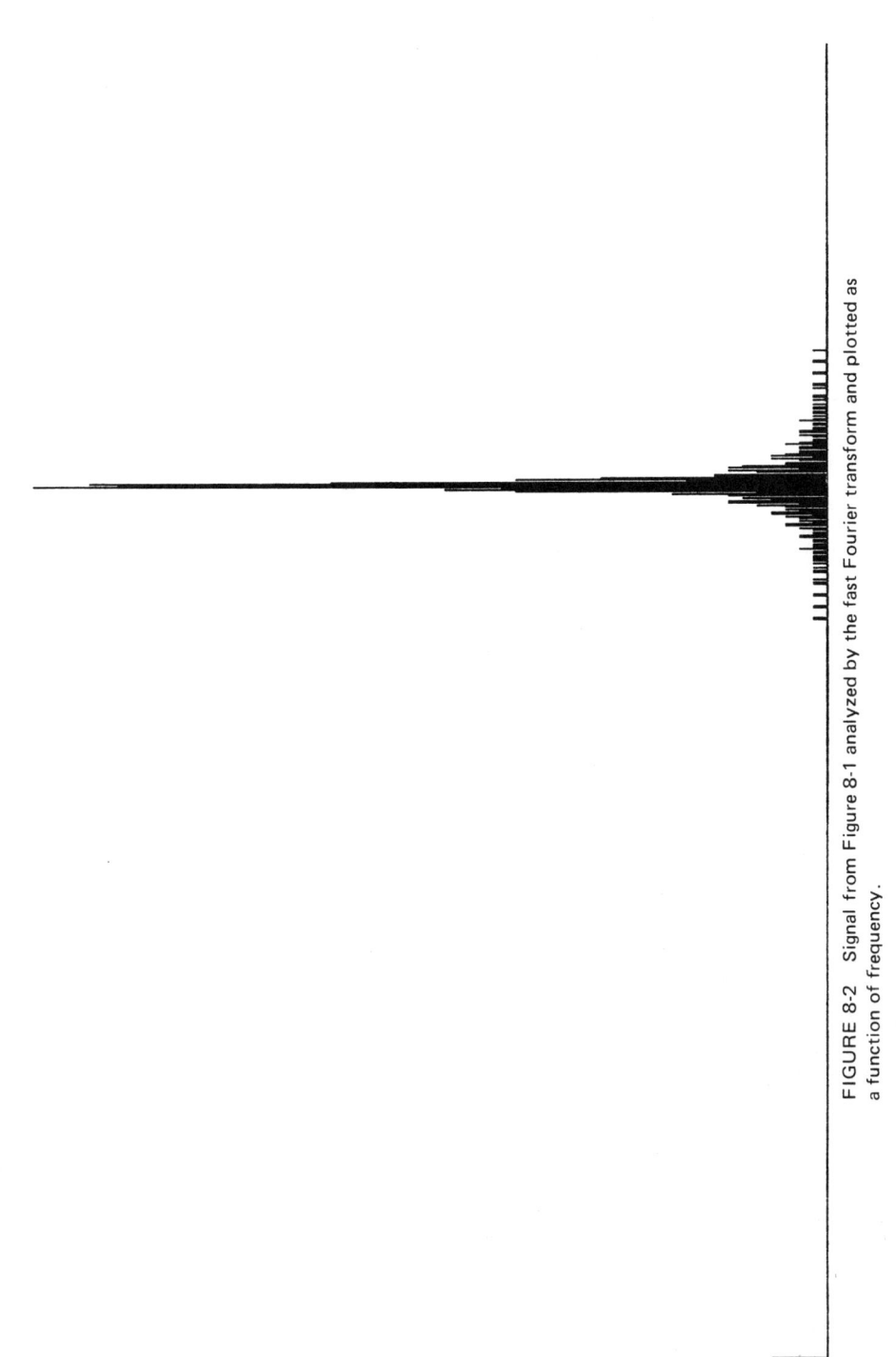

130 Data Analysis

8.2 shows the same waveform transformed into the frequency domain by a fast Fourier transform (FFT). You can easily observe a small dc component at the far left of the plot, and so you can easily make the statement that the complex waveform contains a single, high-frequency signal. In fact, Figure 8.1 is just the plot of a 600-Hz sine wave.

Listing 8.3 shows a program, written in TRS-80 BASIC, that combines the high-speed A/D converter routines developed in Chapter 3 with a fast Four-

LISTING 8-3   BASIC fast Fourier routine.

```
10 REM HIGH SPEED A/D ROUTINE
12 REM R. HALLGREN, MOD III, 6-25-81
22 FOR I=1 TO 55:READ K:POKE (28927+I),K:NEXT I
24 FOR I=1 TO 31:READ K:POKE (29183+I),K:NEXT I
30 POKE 16526,0:POKE 16527,113
31 CLS:PRINT @256,"DATA ARE BEING DIGITIZED"
32 X=USR(0)
33 CLS
34 PRINT CHR$(23)
36 PRINT "******************************"
38 PRINT "* HOW MANY POINTS DO YOU WANT *"
40 PRINT "* TO PROCESS?                 *"
42 PRINT "*                             *"
44 PRINT "*    1. 512                   *"
45 PRINT "*    2. 256                   *"
46 PRINT "*    3. 128                   *"
47 PRINT "*                             *"
50 PRINT "* PRESS THE NUMBER            *"
52 PRINT "* CORRESPONDING TO YOUR CHOICE*"
54 PRINT "*                             *"
55 PRINT "******************************"
60 K$=INKEY$
62 IF K$="1" THEN L=9:N=512:GOTO 80
64 IF K$="2" THEN L=8:N=256:GOTO 80
66 IF K$="3" THEN L=7:N=128:GOTO 80
68 GOTO 60
80 REM FAST FOURIER ROUTINE
101 REM MOD III
102 REM R. HALLGREN   3-5-81
104 CLS
110 DIM X1(N):DIM X2(N)
120 P=3.14159
200 REM DATA FORMATTER SUBROUTINE
202 X=24064
204 CLS:PRINT @256,"DATA ARE BEING FORMATTED"
220 FOR Z=0 TO N-1
222 X=X+2
223 PRINT @384,Z
224 V1=PEEK(X):V2=PEEK(X+1):REM GET DIGITAL DATA
230 IF V1>1 THEN GOTO 300:REM TEST POLARITY
250 X1(Z)=-(511-(V1*256+V2))/100
270 NEXT Z
280 GOTO 500
300 X1(Z)=((V1-2)*256+V2)/100
320 GOTO 270
```

```
500 REM SCALE INPUT TIME FUNCTION
640 CLS:PRINT @256,"DATA ARE BEING SCALED"
642 FOR Z=0 TO N-1
644 PRINT @384,Z
650 X1(Z)=X1(Z)/N
660 NEXT Z
670 REM FFT IN-PLACE ALGORITHM
675 CLS:PRINT @256,"CALCULATION IN PROCESS"
680 I1=N/2:I2=1:V=2*P/N
690 FOR I=1 TO L
700 I3=0:I4=I1
710 FOR K=1 TO I2
720 X=INT(I3/I1)
730 GOSUB 900
740 I5=Y
750 Z1=COS(V*I5)
760 Z2=-SIN(V*I5)
770 FOR M=I3 TO I4-1
780 A1=X1(M):A2=X2(M)
790 B1=Z1*X1(M+I1)-Z2*X2(M+I1)
800 B2=Z2*X1(M+I1)+Z1*X2(M+I1)
810 X1(M)=A1+B1:X2(M)=A2+B2
820 X1(M+I1)=A1-B1:X2(M+I1)=A2-B2
830 NEXT M
840 I3=I3+2*I1:I4=I4+2*I1
850 NEXT K
860 I1=I1/2:I2=2*I2
870 NEXT I
880 GOTO 1100
900 REM SCRAMBLER ROUTINE
910 Y=0:N1=N
912 FOR W=1 TO L
920 N1=N1/2
930 IF X<N1 THEN GOTO 960
940 Y=Y+2[(W-1)
950 X=X-N1
960 NEXT W
970 RETURN
1000 REM MAGNITUDE SUBROUTINE
1010 GOSUB 900
1020 X3=SQR(X1(Y)[2+X2(Y)[2)
1021 PRINT X1(Y),X2(Y),X3
1022 RETURN
1100 REM TABLE OF VALUES
1130 U=0
1140 Z=0
1165 X=U
1170 GOSUB 1010
1190 U=U+1:Z=Z+1
1200 IF Z>9 THEN 1140
1210 IF U>N/2 THEN 1240
1220 GOTO 1165
1240 END
10000 DATA 243,8,217,62,16,211,236,62,0,211,1,62,195,50,18,64,62,0,50,19,64,62,114,50
10001 DATA 20,64,1,0,94,219,224,62,8,211,224,251,0,195,35,113,62,24,50,19,64,62,48,50
10002 DATA 20,64,217,8,51,51,201 62,1,211,1,62,0,211,1,219,2,23,218,8,114,31,230,3,2,3
10003 DATA 219,4,2,3,120,254,112,202,40,113,237,77
```

ier routine. The program first digitizes and stores 1,256 data points. The FFT routine then mathematically separates the complex waveform into the sum of a number of discrete frequencies, and prints the magnitude of each frequency component. The frequency spacing between each component is a function of the digitization frequency and the number of points that you have the computer program process. You have to decide how many of those points you wish to process with the FFT. Using a larger number of points results in greater resolution, but it requires more processing time. For example, 512 points requires 16 minutes, 256 points requires 8 minutes, and 128 points requires 4 minutes. You can calculate the frequency spacing between each component with equation 8.5:

$$F = \frac{1}{t \times N} \text{ Hz}$$

where F = the distance between each component (8.5)
t = the time increment between samples
N = the number of processed points

If we were sampling an input signal at a rate of 1,000 Hz, then t would be equal to 0.001 s. If we then decided to process 512 points, we would expect the distance between components to be equal to 1.95-Hz. So, if we had digitized a 19.5-Hz sine wave, we would expect to see a peak in the magnitude of the output at the eleventh point (the magnitude of the dc component occupying the first point).

You can do several things to enhance the utility of these routines:

1. Write programs to plot both the complex waveform and the Fourier transform with the digital plotter developed in Chapter 5.
2. Convert the BASIC program shown in Listing 8.3 to a machine language routine to greatly decrease the time spent processing the data.

To help assure yourself that you have entered the program correctly, I have included a simple program that generates a perfect 100-Hz sine wave and stores it in memory. After loading the main program, key in the following BASIC statements.

```
20 GOTO 33
90 Y=24064: T=0
91 FOR Z=0 TO N-1
92 Y=Y+2: X=1+SIN (2 x 3.14159 x 100 x T)
94 T=T+7.8125E−4
95 POKE Y,3: POKE (Y+1), 100 x X
96 NEXT Z
```

If everything is working correctly, you should observe a peak in magnitude at the eleventh output.

APPENDICES

APPENDIX A:
CONSTRUCTION TECHNIQUES

Before you start to build, you should have some feeling for the construction options that are available to you. These options will allow you to use appropriate construction techniques for specific circuits that you will be building. I am not going into a lot of detail concerning the actual construction process involved in each option, since this has been covered in detail in other publications. However, based upon my personal experience, I will summarize the advantages and disadvantages of each process.

If you need to construct ten or more boards having the same circuit configuration, you might want to have a custom circuit board constructed. Usually, in any large metropolitan area, a number of small companies can perform this service. Costs will run about $500 for the circuit board layout and about $20 apiece for each circuit board, and the cost is directly proportional to the complexity of the circuit design. Disadvantages include a wait of about four weeks for the boards to be fabricated, the cost of fabrication, and the loss of modification flexibility. The advantages include decreased construction time for each circuit, the increased reliability of operation, and an obviously professional appearance. Figures A.1a and A.1b show examples of this type of construction.

FIGURE A-1a Example of custom circuit board construction; front view.

FIGURE A-1b Example of custom circuit board construction; rear view.

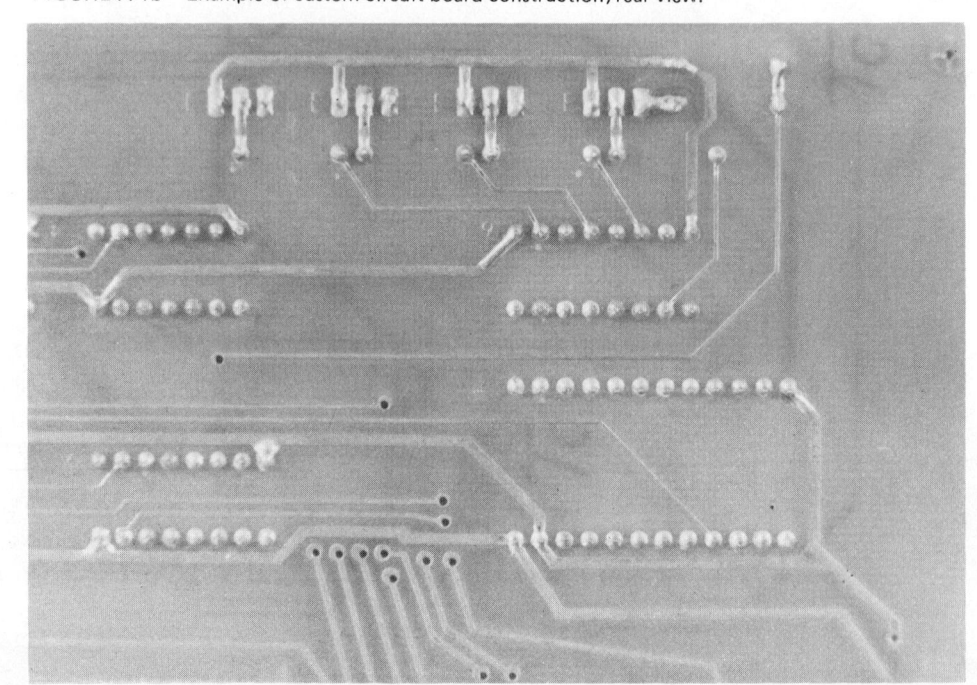

If you need to construct a single circuit that is very simple, I would recommend using Vector board, with a push-in, solderable terminal type of construction (1). Figure A.2 shows examples of this type of construction. Vector board (Vector Electronics Co., Inc., Sylmar, California 91342), and Vector pins, as well as the tool to insert the pins, can be purchased at your local electronics store. It is the least expensive method of construction, and I have used it with success. However, this type of construction sometimes results in undesirable oscillations caused by the close proximity of output signal wires to input signal wires. Another possible problem is the introduction of high-frequency noise, generated by the digital circuitry, into power supply lines. I would discourage its use with DIP packaged integrated circuits unless you are quite proficient with a soldering iron.

If you are adventurous and have an abundance of time, you should con-

FIGURE A-2 Example of Vector board construction; front view.

sider laying out the foil pattern and then etching your own circuit boards (2). This process is limited to relatively simple circuits, but the finished boards are inexpensive to produce and produce a circuit with mechanical properties superior to hand-wired boards.

If the circuit is complex or if you are planning on doing several construction projects over a period of time, I would recommend that you develop your capability to produce wire-wrapped circuits (3,4,5). This type of construction is fast and economical, and it results in circuits that will perform reliably in a variety of applications. Figures A.3a and A.3b show examples of this method of construction. Wire wrapping allows the builder to use point-to-point construction techniques and still obtain a circuit board that is rugged enough to be put into practical use. Construction proceeds relatively fast, and corrections can be easily made. While there is an initial investment, the individual cost of a finished board is comparable to other techniques.

Putting your finished circuit into a cabinet adds a great deal to the personal satisfaction that you will receive from completing the project. Plastic boxes are very easy to work with and are quite adequate for the types of projects that I will be describing. Figures A.4a and A.4b show examples of this type of finished construction.

FIGURE A-3a Example of wire-wrap construction; front view.

FIGURE A-3b   Example of wire-wrap construction; rear view.

FIGURE A-4a   Example of finished project.

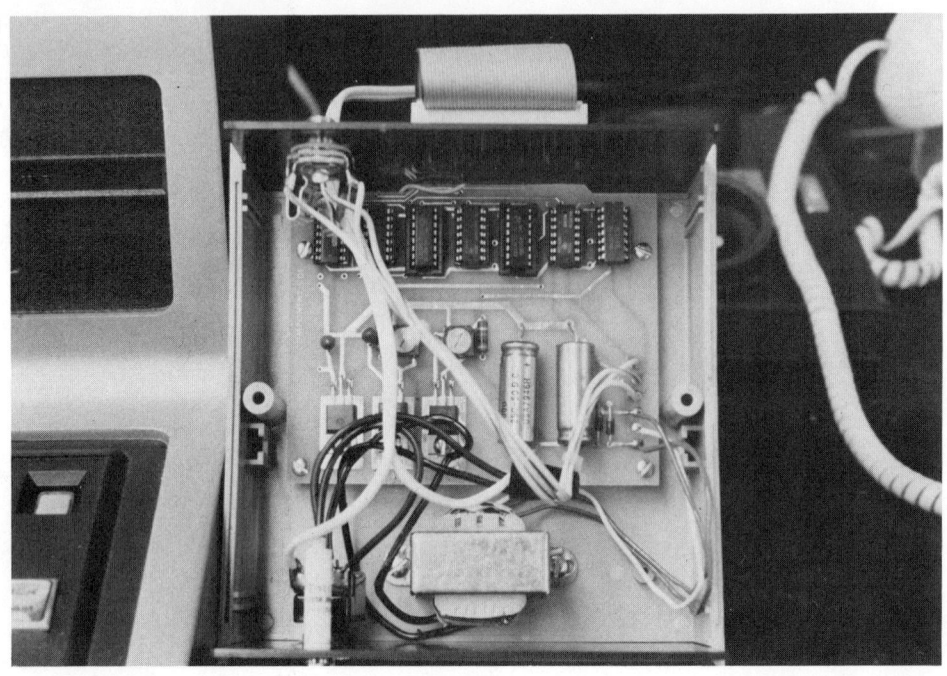

FIGURE A-4b   Example of finished project.

REFERENCES

1. "Perf Board Wiring Techniques For Experimenters," *Popular Electronics,* Vol. 9, No. 4 (April 1976).
2. Houser, M. W., *Circuit Board Etching* New York, NY 10017: Davis Publications, 1981.
3. Sikonowiz, W., *Wire-Wrapping Techniques* New York, NY 10017: Davis Publications, 1981.
4. "Wire-Wrapping Techniques for Computer Hobbyists," *Popular Electronics,* Vol. 12, No. 6 (December 1977).
5. "Wire-Wrapping and Proto-System Techniques," *BYTE* (May 1981).

APPENDIX B: OPERATIONAL AMPLIFIER THEORY

The operational amplifier (op amp) is going to be one of the most important tools that you have at your disposal when it comes time to interface a transducer to the A/D converter. Since most operational amplifiers have one output and two input ports, we can consider them to be a general 3-port device. Their function is to amplify the difference between the two signals that are applied to the input ports. The amplified difference then appears at the output port. The equation that relates the output voltage to the input voltage(s) is a function of the sign and magnitude of feedback, which is supplied by the output to one or more of the inputs. As a result of feedback we can configure our circuit to add, subtract, multiply, integrate, differentiate, compare, rectify, filter, and perform current-voltage conversion. Three general characteristics of the operational amplifier make it a useful tool:

1. It has very high gain from either of the two input ports to the output port.
2. The input impedance at each input port is very high, and the output impedance is very low.
3. It has very low gain when the same signal is applied to both input ports at once. Consequently the amplifier is most sensitive to the voltage difference between the two inputs, rather than to the voltage difference between either input and ground. This allows the amplifier circuit to disregard many signals that would be classified as noise and to respond only to the signal coming from our transducer.

In most of our applications we will need to provide amplification, and possibly filtering, of the transducer signal because most of the signals we will be dealing with are quite small. The operational amplifier will allow us to take a 50¢ integrated circuit and a knowledge of Ohm's law and become proficient at interfacing whatever device we are using as a transducer to our analog-to-digital converter.

Figure B.1 shows the operational amplifier circuit symbol. You should notice the two input terminals and the single output terminal. One of the input terminals has a negative sign associated with it (the inverting input), and one of the inputs has a positive sign associated with it (the noninverting input). We will be using two basic rules to design and analyze op amp circuits:

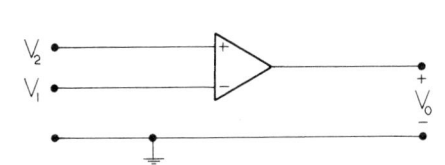

FIGURE B-1

Op-amp circuit symbol. A voltage at V_1, the inverting input, is greatly amplified and inverted to yield an out-of-phase output at V_0. A voltage at V_2, in the noninverting input, is greatly amplified to yield an in-phase output at V_0.

1. When the op amp is operating in a linear region, the two input terminals are at the same voltage.
2. There can be no flow of current into either of the input terminals.

Armed with these two constraints, we can begin our discussion of specific amplifier circuits.

Inverting Amplifier

Figure B.2 shows a basic inverter circuit that is widely used for instrumentation purposes. The input impedence for this configuration is approximately equal to the magnitude of resistor R_i. Note that a portion of the output signal is fed back through resistor R_f to the negative input of the op amp. Reviewing the two

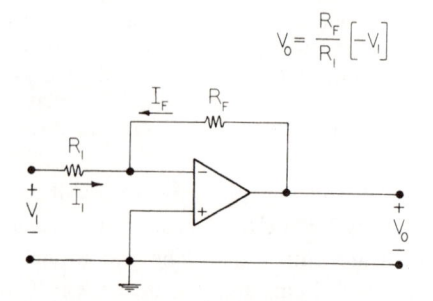

$$V_o = \frac{R_F}{R_I}[-V_I]$$

FIGURE B-2 Simple resistive inverting amplifier. A voltage at V_1, the inverting input, produces a voltage at the output V_O which is a function of the values of R_1 and R_f.

rules previously discussed, we know that both the positive and the negative inputs are at the same potential, which for this circuit is equal to 0V. We also know that the current flowing into or out of each of the two input terminals has to be equal to 0. Using Kirchhoff's current law, we can write the following equation:

$$I_i + I_f = 0 \tag{B2.1}$$

Using Ohm's law we can write the following two equations:

$$V_i - R_i I_i = 0 \tag{B2.2}$$
$$V_o - R_f I_f = 0 \tag{B2.3}$$

Solving equation B2.2 for I_i, solving equation B2.3 for I_f, and then substituting these two values back into equation B2.1, we obtain equation B2.4:

$$\frac{V_i}{R_i} + \frac{V_o}{R_f} = 0 \qquad (B2.4)$$

The voltage gain (K) for the circuit can then be written as follows:

$$K = \frac{V_o}{V_i} = -\frac{R_f}{R_i} \qquad (B2.5)$$

Figure B.3 shows a modification to the basic inverter circuit that allows us to add several input voltages together. Remembering our two basic rules, we know that the inverting and the noninverting input terminals are at the same potential and that there can be no current flowing into or out of either of these terminals. Summing currents at the inverting terminal, we obtain the following equation:

$$I_1 + I_2 + I_3 + I_f = 0 \qquad (B3.1)$$

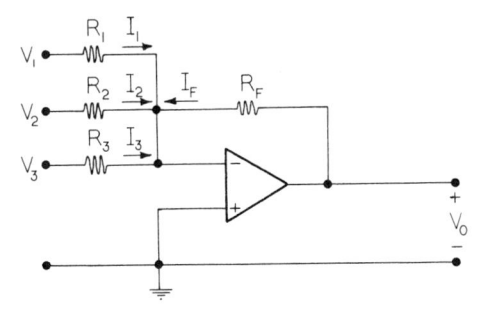

$$-V_o = \frac{R_F}{R_1} V_1 + \frac{R_F}{R_2} V_2 + \frac{R_F}{R_3} V_3$$

Figure B-3 Resistive inverting summing amplifier. Voltages applied to inputs 1, 2, and 3 will sum together to produce a voltage at the output V_o which is a function of the relative values of R_1, R_2, R_3, and R_f.

Using Ohm's law, we can write equations for these currents in terms of the input and output voltages:

$$I_1 = \frac{V_1}{R_1} \qquad (B3.2)$$

$$I_2 = \frac{V_2}{R_2} \qquad (B3.3)$$

$$I_3 = \frac{V_3}{R_3} \qquad (B3.4)$$

$$I_f = \frac{V_o}{R_f} \qquad (B3.5)$$

Substituting these equations back into equation B3.1, we get equation B3.6.

$$\frac{V_1}{R_1} + \frac{V_2}{R_2} + \frac{V_3}{R_3} + \frac{V_0}{R_f} = 0 \qquad (B3.6)$$

Solving for the output voltage, expressed as a function of the input voltages and the resistance values, we get the following equation:

$$-V_o = \left(\frac{R_f}{R_1}\right)V_1 + \left(\frac{R_f}{R_2}\right)V_2 + \left(\frac{R_f}{R_3}\right)V_3$$

Noninverting Amplifier

Figure B.4 shows an amplifier configuration that is sometimes called a *voltage follower* because the output voltage is the same polarity as the input voltage. This circuit is useful because the input impedance is extremely large, and consequently the circuit does not load the circuit attached to its input. Again we have a circuit that has a portion of the output signal fed back to the inverting input through the feedback resistor R_f. The two rules we have discussed state that the voltage at the inverting input will be equal to the voltage at the noninverting input, and that there will be no current flow into or out of either input terminal. Using Ohm's law, we can write an expression that will relate the magnitude of the voltage at point a to the output voltage V_o.

$$V_a = \frac{V_o R_i}{R_i + R_f}$$

FIGURE B-4 Simple resistive noninverting amplifier. A voltage at V_i, the noninverting input, produces a voltage at the output V_o which is a function of the values of R_i and R_f.

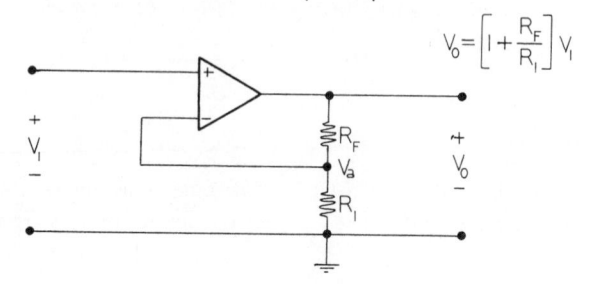

$$V_o = \left[1 + \frac{R_F}{R_I}\right] V_I$$

Since we know that $V_a = V_i$, we can substitute V_i back into equation B4.1 and get the following equation:

$$V_i = \frac{V_o R_i}{R_i + R_f} \tag{B4.2}$$

By rearranging this equation we can obtain an expression that gives the voltage gain of the circuit as a function of the resistors R_i and R_f:

$$K = \frac{V_o}{V_i} = 1 + \frac{R_f}{R_i} \tag{B4.3}$$

By looking at equation B4.3, you should be able to predict what happens to the voltage gain as resistor R_i becomes very large. Figure B.5 shows a circuit diagram where this resistance has been set equal to infinity (open circuit). This is a special circuit called the *unity-gain voltage follower*. Remembering that the voltages at the two input terminals have to be equal to one another, we can see that the output voltage is forced to be equal to the input voltage. This circuit is often used to provide impedance transformation from very high at the input to very low at the output.

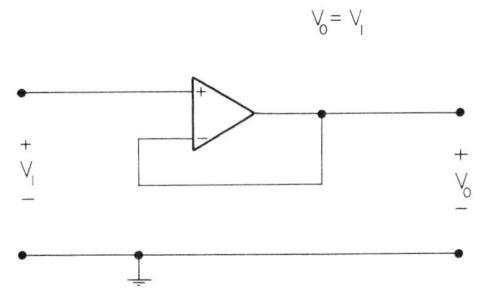

FIGURE B-5 Unity gain noninverting voltage follower. This Circuit reproduces the input voltage, V_1, at the output, V_o, and gives high input impedence and low output impedence.

Differential Amplifier

We found that we could add two or more signals together by using the inverting summing amplifier configuration. We will now take a look at a circuit that will allow us to subtract one signal from another. Figure B.6 shows an operational amplifier used as a differential amplifier. One of the advantages to using this circuit is that the circuit subtracts voltages applied to both inputs, therefore producing an output only when the input voltages are not equal. This is useful when we have a balanced input circuit and need to reduce noise that is common

$$V_o = \frac{R_4}{R_3}\left[V_1 - V_2\right]$$

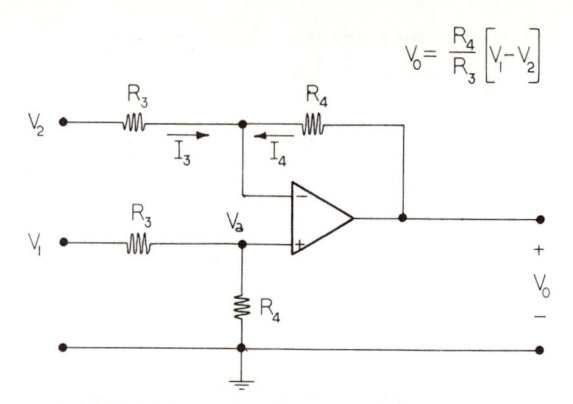

FIGURE B-6 Simple resistive differential amplifier. This circuit is configured so that the output voltage, V_o, is equal to the difference of the input voltages, V_1 and V_2, multiplied by a constant which is a function of the resistors R_3 and R_4.

to both of the inputs. Remember that the voltage at the inverting input has to equal the voltage at the noninverting input and that no current can flow into or out of either terminal. Using Ohm's law, we can then write an equation for the voltage at point a in terms of the input voltage V_1:

$$V_a = \frac{V_1 R_4}{R_3 + R_4} \tag{B6.1}$$

This voltage has to be equal to the voltage at point b. We also know that the following relationship exists between currents I_3 and I_4:

$$I_3 + I_4 = 0 \tag{B6.2}$$

We can write the following equations to relate the output voltage to the input voltages.

$$I_3 = \frac{V_2 - V_o}{R_3} \tag{B6.3}$$

$$I_4 = \frac{V_o - V_o}{R_4} \tag{B6.4}$$

Substituting equation B6.1 into equations B6.3 and B6.4, and then substituting these equations back into equation B6.2, gives the following result:

$$\frac{V_O}{R_4} = (V_1 - V_2)\frac{1}{R_3} \tag{B6.5}$$

Rearranging this equation gives us an equation that relates the output voltage to the input voltages as a function of the resistance values:

$$V_o = \frac{R_4}{R_3}(V_1 - V_2) \tag{B6.6}$$

Integrating Amplifier

The integrating amplifier (Figure B.7) is a circuit whose gain varies as a function of frequency, making it different from the circuits previously considered. Detailed analysis would show that the output voltage will be related to the magnitude and to the frequency of the input voltage by the following equation:

$$\frac{V_o}{V_1} = \frac{-1}{wRC} \tag{B7.1}$$

This equation can also be written as a function of time; this may actually be a more familiar representation for the majority of readers:

$$V_o = \frac{-1}{RC}\int V_i dt \tag{B7.2}$$

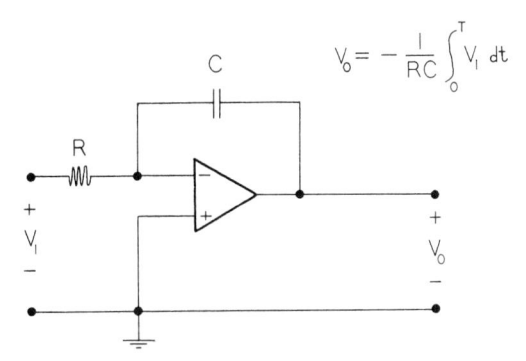

FIGURE B-7 Inverting integrator. A voltage at the input, V_1, is integrated as a function of time and appears at the output, V_o. The time constant for the circuit is a function of the ratio of resistor R and Capacitor C.

Figure B.8 shows an integrator that has had a resistor added in parallel with the capacitor. This arrangement provides us with a circuit, called a *low-pass filter*, that is useful for attenuating high-frequency noise. As with the integrator, the

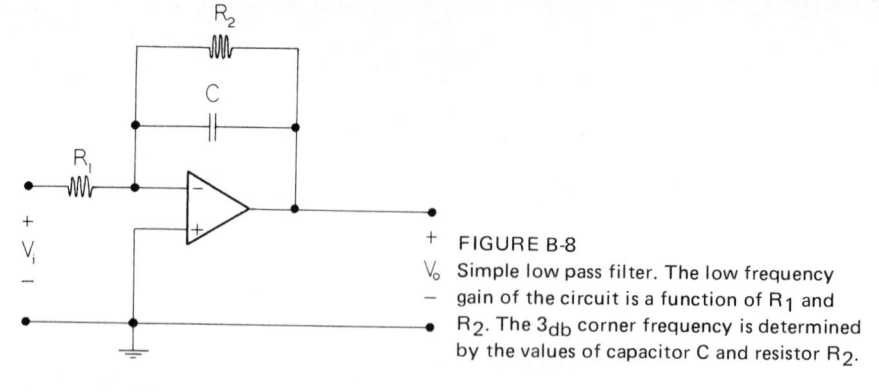

FIGURE B-8 Simple low pass filter. The low frequency gain of the circuit is a function of R_1 and R_2. The 3db corner frequency is determined by the values of capacitor C and resistor R_2.

frequency response is given by the ratio of feedback to input impedance. However, at low frequencies the circuit behaves like an inverter because the impendance of capacitor C is large when compared to that of the resistor R_2. At higher frequencies, the circuit behaves like an integrator because the impedance of C becomes smaller than R_2. Equation B8.1 expresses the gain of this circuit as a function of frequency:

$$\frac{V_o}{V_i} = -\frac{R_f}{R_i} \frac{w}{R_2 C} \frac{1}{1 + \frac{w}{R_2 C}} \qquad (B8.1)$$

At low frequencies this equation reduces to the following equation, which will be recognized as the equation for the simple inverting amplifier:

$$\frac{V_o}{V_1} = \frac{R_2}{R_1} \qquad (B8.2)$$

At high frequencies equation B8.1 will reduce to equation B7.1. When a circuit designer needs to limit the frequency response of a wide-band amplifier, there is no need to add a separate stage but only to add the correct-sized capacitor to the existing circuit.

You could use many types of operational amplifiers in the circuits which we have discussed. An op amp that is commonly available, low in cost, and easy to use is the 741. This general-purpose device provides output short circuit protection, internal phase compensation, and latch-free operation. Another readily available device is the CA3140. This operational amplifier differs from the 741 by having MOS/FET input stages, which provide high input impedance. The pin configuration for both of these devices is shown in Figure B.9.

FIGURE B-9 Pin assignment for the 741 and CA3041 operational amplifiers.

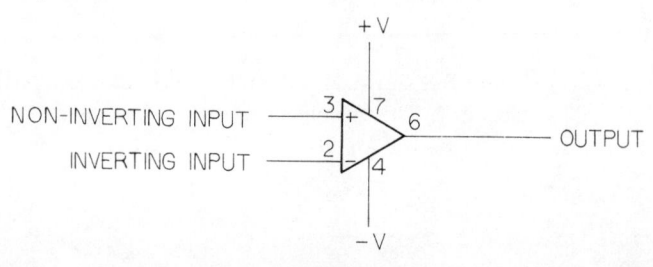

APPENDIX C:
POWER SUPPLIES

The widespread availability of three terminal regulators makes the design and construction of power supplies for digital and analog circuits almost a simple task. In the past, power supplies were generally made from a number of discrete components. Today, advances in fabrication techniques related to monolithic semiconductors have enabled a number of discrete components to be incorporated onto a single chip. The result has been a series of low-cost, positive and negative voltage regulators that are extremely easy to use and difficult to abuse. Monolithic voltage regulators usually have a series pass transistor power control element, a reference source, and current overload protection—all on the same chip. As a result, no adjustments are required to set up the output voltage, and it is virtually impossible to destroy the regulator.

Figure C.1 shows a schematic of a +5-V power supply that can provide up to 0.5 A of current with adequate heatsinking.

Figure C.2 shows a schematic of a +12- and −12-V power supply that can provide up to 0.5 A of current with adequate heatsinking.

FIGURE C-1   Positive 5 volt power supply.

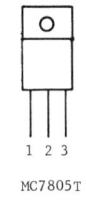

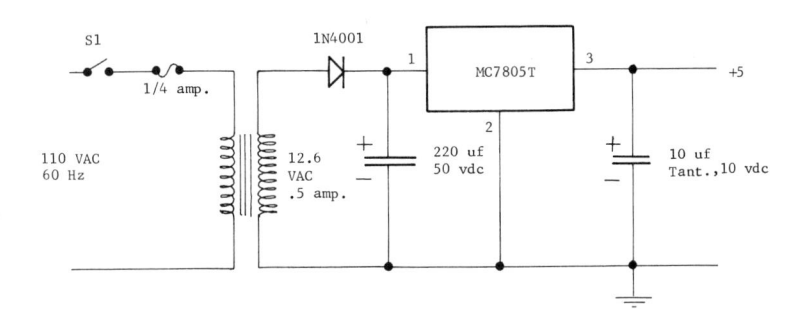

147

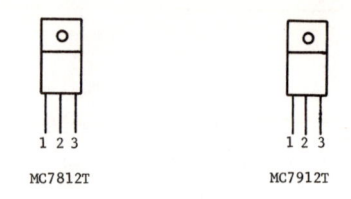

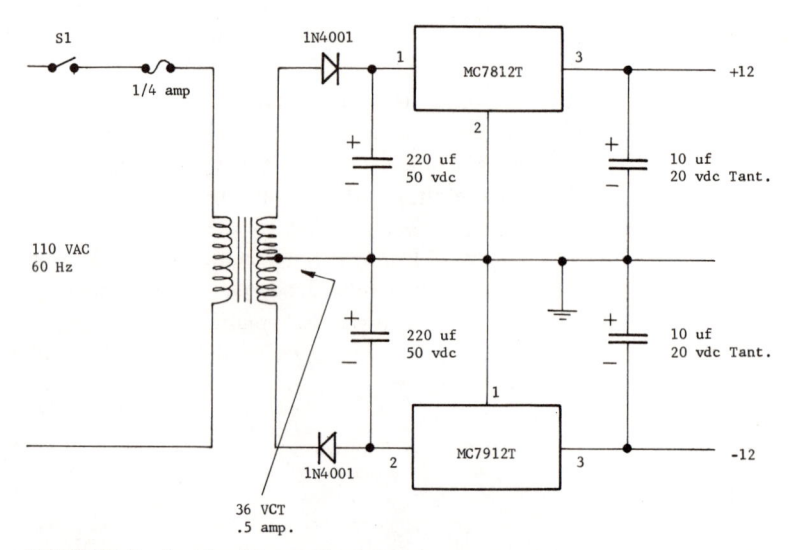

FIGURE C-2 Positive 12, negative 12 volt power supply.

Once you have constructed either of the supplies, you should check to make sure that the output voltage is what you were expecting it to be. You should be concerned about the following items:

1. Treat the 110-V line voltage with care.
2. Make sure that the poliarity of the filter capacitors is correct.
3. Make sure that the polarity of the diodes is correct.
4. The positive and negative regulators do not use the same pin configuration. Be sure that you have used the correct pins for input, output, and ground.

INDEX

A

AD 558 Dacport, 62
Amplifiers, 140-46
Analog-to-digital conversion:
   accuracy, 24
   aliasing, error type, 24, 25
   analog signal, nature, 23
   background, 21
   discrete signal, defined, 23
   rate of sampling, 24
   relative system error, 24
   resolution, 23-24
   sampling theorem, 24-25
   waveforms, 23
Analog-to-digital converter, 8-bit low-
     speed, 31-48
   BASIC program #1:
     flowchart, 43
     routine, 44
   BASIC program #2:
     flowchart, 47
     routine, 45-47
   block diagram, 34
   clock frequency, 37
   clocking of, 45
   checks to make, 44-45
   digit selection timing, diagram, 38
   DISPLAY UPDATE, 37
   dual slope conversion process, 33
   END OF CONVERSION, 37
   function of converter, 39
   integrator output, 34
   joystick game, 32-33
   machine language program:
     flowchart, 41
     routine, 42
   MC14433 chip:
     block diagram, 35
     discussion, 31, 33
     pin assignment in, 36
   noninverting amplifier, 36
   output, nature of, 38
   ratiometric measurement scheme in, 33, 35
   resistive voltage divider, 36
   schematic diagram, 40
   series R/C circuit, 48
   software, division of, 41
   truth table, 39
   voltages in, 35
Analog-to-digital converter, 10-bit high-
     speed, 48-61
   AD571, nature, 48-49

149

Index

BASIC program:
  flowchart, 60
  program, for output format, 60
bipolar offset control, 50
bit configurations, 52
block diagram, 49
buffer amplifiers:
  inverting adjustable gain, 52
  noninverting unity gain, 52
  input lines, 54, 56
  input resistance, 50-51
  machine language:
    flowchart, 58
    program, 59
  memory map for, 58
  operation sequence, 56-57
  oscilloscope, tests with, 57
  resolution, 52-54
    measurement of, 54
  schematic diagram, 55
  software, handling of, 58
  successive approximation, 49
  test sequence, 51, 57
  time base, crystal-controlled, 56
  voltage division, 50
Analog interface, low-cost, 25-31
  joystick in:
    demonstration, flowchart, 30
    demonstration program, 31
    interface circuit for, Mod III, 27
    modified, schematic, 28
  modification to connections in, 27
  NE556 dual timer in, 26
  program:
    sample, 29
    tests for, 29-30
  resistance, measurement of, 26
  resolution, 30
  software driver, flowchart, 29
  tests to, 28

B

BASIC, programs in, 21-22, 44, 45, 47, 60, 66, 70-76, 83, 87-89, 96-97, 112-21, 123-24, 125-27, 130-32
Betamax, (video cassette recorder), 102-5
Bidirectional serial interface, machine language program for, 81-82
Binary signal, status of, 19-21
  BASIC program about:
    flowchart of, 21
    for switch status display, 22
  switch status input port, schematic, 20
  switch testing, 19-20
  use, 20

Biofeedback, 84-85
  and body, 84-85
  and brain, 84
  feedback, nature of, 85
  learning, 84
Board construction techniques, 133-38
  costs, 133
  discussion, 133
  etching, 136
  finished projects, examples, 137-38
  front view, 134
  rear view, 134
  Vector type:
    discussion, 135
    front view, 135
  wire-wrapped technique, 136-37

D

Differential amplifier, 143-45
  diagram, 144
  equations governing, 144, 145
  use, 143-44
Digital-to-analog conversion, 62-67
  AD558 Dacport, nature of, 62
  BASIC routine for lamp test, 66
  block diagram, 63
  lamp, output tests of, 63-64
  lamp power supply, schematic, 65
  lamp tests, BASIC program for, 66
  lowpass filter, frequency response test, 65, 67
  lowpass test, block diagram, 67
  interface, schematic for, 64
  tests, 63, 65
    arrangements, block diagram, 65

E

Exponential regression, 125-27
  BASIC routine for, 125-26
  example, 127
  general formula, 125

F

Fourier analysis, rapid, 127-32
  analog signal, 128
  analyzed signal, 129
  BASIC routine, 130-32
    discussion, 132
    enhancement, 132
    frequency spacing, 132
    100-Hz program, 132
    program for, 130-31
  discussion, 127, 130

Index

H

Handshaking, 3
Heart rate, control of, 91-99
   analog circuitry, schematic of, 92
   BASIC program:
      for experiments, 95-96
      flowchart, 97
      machine language routine, 96-97
      for set-up, 94
   circuitry, action of, 93
   diagram of feedback, 92
   factors in, 91
   finger, observation of, 94
   graphic displays, 98
   and lamp, 93
   measurement method, 91
   photocell in, 91, 93
   self, experiments for, 98-99
   tests, 93, 94, 95
   tools for, 91

I

Input-output port, defined, 3
Integrating amplifier, 145-46
   diagram, 145
   equations, 145, 146
   high frequencies, 146
   integrators, 145-46
   low pass filter, diagram, 146
   pin assignment, 146
   use, 145
Inverting amplifier, 140-42
   action, 140
   currents at terminal, 141
   equations governing, 140-41, 142
   resistive summing type circuit diagram, 141
   simple resistive, circuit diagram, 140
   voltage gain, 141

L

Linear regression, for curve fitting, 122-25
   example, 124-25
   general formula for, 122
   least squares method, BASIC routine for, 123-24

M

MC14433, 35-36
Microprocessors:
   early, 1
   input/output set of, 7
Mod III, 10, 11, 69, 102, 104, 105
Modem, nature of, 78

N

Noninverting amplifier, 142-43
   diagram, 142
   equations, 142, 143
   unity-gain type, 143
      diagram, 143
      use, 143
   as voltage follower, 142

O

Operational amplifier theory, 138-40
   characteristics, 139
   circuit symbols, 139
   design rules, 140
   use, 138-39

P

Parallel data format:
   and commands, 10, 11
   input circuit, action of, 12
   input port for, diagram, 12
   output circuit, action of, 10
   output pins, configuration of in Mod III, 10
   output port, diagram, 13
   pins in Mod III, functional description, 11
Parallel transfer, defined, 3
Plotting, high-resolution digital, 68-77
   BASIC program for operation, 70-76
   demonstration, program for, 70
   digital plotter program, flowchart, 77
   HIPLOT:
      command characters, 76
      device for, 68
      vector notations, 76
   and Mod III interface connections, 69
   RS 232C output, bit pattern and spacing in, 76
   tests, 69
   and TTL-to-RS 232-C conversion, 69
Ports, nature of, 3
Power supplies, 147-48
   discussion, 147
   points to remember, 148
   positive 5-volt, 147
   positive 12-volt, negative 12-volt, 148

R

References, 138
Regression, 122-25, 125-27
RS-232C, 15, 16, 18

152   Index

S

Serial data format:
   asynchronous format, 13-14
   bit pattern, example, 14
   flowchart, TTL-to-RS 232-C, 16
   interfaces:
      RS 232-C-to-TTL, flowchart, 17
      TTL-to-RS 232-C, 15
   logic levels, 14
   and noise reduction, 12-13
   RS 232-C-to-TTL converter, flowchart, 18
   START bit, 14
   subroutines:
      conversion to parallel, 16
      conversion to serial, 15
   TTL voltage levels, 14-15
Serial transfer, 4-5
   EIA standard, 5
   mark, 5
   space, 5
Skin temperature, control of, 85-91
   analog circuitry for, schematic, 86
   BASIC program:
      flowchart, 89
      routine, 87-89
   diagram, 90
   graphic display, 90
   heat in body, 85
   peripheral temperature, factors in, 85
   practice, 90-91
   tests, 87
   thermistors for, 86

T

TTL, 14, 15, 16

V

Video playback device, control of, 100-21
   advantages, 101
   Betamaxes:
      design, 102
      functions, 102, 104-5
      interface, diagram, 103
      interface, to Mod III, 102
      signals from for control, 102
      software commands for, 104
      tests for, 105
   controller software, parts of, 107
   demonstration program:
      BASIC flowchart, 111
      BASIC routine, 110, 112-21
   location count, decrement of:
      flowchart, 109
      machine language program, 110
   location count, increment of:
      flowchart, 108
      machine language program, 108-9
   Mod III cassette output, program for, 104
   and personal computer, 101
   programs, functions of, 107-8
   slide/audio cassette systems, 100
   and TV, 100-101
   test program, Betamax/Mod III, 105-7
   VCRs, 101
   visual aids, importance of, 100
Video terminal, 77-83
   BASIC program for, 83
   flowchart program, 83
   interface circuit for, 80
   modem:
      block diagram, 80
      for terminal, 78
   plot dimensions, range, 79
   startup of, 82
   tests for serial interface board, 79
   time constant, exponential plots for, 78

Z

Z-80 chip:
   address decoder in, 4-16 type, 8
   architecture of, 5
   control signals, 7-8, 9
   data processing in, 5, 7
   input/output–peripheral decoding, 9
   instruction set in, 7
   pin configuration, 6
   16-32 address decoder, 9